THE MODERNS

THE MODERNS

ESSAYS IN LITERARY
CRITICISM

By

JOHN FREEMAN

Essay Index Reprint Series

BOOKS FOR LIBRARIES PRESS, INC.
FREEPORT, NEW YORK

First Published 1917
Reprinted 1967

LIBRARY OF CONGRESS CATALOG CARD NUMBER:
67-30213

PRINTED IN THE UNITED STATES OF AMERICA

CONTENTS

THE MODERNS

GEORGE BERNARD SHAW

I

MR. SHAW has told us so much about himself, and told it so often, that any commentary by another may seem superfluous. But since all that he has said in this way has been said for the avowed purpose of calling attention to his work and advertising its merits, we may be pardoned for considering the work and the commentary together. He is accepted as an oracle, he would have us believe, only because he has so insistently claimed oracular authority ; but to take this without question is to neglect the modesty lurking in his defiant egotism, and to overlook the fact that for many people the simplest truism glittering with his phrase seems inspired. Naturally he deals much in truism, though he often contrives an elusive disguise for it ; and we have his own urgent repudiation of originality in regard to a dozen things of which the discovery is flatteringly attributed to him. Some of these things we shall be considering in a moment : here it need only be said that Mr. Shaw, like many less egotistical authors, is not a wholly impartial witness. With his hero, Richard Dudgeon, he seems to desire exceedingly an opportunity of kicking his heels in the air, hanged by his own false testimony.

But there is no need to be deceived. We need not spare Mr. Shaw the praise he has so long protested against. Ruskin complained of admiration given to his prose style, while his sermon was politely ignored. We have never known anyone praise Mr. Shaw's prose style, but we do join most cordially with those who think gratefully of the amusement they receive from his high spirits and gay love of paradox, even while we linger only half convinced by his infinite argumentativeness.

II

Long before the larger public knew him as a dramatist, the smaller public which reads the superior weeklies knew him as a critic. None could read him, on music, pictures, or plays, without being arrested by the sharp tone of his briefest notices. His interests have been almost equal in diversity and activity ; and his activity is most clearly shown in the *Saturday Review* articles which have been collected into two volumes and " introduced " to those who had read them already by Mr. James Huneker, an American gentleman whose style is that of a literary sharpshooter. Mr. Shaw is intensely interested in the theatre, and this alone is sufficient to separate his work from the otiose articles of critics who are intensely interested in nothing at all. Surely nothing can be mustier than revived notices of plays which were born in grave clothes, and became old-fashioned the moment they were produced. Trash and master-piece alike receive Mr. Shaw's assault—for assault is his invariable method, even at his friendliest. Petu-lant, perverse and sometimes savage, his freedoms may have offended actor and play-maker, ever inclined to regard their work a little too piously : they could only delight his readers. Mr. Shaw did much to achieve that primary miracle—the creation of an acute and honourable minority who would regard the theatre with the same seriousness as others would give to a novel of Turgénev or a portrait of Holbein. That it remains a minority is only partly his fault. Vio-lently impatient as they often are, his criticisms yet bear a hint of restraint and compassion. It may hardly gratify a victim to be told, Why, man, think of the things I wouldn't say ! but this casual forbearance is pure virtue in the critic, and the sense of it sheer amusement to the intelligent reader of these few hundred notices—this extraordinary mixture of rail-lery, contempt, perversity and despair. Mr. Shaw has, in fact, the critical faculty unusually well deve-loped, together with a great natural combativeness. He not only sees clearly what he wants, but he sees clearly what is offered to him ; and this is a gift not too common. So far as the theatre at any rate was concerned, he was as unmerciful as an impassioned theorist must needs be, and made no claim to serene impartiality. His interest in the theatre showed, it must be said, more of difficult faith than of easy hope; —I mean that, taking his collected criticisms as a whole, and recalling with their aid one's impressions of some of the plays dealt with, it is hard to see what but a splendid and audacious faith could have left him after four years with a shred of hope for the national drama.

He avers that the theatre nearly killed him as a man, but it wonderfully failed to kill him as a dramatist. Mr. Pinero was Mr. Pinero at the end of those four full years, just as he was at the beginning, and just as he is still—save for the distinction of a knighthood; Mr. H. A. Jones was the same Mr. H. A. Jones, in fact everybody connected with the theatre was the same when Mr. Shaw sighed *Finis* as when he shouted *Fiat Lux.* Only, Mr. Shaw was more obstinately Mr. Shaw, except that he learned from his inferiors, revenging himself for long submission to their frivolity and debility by crunching whatever bones were hid in their unfortunate bodies. For us, now, his work as a critic has this significance, that it showed him, if not the way of success as a dramatic writer, at least a hundred avoidable ways of failure.

III

Now, although the concern of this appreciation of Mr. Shaw as a modern influence is naturally with his ideas,

as presenting the essence of his mind, a brief survey
of his adventures in drama is necessary not simply to
the justice of our estimate, but also to an understanding
of those ideas in their development. And in the first
place it must be said that his work in the theatre has
made a considerable difference to the theatre. He has
sought to turn it—and partly at least has succeeded
—into something other than a shop of frivolousness
and sensuality :—at any rate, if this be an extravagant
claim he has assuredly put a shoulder to the wheel
which others are moving. If the vast inertia of the
theatre has been stirred, he has helped to stir it. For
myself, I must confess that the theatre is still in the
main an intolerable bore ; the exceptions are so
brilliantly conspicuous as to need no more than a
general thanks. It is hard to endure on the stage the
nonsense which one would never dream of enduring
in a book. That is to say, it is hard indeed to turn
from Mr. Hardy, Mr. Henry James or Mr. Conrad to
the varnish of Mr. X., the salacities of Mr. Y. and the
morality of Mr. Z., without a sense of unutterable
languor and despair. Mr. Shaw has complained
long and loudly against this divorce of the writer of
genius from the beloved stage, and has certainly done
all that his own bright talent could do to repair the
breach. That he has not wholly succeeded is due
perhaps as much to a misapprehension of the task, as
to the inadequacy of the effort. For the plain fact
is that while these prodigious agitations have been

stirred on the stage and in the auditorium of the English theatre, it is the music hall that has come quietly in and captured the prize. The intelligent people whose interest the dramatic reformers sought to arouse have responded by rubbing their eyes, and turning in long immense queues to the *Palace* and the *Coliseum*. The campaign has overrun the suburbs and the provinces; and in provinces and suburbs alike theatre after theatre has been turned into a music hall.

It is a phenomenon which I cannot pretend to explain. On the one hand it will be said that people go now to the music hall who never went before, because the fare is vastly improved; and on the other that the fare is vastly improved because more people go. But at least one can see pretty clearly that the phenomenon is due to other than merely superficial causes: it may even be due, in the final analysis, to the fact that we are essentially an un-dramatic people; and the contention would hardly be answered by naming Shakespeare. Mr. Shaw, no doubt, will explain it easily enough, if he has not explained it a dozen times already in those loud newspaper asides which one is always missing in an unaccountable way. His lieutenant in what is carefully termed the Normal theatre, but which normal people persistently regard as the Abnormal theatre, even Mr. Granville Barker has gone over to the enemy—for it is as an enemy that the theatrical manager surveys the more prosperous music hall manager—so far as to appear himself on the stage of a theatre of " varieties." Nay, Mr. Shaw too has taken his wares to the vaudeville theatres, which is indeed carrying not war but ammunition into the enemy's camp.

But, otherwise, this is not Mr. Shaw's fault. As a comic playwright he has done all that a comic playwright who is not a poet can humanly achieve. Foolish critics in the haste of their pens and the hate of their hearts have contemned him because he will not be serious ; more justly would they deplore the occasion when he is. He brings to comedy a broad natural portion of the comic spirit.. Meredith reminds us of Landor's wise word :—" Genuine humour and true wit require a sound and capacious mind, which is always a grave one. . . . Few men have been graver than Pascal. Few men have been wittier." Elsewhere in his famous and luminous essay Meredith insists on the justice of the common distinction of wit from humour ; and of this Mr. Shaw is a capital example. Of humour he has probably as little as any comic dramatist, who was not also a poet, ever rejoiced in. Meredith, in another valuable passage, estimated the capacity for comic perception by the ability to detect the ridicule of those you love without loving them less ; but, he proceeds, if you detect the ridicule and your kindliness is chilled by it, you are slipping into the grasp of satire. Kindliness, tenderness,—these are words which seem almost ludicrously inapplicable to Mr. Shaw's work ; they are forgotten in the fierceness of his romance-renouncing satire. The whole of his characters move in a peculiarly rare atmosphere of inhumanity.[1] They have movement, but they do not live :—rather should we say they are galvanically active. They are inhabitants of a country as essentially unreal as the country of Mr. Henry James's characters ; they are citizens of a city where the unexpected always happens, and nothing is impossible but the normal. I do not think it would be true to say, as I was about to say, that they are unnatural, since unnatural persons are not uncommon : they are lifelike but unliving ; they may be freakishly true portraits of certain actual persons, but they are not true within nature ; they are cinematographic pictures of aberrations. And the reason of this is, I think, that his plays have not a " natural " origin : they are all illustrations of ideas. The folly of romance, the crime of criminal punishment, the economic

---

[1] It is a truism that no one can be so inexorably inhuman as a convinced humanitarian. Mr. Shaw would sacrifice a nation for a theory put forward in humanity's behalf. His plays are, usually, inhumanly frigid and, for all their liveliness, unemotional ; and it is notable that the play of which this is but slightly true, *John Bull's Other Island*, is one of his best and ripest dramatic experiments. Here his gift for seeing two sides of a subject, and seeing them, in spite of exaggeration, to some extent sympathetically, finds an excellent opportunity. It is notable, too, that it is his only play dealing with his native country.

oppression of woman, the cupidity of doctors, the prosaic reality of florid history—these are his theme. Some of his subjects he thinks unpleasant and calls the plays unpleasant ; but it is the conduct of the play which is unpleasant, as, for example, in the excitement of sexual desire described in *Widowers' Houses* and glimpsed in *Mrs. Warren's Profession* ; the unpleasantness, in short, is incidental and not inevitable. And so it becomes significantly easy, with some of the later plays, to describe them in a brief phrase. *Man and Superman,* for instance, is simply a comedy of inverted sex-pursuit ; *John Bull,* a brisk political satire with a sweetening of sentimental passages ; *The Doctor's Dilemma* a mere anti-medical philippic with remarks upon the immorality of genius ; *Major Barbara* a mere anti-poverty philippic, with remarks upon the immorality of progress.

Nothing could have saved plays thus conceived but what has actually saved them—their author's high spirits. An intellectual buoyancy of remarkable pitch carries him through. With less of liveliness his plays would be detestable ; with more of humanity they would be absurd. Take a few passages of *Arms and the Man, Getting Married,* or *Man and Superman,* and, looking a little closely, you will find that the pleasure you receive is in a large degree precisely the pleasure you receive from a " knockabout " turn at the *Empire.* At the *Empire* the excitement is that of blows—more or less real and noisy—deftly delivered and stockishly endured ; at the *Court* or *Criterion* it is exactly the same, only the blows are verbal. Be it said at once that Mr. Shaw's blows are very dexterous. He has the literary gift as only a " born journalist " (the claim I fancy, is his own) can have it. Other comic play-makers have usually reserved their surprises for their " situations " ; Mr. 'Shaw scatters his bewilderingly over all his dialogue. He has explored the unexpected as no man has explored it before him. So systematic has been his cultivation of this nebulous freehold that you can almost certainly calculate his surprises by the simple process of inverting the normal or natural. This inexpensive unexpectedness is so often made to pass for wit that you may even fall indulgently into the author's persuasion and accept it as wit. . . . Remember, too, that his briskness and agility usually achieve a great pace in the dialogue, and you will hardly wonder that his plays seem so witty on a first acquaintance. Only, you wonder how they can seem so tiresome on a further acquaintance. The clash and contrast of which the dramatic moment is born are too often only verbal and rhetorical. His dramatic moments do not arise from the opposition of suddenly revealed character, but at best from characters perfectly definite and limited, faced with the arbitrary unexpected. There is no development of character on the one hand ; the unexpected is seldom inevitable on the other : and so for all the high spirits, genuine dramatic surprise is rare. You have, instead, such a typical scene as this from *Man and Superman* :—It is the scene where Violet's supposed delinquency is discussed, or rather denounced, by all save the paradoxiçal Tanner. (I take the liberty to condense slightly.)

TANNER. I have something to say which I beg you to hear. I am altogether on your side in this matter. I congratulate you, with the sincerest respect, on having the courage to do what you have done. You are entirely in the right ; and the family is entirely in the wrong.

VIOLET (*sharply to Tanner*). Who told you ?

TANNER. Why, Ramsden and Tavy of course. Why should they not ?

VIOLET. But they don't know.

TANNER. Don't know what ?

VIOLET. They don't know that I am in the right, I mean.

TANNER. Oh, they know it in their hearts, though they think themselves bound to blame you by their silly superstitions about morality and propriety and so forth. But I know, and the whole world really knows, though it dare not say so, that you are right to follow your instinct ; that vitality and bravery are the greatest qualities a woman can have, and motherhood her solemn initiation into womanhood ; and the fact of your not being legally married matters not one scrap either to your own worth or to our real regard for you.

VIOLET (*flushing with indignation*). Oh! You think me a wicked woman, like the rest. You think I have not only been vile, but that I share your abominable opinions. Miss Ramsden : I have borne your hard words because I knew you would be sorry for them when you found out the truth. But I won't bear such a horrible insult as to be complimented by Jack on being one of the wretches of whom he approves. I have kept my marriage a secret for my husband's sake. But now I claim my right as a married woman not to be insulted.

OCTAVIUS (*raising his head with inexpressible relief*). You are married !

The Moderns

In this easy device is Mr. Shaw's contempt for his audience made manifest. Years of endurance, as a dramatic critic, of the paltry or prurient plays of other writers, have taught him to despise his own public as well as theirs. Else, surely, he would risk a trifle more on his reader's or auditor's intelligence. How little he cares to trust it is shown on almost every page by his profusion of square brackets. In the preface to *Plays Unpleasant* he is careful to explain that these ample stage-directions are necessary for the comprehension of his work : the effect, however, is that of underlining capital letters. I say nothing of the meticulous descriptions of scene and person which he loves to give, and gives often so excellently : these at worst are superfluous and amusing. But what is the author's estimate of his poor reader's wits when he feels obliged to shout like a Hyde Park Sunday evening orator engaged to gather, by pure force of lungs, the crowd that shall listen to the real star of the meeting ? Ironic remarks, for example, invariably carry the square-bracket signal, lest you should fail to discover the irony. An interruption which the dullest could not help remarking for an interruption has nevertheless to flap its label pathetically before your eyes. You must not perceive these things for yourself, you must not trust to your own sense of the dialogue. You are pedantically told that this is meant for irony and that for resentment. Every colour or tone has its label ; and as the labels

are necessarily few, you come to perceive that the
colours or tones are few. Since everything is capable
of such brief and clear indication, you are hardly
disappointed of any delicacy of thought or any subtlety
of apprehension. Mr. Shaw's armoury holds nothing
more subtle than a mace, nothing more cleanly pene-
trative than a shillelagh.

And if he gives his readers credit for little intelligence, he gives them credit for much simplicity.
Consciously or unconsciously, he views his *dramatis
personæ* as merest puppetry and, wise and fool alike,
permits them to be overwhelmed, shocked, disgusted
and so forth through the narrow range of a dozen
simulations at the very tamest epigrammatic onset.
But this, I must hasten to point out, does not spring
so much from his fierce contempt of his docile public,
as from the simple necessities of the Shavian drama.
Since his plays do not arise from the development
and opposition of character, but are mere illustrations
of ideas, he cannot afford to let his characters speak for
themselves. They have no proper speech of their
own, for they must perforce play into each other's
hands, exactly as, with Cinquevalli juggling, one ball
is whipped from his palm in time for another to be
received. So you find that one after another presents
himself like an ignition strip, for the Shavian incarna-
tion to rub the match of his wits upon. In *Getting
Married* General Bridgnorth displays a capacity for
being overwhelmed which is surely beyond parallel.

Who but a general of Mr. Shaw's would succumb to such paper cartridges ?—

THE BISHOP. Shakespeare pointed out long ago that a woman wanted a Sunday husband as well as a weekday one. But, as usual, he didn't follow up the idea.
THE GENERAL (*aghast*). Am I to understand——
THE BISHOP (*cutting him short*). Now, Boxer, am I the Bishop or you ?
THE GENERAL (*sulkily*). You.
THE BISHOP. Then don't ask me are you to understand. " Yours not to reason why : yours but to do and die "——
THE GENERAL. Oh, very well : go on. I'm not clever. Only a silly soldier man. Ha ! Go on. (*He throws himself into the railed chair, as one prepared for the worst.*)

Or take the first of his plays, *Widowers' Houses*, and you will find already the same immense capacity for succumbing to a portentously feeble attack ; only here it is not a single surrender but the capitulation of a whole group. Sartorius, slum landlord, pities his slum tenants and explains to the honest fool of the play how hopeless it is to help them. Here is the conclusion :—

No, gentlemen : when people are very poor you *cannot* help them, no matter how much you may sympathize with them. It does them more harm than good in the long run. I prefer to save my money in order to provide additional houses for the homeless, and to lay by a little for Blanche. (*He looks at them. They are silent : Trench unconvinced but talked down ; Cokayne humanely perplexed. Sartorius bends his brows ; comes forward in his chair as if gathering himself together for a spring ; and addresses himself with impressive significance to Trench.*)

14

It means, of course, that the rhetorical impulse has overcome—and with how swift and easy a movement ! —the dramatic. The poor author simply daren't give his creatures a free tongue to answer this puerile tirade. . . . You come to remark that there is no natural propriety in the language which his characters use. Take a page of almost any play, strike out the names of the speakers, and it is doubtful, if your familiarity with the play be not uncommonly close, whether you will be able to visualize for yourself, merely from the printed utterance and without the emphatic directions, the persons speaking, or perceive for yourself the dramatic situation as presented in them. It is true that some of the characters (as, for example, in *You Never Can Tell*) have their peculiarities so unfailingly proclaimed that they could not be mistaken, any more than a man with a false nose or a black-patched eye. Artifices such as these apart, the distinction of persons speaking in ordinary life is lost in these plays, where all are speaking the same smart, strident impromptus. Candour compels the remark, nevertheless, that in all but the earliest and latest plays the impromptus really have a certain antiphonal sound, and a semi-dramatic effect. Where this is wanting, as in *Plays Unpleasant*, the result is tediousness. . . . *Widowers' Houses* is a poor start for a play-maker who set out upon so large a mission ; its virtue—almost a solitary one—is that the subject of the play (slum landlordism) seemed in 1892 fresh and novel as a dramatic subject, even though *An Enemy of the People* had been translated a good many years previously.

I said just now that Mr. Shaw's plays are mere illustrations of ideas ; and of the difficulty of presenting ideas in dramatic form *Mrs Warren's Profession* is a fair example. His assertion in this play is that the modern economic pressure upon women is so sore that between prostitution and labour-tortured days and nights there is no choice for poor girls. One needs but small knowledge of the poorer classes and their social conditions to see that this is not the whole case. And more : is it quite wise (even if it be your sorrowful conviction) to tell poor girls that the only alternative to the coarsest uncertain physical drudgery is the moral drudgery of that subtle, convenanted octopus, prostitution ? But Mr. Shaw must needs do this dangerous thing, to prove dramatically the economic oppression of women.

He has mastered the trick of showing up one character vividly at the expense of another, but he has not mastered the trick of letting one character speak for itself and by itself, and without this visible foolish act of friction. His failure simply means that his characters never burn from within, but are artificially kindled from without ; and the whole innocent conceit shows as clearly as has ever been shown the difference between vital and mechanical work, between the living creature and the galvanized puppet. Emptied of romance as he professes to be, and full of natural hatred of its enchantments, there is one intensely romantic strand in Mr. Shaw's personality. He is a devout hero-worshipper, when himself has erected the hero. A favourite is the youthful Shaw disguised as John Tanner, Richard Dudgeon, Hotchkiss, Napoleon. With infinitely insistent gaiety this " hero " dances through three or four acts, sparkling, flashing and sputtering in an immense assurance of his own amusingness or impressiveness. For him only does Mr. Shaw reserve a tenderness with which he is seldom credited. He is proof against the thrusts of others, but none is proof against his. Others he disarms lightly with an inverted platitude, charming them from answering with any obvious effective jibe. His are the newest phrases, the promptest paradoxes. Even his humiliations and confusions are figures of wit, and he recovers as easily as Mdlle. Genée from a cataract of applause which (she prettily affects) has shocked her into self-consciousness. The Shavian hero, unhappily, can never be shocked out of it. Mr. Shaw, when he is most genial, as with John Tanner, laughs at himself ; and Tanner is probably the flower—or shall we say the hub ?—of his author's characters. But usually he is so intent upon mockery at his audience and their quasi-prototypes upon the stage ; so concerned to shock them into surprise ; and so resolved to add surprise to surprise (where another writer would unfold the normal consequences of a single surprise), that he cheerfully sacrifices everything so only he achieve the shock. And since the hero, too, must never be at a loss for quarry, that favourite game of childhood must be revived, and his prowess in demolishing Aunt Sallies demonstrated in every act. Let me beg the reader not to contemn this as an inexpensive excitement. It is only humour that is rare, and Mr. Shaw can hardly claim the endearing title of humorist. And so you laugh gladly as, with tremendous fury, the same epigrammatic missiles are flung at conventionality (poor ancient victim !) nonconformity, missionaries, education, home-life, and all other things as familiar as the stones jerked against them. More : Mr. Shaw will frequently improvise, in a single breathless sentence, the very Aunt Sallies which he means in a flash to shatter. The gain in precision is obvious ; there is no possibility of mistake ; and you are left with a feeling of astonished gratitude that the author has spared you all intellectual effort, even while calling attention to the truth or falsity of an intellectual conception.

IV

Let us look a little more closely. Mr. Shaw's influence upon our time is not confined to the public that sees or reads his plays. His own claim is to deal with ideas, and than this no man can make a larger or nobler claim. To this, as we have seen, his plays owe their birth, and he himself has made the case clear for us. The drama, he tells us authoritatively in *Three Plays*

George Bernard Shaw

for Puritans, can never be more than a play of ideas. This is true, in the precisest sense of the words, but I do not think Mr. Shaw is using them with the precision we expect from him. He has always wanted, he says, a pit of philosophers, and he points to *Man and Superman* as the play for such a pit. He complains, in the vigorous dedication of that play, that Shakespeare and Dickens have no constructive ideas ; that they lack compelling thought and inspiration ; and that their sanity and shrewdness are to the philosopher's as Sancho Panza's to Don Quixote's. Shakespeare has always much to show and nothing to teach, never understood courage and virtue, was utterly bewildered in the world, and could do nothing with a serious positive character. I am not concerned to explain or vindicate Shakespeare, for I think Mr. Shaw is simply jumping agilely upon a shadow. If *Hamlet*, to take Mr. Shaw's favourite instance, is not a play of ideas, nor *Othello, Macbeth, The Winter's Tale*, nor *Troilus and Cressida*, then the term has no exact apprehensible meaning. The *idea* of love and its soilure by passion, the *idea* of treachery, the *idea* of inward falseness—these surely shine like seaward beacons out of the splendid mystery of the plays. The plays are born of moral ideas—ideas so profoundly conceived and so tenaciously held that they burst the narrow bonds of traditional story which was all that Shakespeare needed for their indication or background.[1]

[1] Mr. Shaw's dealing with Shakespeare may be appraised

But Mr. Shaw, as his prefaces and plays clearly show, does not mean ideas in this exact sense. He means ideas in the current loose sense. As a man has advanced " ideas " (meaning notions) upon marriage, divorce, submission to law, etc., so Mr. Shaw, himself restless with these ideas which are simply notions with a nicer name, can perceive no ideas but notions. And since Shakespeare, ignoring notions, was so spiritually intent upon ideas, it is plain he would never agree with Mr. Shaw upon the scope and subject of the drama. But Shakespeare goes his own way, and Mr. Shaw

from the single instance of Henry V, whom he compares with Bunyan's fine imaginations. " Put your Shakespearian hero and coward, Henry V, and Pistol or Parolles beside Mr. Valiant and Mr. Fearing, and you have a sudden revelation of the abyss that lies between the fashionable author who could see nothing in the world but the personal aims and the tragedy of their disappointment or the comedy of their incongruity, and the field preacher who achieved virtue and courage by identifying himself with the purpose of the world as he understood it. The contrast is enormous : Bunyan's coward stirs the blood more than Shakespeare's hero, who actually leaves you cold and secretly hostile. You suddenly see that Shakespeare, with all his flashes and divinations, never understood virtue and courage, never conceived how any man who was not a fool could, like Bunyan's hero, look back from the brink of the river of death over the strife and labour of his pilgrimage, and say ' yet I do not repent me.' " . . . The assumption that Henry V was Shakespeare's hero is merely unreflecting. Mr. Masefield has put the plain view of him in a few just words. " Prince Henry is not a hero, he is not a thinker, he is not even a friend ; he is a common man whose incapacity for feeling enables him to change his habits whenever interest bids him."

goes his, and the play of notions has the day ; and the Bardolaters, as Mr. Shaw wittily calls us, are very well content to remember that a notion is not an idea.

To consider in detail Mr. Shaw's ideas (the term must be allowed for convenience) is to undertake a difficult task. They are not really strange, they are not really alarming ; but they are presented with so much vigour, with so much insistence and various repetition, with such perplexity of illustration, that I feel an impossible nimbleness is required of a commentator. And, too, the fact of their double present-ment, in the play and in the preface,—the preface hanging on the play like the albatross around the neck of the Ancient Mariner,—adds somewhat to the diffi-culty ; since you find yourself faced with apparent contradictions which really spring only from the necessity of the play. Not that there is the least obscurity : only you come to see that confusion may arise without obscurity, as surely as with it.

Let us take the volume containing *The Doctor's Dilemma*, *Getting Married* and *The Showing-up of Blanco Posnet*. Each of these has an inordinately long preface ; the first, of ninety-four pages upon doctors and their abuse of public confidence ; the second, of eighty pages upon marriage and divorce ; and the third, of seventy-four pages upon the censor-ship. More than half the book, in fact, is occupied with strenuous dissertations upon subjects connected with the plays. As to the first play and preface,

the subject is one in which it is almost superfluous to
follow the author.   Not all Mr. Shaw's vehemence can
persuade us that what he says is new, or conspicuously
untrue, or anything but conspicuously unjust; he
fails, in short, to shock us, which is only to say that
he succeeds in boring us.   But when he comes to the
subject of the second play, *Getting Married,* he is on
more accustomed ground.   To no feature of common
welfare has he given more constant and impetuous
attention than to this of marriage and divorce.   Mr.
Shaw must have grown tired of hearing, when he
produced *Getting Married* at the Haymarket, that it
was not a play at all; though in justice to his critics
it might be admitted that he did not anticipate the
objection by calling it a conversation.   Questions of
technique apart, what do we find here ?   We will take
for granted all the usual qualities—high spirits, face-
tiousness, verbal fence and the rest—since we have
already dealt generally with these.

Well, to summarize the action of the play does not
help us very much, for a reason which is as weighty
as it is curious.   It is this : that after a discussion of
marriage and divorce with such freedom and wanton
unconventionality as may suffice to make Mr. Shaw's
favourite Tooting stare and gasp, the marriage rite is
nevertheless faithfully observed, though with a farcical
accompaniment not unwholly unexpected.   It is perfectly possible that people in what he calls " real life "
would hold extreme views of the current conventions

of society, and yet themselves pay seemingly devout tribute to those conventions. But then, *Getting Married* tacitly claims certain immunities from the obligations of real life. Since the characters and dialogue are contrived—albeit so cunningly—for the disparagement of the sacramental view of marriage and the annihilation of ordinary married relations, surely the earnest dramatist with " views " would secure the consistency of dialogue and character in the ultimate development of his play. Mr. Shaw is so utterly against that rose-red sentimentality which follows all manner of divagation and wantonness in two acts with tame recognition of conventional morality in the third, that we wonder to find his clamant onslaught upon obdurate sentiment culminating in dull acquiescence in the very code he revolts against. For the unthinking, of course, the admirable result is just this : they have the excitement of dalliance with " advanced " anti-conventional notions, and the comfortable opiate for their conscience of old-fashioned acceptance of convention. To secure the anti-conventional public—an alert and intelligent public—is a fine thing ; to secure the vast conventional public—perhaps not so alertly intelligent—is a profitable thing ; but to attract both is the very summit of success.

Now *Getting Married* is a tangle from which I can only trust myself to take one or two little plain strands. The Bishop of Chelsea's daughter is on the point of marriage, but refuses to proceed—though the guests

are waiting at the church—because of a pamphlet
which comes into her hands on the wedding morning,
exposing the dismal truth that she will have to take
her husband for better or worse, and that women have
sometimes taken their husbands for worse. Edith is
shocked to discover that if Cecil murders, drinks or
steals, she cannot get divorced from him. And just
when she declares that she will not marry Cecil on such
preposterous terms, Cecil declares that he will not
marry Edith save under protest. He too has been
reading a pamphlet, Mr. Belfort Bax on *Men's Wrongs*,
and he is stupefied at the thought that Edith—a social
reformer who has the usual hearty gusto in denouncing
furiously those who do not please her—might by her
censorious licence involve him in a slander action.
The Bishop is airily indifferent, his only concern being
to give the devil his due ; while his brother, General
Bridgnorth, hopelessly in love with a lady who des-
pises him, is a target for the spare shots of every one
of the party. Another brother, Reginald, is in process
of being divorced from his wife for the benefit of her
lover, St. John Hotchkiss, who is something short of
appreciation of his kindness. There is also an alder-
manic greengrocer (chief adviser to the Palace family),
and his sister-in-law, mayoress of Chelsea and wife of
a local coal-seller. She is in love with the Bishop.
Hotchkiss, the bold bad man of this agreeable gathering,
is the mouthpiece of the old familiar Shavian defiances
of an indifferent world. He believes in nothing but

his own will and pride and honour, prophesies the early adoption of a reformed Mahometanism, and indignantly asks Father Anthony (ascetic solicitor and confessor) :

Who are you, anyhow, that you should know better than Mahomet or Confucius or any of the other Johnnies who have been on this job since the world existed ?

He is, in fact, brother to John Tanner, Ann Whitfield, Richard Dudgeon and Blanco Posnet, and at times speaks like a maiden aunt determined to be shocking.

Even from this brief summary one can imagine Mr. Shaw's opportunities. He very ingeniously assigns the utterances of some of the most revolutionary notions, not to Hotchkiss, but to the bland Bishop ; knowing surely with what additional force these notions will sound from the lips of a shepherd of souls. A bishop is the very man to recommend most startlingly the convenience of polygamy. True, many readers may think the whole play indecent ; true, others may think it pervadingly though not specifically blasphemous ; but they of course forget that gaiety beclouds indecency, and brilliance atones for blasphemy. Yet even the devout student of Mr. Shaw may feel a little perplexed at the contrast in this play of theory and practice ; though whether the preface was written to mitigate this perplexity, or the play to dull the edge of the preface, I am loth to guess. But at any rate after the badinage, vigorous rather than delicate, after the customary attacks upon snobs, conventions, suburbs, middle classes and so forth, after the tedious unpleasantness of the love-making of Hotchkiss and the mayoress, you are left dubious before the altar.

Turn now to the preface. Mr. Shaw pleads there for the rationalizing of marriage. He appears to consider that marriage means but the secure activity of the sex-relation. Marriages are seldom ideal and are often disastrous; even the best of husbands irritate the best wives; children are ruined by domestic affection; many people find themselves unfitly mated, and are driven by the strictness of the bond to avowed or furtive evil courses. These are some of his shots at this institution. He thinks the alteration of the marriage laws must necessarily proceed together with the reform of the divorce laws; and in the simplification and extension of divorce, discovers a remedy for most of the ills of married life. He believes in the existence of a class of women—a large class—who would find the concession of conjugal rights to any man intolerable, but who yet thirst for what he terms the sexual experience :—women, he means, who would make the most admirable mothers, but who are denied the right of maternity because of their delicate abhorrence of the male creature. And, too, he finds a vast class of potential mothers whom no man desires; wherefore he urges the desirability of polygyny, although at the same time he recognizes that—" there is no way at all out of the present system of condemning superfluous women to barrenness, except by legitimizing the children of women who are not married to the fathers." He appears to regard with favour a household which consists of three families, and where the children have had the " advantage " of a change of both fathers and mothers and learned in consequence " superior sociability."

These, as far as I can ascertain, are the characteristic views of Mr. Shaw upon marriage and divorce. Remember that the problem of the future is the problem of present sound births and wise nurture, and you will recognize the necessity of considering closely the attitude of our prophet on these questions. That it is not expressed quite without premeditation is to be gathered from the fact that *Man and Superman*, published eight years previously, contains something similar in curiously Shavian jargon :—

It cannot be denied that one of the changes in public opinion demanded by the need for the Superman is a very unexpected one. It is nothing less than the dissolution of the present necessary association of marriage with conjugation, which most unmarried people regard as the very diagnostic of marriage.

And when he comes to consider, with more than ordinary precision, what reform of the divorce laws is required, he summarizes his position under eight heads, of which the chief may be stated shortly thus :—

Divorce to be easy, cheap and private as marriage ; to be granted at the request of either party, with or without the

consent of the other, and no ground for the request to be
stated. Power of dissolving marriage for misconduct to be
confined to the state. State may intervene at request, but
only in regard to alimony. Work of wife or mother, to
be on the same footing as other work.

We must, our reformer humorously concludes, adapt
our institutions to human nature ; but the odd thing
is that after ninety pages of theoretical probing and
adaptation, you are left with a dark misgiving that
Mr. Shaw's understanding of hunan nature is of the
cloudiest.   Leslie Stephen said that whenever he came
across the word nature he prepared himself for loose
thinking ; and Mr. Shaw seems to be betrayed by the
term human nature into mere easy vagueness.   Not
that he is bound very strictly by his own observations
of human nature ; he loves to be inconsequential.
Repudiation becomes easy, or definition at any
rate difficult.   But of one thing we may be sure : he
does plainly lack the least sense of the delicacy of what
he calls the sexual or married relation.   That under
the restraint of this relation men and women are
conscious of any change he loudly denies ; love he
regards simply as sexual passion.   He objects to the
" intolerable indignity " of married life as ordinarily
conceived, and proceeds to erect an image of suburban
people—" a black-coated army of calamity "—in order
that he may have the satisfaction of spurting contempt
at it. . . .   An inexpensive pleasure, you remark
again !   And these suburban people are produced by a

system of which the family and institution of marriage form the corner-stone.

Nor is this all : from his detailed brilliant description of these suburban tame ones, he goes on to declare that English home life to-day is neither honourable, virtuous, clean nor, in any creditable way, distinctively English ; it is, in short, unnatural. Unhappily, he omits to tell us what is his own ideal, unless it be indeed the triple household already mentioned. We are not sure (one never can be so sure of our author's meaning as he appears to be) whether he deems the union of three families in one household, with the ensuing inextricable perplexity of parentage, blessed above all other unions ; or whether a double household might not secure an equal degree of felicity ; or, again, whether, since he has not utterly denied the possibility, even a mean monogamous union may not stumble upon happiness. . . . But this is to be merely heavy. For all his emphasis he is not so precise as he might be : the effect of his vagueness is sometimes like that of reading Plato in a pretentious mistranslation. He complains of the excessive intimacy into which home life plunges its victims, yet avers that " a man as intimate with his wife as a magistrate with his clerk, etc., is a man in ten thousand. The majority of married couples never get to know each other at all." (It is Mr. Shaw's excellent statistical habit of mind which leads him to imagine that personal intimacy is proportionate to personal proximity.) Another inconsistency may be seen in the statement that the revolt against marriage is a revolt " even against its enervating happiness." Even reformers, one gathers, have their reckless moments.

Let us not turn too impatiently from Mr. Shaw's genial nonsense. One advantage of this method of merely stating his arguments is that, in this " frightful neighbourhood " of one another, they often answer one another. Their author is far too much amused by his own swift wit to be incapable of amusing others ; and he really has a serious conception of common things. He points to many unsatisfactory features of which we are all aware, but he loves to leap farther than others can see, with a smart and alarming " whoop." Since marriage, in its sacramental aspect, is a Christian ordination, its failure at various points is to be charged upon Christianity. To suggest, in response, that the failure of marriage results from the fault and folly of human nature, and will persist while human nature remains foolish and faulty, is to be too absurdly obvious. It is Mr. Shaw's long inexperience of human nature, and his too-great experience of an exotic, super-subtle nature, that lead him to overlook a general fact, viz., that under what conditions soever the social intimacy of men and women is maintained, some friction is inevitable and distress only too probable.

For all these ills and errancies his sovran panacea is change of partner. Seeing so sharply (to repeat once again) the sorrowfulness of some marriages, and guessing that the most excellent " regular " unions have moments of exasperation, he concludes that change, and frequency of change, will redress many miseries and save the institution of marriage itself from desuetude. Hence his generous proposals for the reform of divorce. What he seems not to see is the full force of the very simple question, if divorce is to be as easy as marriage, why marry ? He thinks that by granting divorce at the request of either party to a marriage, without statement of reasons, divorce will be as easy as marriage. He wonderfully fails to see that it will be a great deal easier, as well as (to take his other points at the same time) a great deal cheaper and more private. He amazingly fails to see anything so baldly obvious as that, while it takes two to make a marriage, it will need only one to break it. For thousands of people marriage is by no means easy, cheap or private. A man cannot arrest a woman nor a woman a man with a peremptory order for immediate, unconditional marriage ; yet this is a logical corollary of Mr. Shaw's ingenuous proposition. But his logic, I am afraid, is often imperfect. He is more imaginative than he cares to believe.

From the gaily simple solution of the marriage problem Mr. Shaw proceeds, in the volume called *Misalliance*, to the exposure of another domestic ugliness, the parental relation ; offering what seems to be his solution of that also. He has discovered what I have for some years been so frankly and so deliciously confronted with—the fact, namely, that parents are unfit to " bring up " their own children ; and with this couples an opinion that children in other hands than their parents' are even worse off. The briefest experience of children is sadly sufficient to grapple, as with hooks of steel, the first of these facts to the bewildered minds of most fathers and mothers. The dilemma illustrated by this volume of three plays and two prefaces is so common and so huge that it has escaped discussion as wild beasts escape vaccination. But Mr. Shaw is possessed with it. The child's " political rights "—so highly prized by his newest paladin —are kept from him ; he is nursed and fed and clothed, and sent to school, and flung into a career, humiliated, with scarcely an expostulation except from Mr. Shaw. But what Mr. Shaw is so strangely unaware of is the case for the parent. I do not remember that he has anywhere guessed the humiliation of the parent, who knows that he holds beneath his hand this delicate, extraordinary, darkly prophetic being, to make or to mar, to enrich or to starve, to bless or to curse, with nothing to guide but vague memories, fascinated affection, and a daily attenuating common sense. It is alas ! the blind that lead the blind, and the leaders deserve a fragment of humorous pity for *their* dilemma. Common life is crammed with dilemmas. What a dilemma is a human creature placed in, suspecting in himself a lonely and immortal soul, yet driven to toil

for bread ? What a dilemma, striving to preserve
some shadow of himself amid the darkening pressure
of external relations with men and things ?

Mr. Shaw has discovered that a parent may be
brutal, sometimes through ignorance, sometimes
through passion ; but he has not discovered that a
parent may be simply affectionate, bathing a child
with a love as entire, as natural, and as unnoticed,
as the circumambient air ; or that the child may
respond to this subtle stimulus as naturally and entirely as leaves lifting to the light. Because in one
class social ordinances, and in another social privations,
have been permitted to defeat this general miracle,
he ignores its persistent triumph in the other classes.
His own idea of the truer parental relation is illuminated
in the play *Misalliance* as distinct from its tremendous
preface. What the young generation must needs
achieve is total emancipation—from control, affection,.
homeliness ; better than the company of parents is the :
company of harlots and rioters. Let the daughter gaily
taunt her father with decrepit infidelities—so gaily that
he need not feel ashamed and cannot feel resentful.
Self-assertion, strident, wanton, wearisome,—that is the
aim and the achievement. There is no least touch of
love, nor so much pity as you give to a homeless dog :
for is not family affection a disgusting pretence ?
When I recall the exciting scenes of *Misalliance* and
Fanny's First Play and hear again this infinite babble,
I see, by an odd freak of the mind, John Bunyan

33

rushing from some knavish porch stuck over with malicious grotesques, his fingers stuffed in his ears and the wind wrestling with him as he goes by crying, " God, God, God ! "

No fallacies are so pathetic as the fallacies of a clever man. I believe that Mr. Shaw's erratic improvisations upon the great and serious themes of marriage and the nurture of children are hardly more erratic and pathetic than his improvisations upon other themes. But to take with equal seriousness all the points of his campaign against the time—points obviously urged in so many cases merely for fun—would be to prolong tediousness into infinite boredom ; and Mr. Shaw, who often amuses and not often bores his readers, ought not to be made dreadful in a new way. When he expands the third act of *Man and Superman* with fifty-six pages upon the respective attractions of Heaven and Hell, the pursuit of men by women, the superman, etc., it is only his fun, though it must be confessed sad and tedious fun. Even vivacity can become tiresome, and the gratuitousness of epigram painfully evident.

Upon one particular opinion he insists for its novelty as well as for its truth. " What is new, as far as I know," he says of *Major Barbara*, " is that article of Undershaft's religion which recognizes in money the first need and in poverty the vilest sin of man and society." A little earlier (First Aid to Critics) he writes :—

34

George Bernard Shaw

The crying need of the nation is not for better morals, cheaper bread, temperance, liberty, culture, redemption of fallen sisters and erring brothers, nor the grace, love and fellowship of the Trinity, but simply for enough money. And the evil to be attacked is not sin, suffering, greed, priestcraft, kingcraft, demagogy, monopoly, ignorance, drink, wars, pestilence, nor any other of the scapegoats which reformers sacrifice, but simply poverty.

Resuming a favourite attack, he charges Christianity with much that is evil in our own day, accusing its submission to oppression : " Christianity, in making a merit of submission, has marked only that depth in the abyss at which the very sense of shame has been lost." He speaks of " soul-destroying Christendom," and objects to the Cross as to all gibbets. The Christian idea of Atonement he perceives to be " that central superstition—salvation of the world by the gibbet." Mr. Shaw's familiarity with Christian doctrine, it will be noted, is not quite exhaustive. " Popular Christianity," he repeats more shrilly, " has for its emblem a gibbet, for its chief sensation a sanguinary execution after torture, for its central mystery an insane vengeance bought off by a trumpery expiation." As Newman remarks, " The blind teacher in morals can ensure himself a blind audience, to whom he may safely address his paradoxes." Mr. Shaw has apparently been touched with the fine freedom of a paper which he alludes to in this preface, *The Freethinker*, a paper which used to amuse its readers with puns upon the names of the Prophets. To state his position in these

matters is in itself sufficient, since such grotesque
misapprehension of the "central" truth of Christianity (whose centre is everywhere), or such grotesque
misrepresentation of it, leaves no room for argument.
One is forced to fall back upon the purely esoteric
position, not simply because other positions are un-
tenable, but because the dispute is in its nature fruitless. But where a correction might be suggested is
in regard to a point concerned less with dogmatic
theology than with human nature. The sense of sin
(to reduce to its simplest term what is often confused
in wider terms) is part of the general experience of men
and women. Probably no man, save he who has
never discovered or suspected in himself abysses of
weakness, follies and treacheries, can forget the sharpness of that consciousness, the depth of that recognition, the intensity of that conviction, which we call
the sense of sin. This, I repeat, is so plainly not
a matter of mere theology but of universal experience,
that Mr. Shaw's blindness to it—star-proof in serene
density—can only be taken as a sign of his acute ignorance of general human experience. Be it far from us
to regard lightly the privations of poverty, far from us
to suggest tame acquiescence in those social ills whose
present existence is witness of our past indifference.
Only, let us recognize the whole problem ; or if the
recognition be difficult, let us frankly say that the
spiritual world holds mysteries which the material can
never comprehend, and throbs with desires it can never

satisfy. Mr. Shaw builds his play upon this thesis of the supremacy of money, and may be excused for thinking it new : it is old enough to be forgotten and taken for new again. All that he gives it is a quasi-philosophical guise, which might half induce the reader to think the play much more than a play, being obviously rather less. A very good play may be built upon the thesis, or a very plausible theory of political economy : but to expatiate upon a theory of political economy in a play, or to make a play of the theory, is hardly the way of success for dramatist or economist. The effect is to leave the reader sadly unconvinced by both play and theory. . . . And if the crying need of the world is money, and Undershaft be the type (as he dramatically is) of the man whose need is wholly satisfied, the theory bears for exemplar a boastful and cold automaton, who will roll out the old dull paradoxes as surely as a machine when the penny is thrust into the slot. Undershaft is, in fact, only our old friend the Superman turned factory-owner, a John Tanner whose wits have outrun his intelligence.

To what event, it may now be asked, do Mr. Shaw's anticipations move ? He is not so determinedly " practical " as to permit himself no speculations upon the future. In the airily entertaining pages of "The Revolutionist's Handbook " he has given his judgment upon the history of progress, and is as dismal as any perplexed Tory can be. Naturally he cannot spare his customary gibe at Christianity, nor his long antithetical paragraphs upon the practical falsification of its profession. These we will pass and turn to the following :—

> We must frankly give up the notion that man as he exists is capable of net progress. There will always be an illusion of progress, because wherever we are conscious of an evil we remedy it, and therefore always seem to ourselves to be progressing, forgetting that most of the evils we see are the effects, finally becoming acute, of long-unnoticed retrogressions : that our compromising remedies seldom fully recover the lost ground ; above all, that on the lines along which we are degenerating, good has become evil in our eyes, and is being undone in the name of progress precisely as evil is undone and replaced by good on the lines along which we are evolving. This is indeed the Illusion of Illusions ; for it gives us infallible and appalling assurance that if our political ruin is to come, it will be effected by ardent reformers and supported by enthusiastic patriots as a series of necessary steps in our progress . . . Whilst Man remains what he is, there can be no progress beyond the point already attained and fallen headlong from at every attempt at civilization ; and since even that point is but a pinnacle to which a few people cling in giddy terror above an abyss of squalor, mere progress should no longer charm us.

Laodiceanism could ask for no sweeter anodyne. In sober truth, if this is the conviction of Mr. Shaw himself he deserves hearty praise for that his own impulse towards the amelioration of the world has not failed. He would probably say—he has said most of the smart things—that despair will serve a reformer as well as hope. But in an earlier sentence from the " Handbook " he has uttered the true secret, one of the few old simple truths that his restless acute mind has permitted him to express. " Man will return to his idols and his cupidities in spite of all movements and all revolutions, until his nature is changed." How comes it that our superman, our intellectual corrosive, utters so true and eternal a thing ? Have we not heard this before, even in the despised scriptures ? Is this the simple end of all those flashing plays, those lectures and interminable letters to the press, those fatiguing prefaces ? . . . It has here the suddenness of a revelation, the inexplicableness of a betrayal. After a lifetime strenuously spent in exhorting men to change their views, he abruptly tells them instead to change their hearts. His wondering adherents may not unreasonably feel aggrieved at hearing from Mr. Shaw the very advice they have heard, unregarding, from the preacher at the street corner ; and the few who are not his adherents may feel bewildered to hear the Lord's songs in so strange a land—" A torrid waste of water-mocking sand "—and suspect their own ears. But it is the fate of reformers, when they stumble upon an accepted truth, to experience the resentment of their followers and the suspicion of their critics. It is the fate of this reformer—none regrets it more sincerely than I—that when he is lucidly and irrefragably right (as upon criminal punishment, Ireland, Egyptian tyranny, etc.) he rouses a profound suspicion of the truth itself, and almost drives you by a paradox of mistrust into the wide arms of crazy error.

The Moderns

It is significant that from Mr. Shaw's earlier books are his doctrines most clearly ascertained ; the later merely adding weight by accretion not by development. And this is unfortunate, since the war offered him a natural opportunity of which he became promptly aware but which, I am afraid, he did not in any sense of the word " improve." " *Common Sense about the War* "—what better could we desire when the war had run its bewildering course for three months ?— but it was precisely what Mr. Shaw avoided giving us. An unfriendly critic, whose office I shall not attempt to seize, might conceivably have anticipated much that Mr. Shaw tells us ; and indeed, anticipation would be too easy to be intelligent. Mr. Shaw himself is careful to recall prognostications of his own which the war has seen in fruition, and it would not be quite impossible to detect on the other hand some which have proved incorrect. Pointless, however, must all such small matters appear in face of the affront which Mr. Shaw has flung at those for whom England—to speak immodestly—is in truth a mother, loved, forgotten, betrayed and loved the more. Such intense feeling, so intense that words fall to a whisper, as inspires, for instance, Swinburne's *The Oblation*— written not explicitly of England yet written for England—finds neither expression nor recognition in this enormous tract.

> Ask nothing more of me, sweet ;
> All I can give you I give

George Bernard Shaw

> Heart of my heart, were it more,
> More would be laid at your feet :
> Love that should help you to live,
> Song that should spur you to soar.

You cannot blame Mr. Shaw for this ; the limitation is avowed.

> " I shall retain my Irish capacity for criticizing England with something of the detachment of a foreigner, and perhaps with a certain slightly malicious taste for taking the conceit out of her."

Unnecessary warning, for that detachment, that " slightly " malicious taste, are conspicuous everywhere. Everywhere is the old rasping querulousness, the sparkling cleverness—and now the flatness following effervescence. It is a pity, for in November 1914, scarcely less than now, wise words were needed ; but wisdom herself would cry but exasperatingly if she took the trick of a scold. Once again to state his position would be, I think, to answer it, although Mr. Shaw himself, having devoted some hobby-horsical energy to the presentation of his case, might object to such an answer as a mere evasion. He finds the Junker class predominant in England as in Germany ; the Foreign Office is, like Germany's, a Junker club. Here, not in Germany, was begun " the propaganda of Militarism and of inevitable war," and the Kaiser himself was the victim of English Junkerdom. Sir Edward Grey is a Junker,—but then, in another place (good easy man), is only a figure-head, and in yet another the popular but confused " instrument " of the Foreign Office. Our Admiralty and our Foreign Office both were deliberately bent upon war with Germany. Yet England and her Junkerdom did not act at cross purposes : the nation too wanted to strike at Germany, " the monster all freedom-loving men hate." All that lacked was the pretext, and this Mr. Asquith, for all his ignorance of foreign politics, was able to find in " the obvious barrister's point about the violation of the neutrality of Belgium " ; for Mr. Shaw in his swift imaginative way sees in the Prime Minister merely a Yorkshire Kaiser, a lawyer Hohenzollern. One sighs for the pen of Mr. Max Beerbohm. Belgium, in short, gave *our* militarists their excuse for " attacking " Germany, although elsewhere Mr. Shaw thrusts solely upon Russia the responsibility for the " outrageous absurdity " of the war. " *Six of One : Half-a-dozen of the Other* " is one of the headlines of this tract, and when its author touches the question of " damages " at the end of the war he dismisses it with an airy confessional note, " God forgive us all ! " and the suggestion that Belgium's indemnity should be paid not only by Germany, but by all the entente powers as well ; for England, France and Germany are seen alike as crucified Belgium's " guilty neighbours." Yet, surely with a fleck of humorous inconsistency, he avers that the neutrality of Belgium had no real existence for the Germans, since it was known that if the Germans invaded Belgium, England and France would be invited to defend it. . . . So might the super-subtle burglar maintain the necessity of breaking into Adelphi Terrace since the police will arrest him there if they can.

So much there is that is trifling, captious, maliciously perverse, that what is true in this tract is scarcely likely to be regarded. Mr. Shaw perceives quite clearly and says quite frankly what our national aim is—to rid the world of " Potsdamnation," but nevertheless sees all the tragic protagonists in the same guilty light. Put plainly, the answer which must be given even if so superfluously is merely this. How can a war against " Potsdamnation " be waged and justified by the " Potsdamned " ? For his own share in this warfare Mr. Shaw has sought ingeniously to disarm England of her moral weapon and thrust it into Germany's hand. No one was better qualified for this eminent disservice to England. As for Germany, with the words *Louvain*, *Lusitania* and *Wittenberg* clanking round her like a leper's rattle, her thanks should make up for the coldness of ours.

V

Mr. Shaw has risked the reputation of comic dramatist, to gain that of comic philosopher. If, by an impossible freak of wilfulness, he should take—and strangely keep—a vow of silence and we—

" More at the wonder than the loss aghast "—

should consider what he has given us, apart from the amusement of brisk comedy, what should we find ?—Theories of marriage, divorce and family life, crime and punishment, government, wealth and poverty ; theories of Irish and English character, theories of the shame of women, which is the shame of men ; theories of the pursuit of sex by sex, theories of history and art. The theories are many and not very new ; but they are recommended with such natural vivacity, such affluence of analogy, such energy of repetition, as to dazzle even when they are far from convincing. As Johnson says of Pope : " The reader feels his mind full though he learns nothing." Our author has a great love of Bunyan—and who could be more unlike Bunyan ? What do we feel in *The Pilgrim's Progress*, if not the presence of a character of large and delicate simplicity, a character whose very boldness is a kind of sharper sensitiveness, a character of unmatched vigour, sincerity and integrity ? and the medium of that imperishable portrait is a prose as plain and supple, powerful and responsive, as the body and soul of Christian himself. . . . How unbridgeable is the gulf between Bunyan and Mr. Shaw ! Mr. Shaw's mind is active yet inflexible, positive yet changeable, alert yet insensitive. That intemperance of language, that constant freedom of abuse, that reluctance to let words speak for themselves—what is behind it all but mere insensibility ?

When I think of Mr. Shaw I am reminded not of

Bunyan but of Cobbett. Mr. Shaw and Cobbett have the same gusto, the same inordinate love of talk, the same native pugnacity, the same readiness of explanation, the same volatility, the same brief flashes of indignation and fine scorn, the same passion for reform, the same autocratic insistence upon it, the same underlying disbelief in it. Cobbett's great advantage over Mr. Shaw is one which the latter would naturally contemn—the advantage of style. Who needs praise Cobbett's prose now, save by sedulous imitation! But let no one dream of imitating Mr. Shaw's. Assuredly, if " the whole man, the very whole of him is his style," this is singularly true of Mr. Shaw's prose style. It is clear, hard and bright like varnished wood. By some miraculous and deadly chemistry he has emptied his vocabulary of all but obvious meanings, and denuded his sentence of every associative value. Never did words so serviceable serve their master so meanly. They shout, scream, and leap in a stony chatter with urgent speed; they seldom merely speak. They are like words which we have heard gladly from the lips of another, but which seem utterly different when we repeat them to ourselves. It is the voice, we reflect, that makes the difference. Lacking that charm the poor words seem devitalized, even at times decivilized.

*　　*　　*　　*　　*

Postscript concerning " Androcles and the Lion " (1916).

It may seem merely perverse to differ from Mr. Shaw

and his critics in almost equal measure, but with some of the critics of this book only a very humorous man could be patient. They complain of Mr. Shaw's levity, of his self-assertiveness, and so forth, and seem not to see the unusual if not quite unqualified sincerity of his survey of Jesus Christ. I had nearly written, of the Founder of Christianity, by a heedless habit of the pen, and careless of the fact that Mr. Shaw's entire campaign is meant to show that He is not the Founder of Christianity as Christianity now exists.

Androcles is one of the simplest and soberest pieces of criticism that Mr. Shaw has written. It has occurred to him (as to Mr. George Moore) to read the Gospels, and he frankly confesses unanticipated delight and stimulation. Almost for the first time in his life he is naïve, and so suggests more than he says—things indeed quite different from the things he says. He has gone to the Gospels for the Portrait of Jesus Christ, and I imagine that it is with something as like to genuine pain as any sensation he has ever felt that he hears the charge of flippancy. Why, his answer is, I have simply treated Jesus as a real person—as real as myself. And it is indeed a deadly and deadening " reality " that has been imparted to the portrait. A little here, a little there, this from Matthew, that from Mark, this charming sentiment from Luke and that egotistic outline from John—and the portrait is done, neat and compact and complete and empty as a box. Nothing could surpass the ingenuousness with which he glides

46

over inconsistencies and ignores whatever is not so
neat and smooth as his theory, or the strange facility
with which he denudes the character of Jesus Christ
of every suggestion of mystery, every echo of depth,
every reflection of love, every hint of anguish. But
of deliberate flippancy not a trace in the whole study.
True there is an amazing and ghastly attitude of
patronage ; true that it is from a by no means unconscious elevation that this elaborate portrait is dabbed
in ; true that it is full of comparisons which may be
gently called odious ; true that the whole thing is
done without reverence as without affection ; but
that there is anything wanton in all this, anything
consciously amiss, cannot be sensibly urged; and that
is Mr. Shaw's praise—and deepest fault. There are
revelations sadder than any intended revelations.

Mr. Shaw has asserted somewhere that he could
have given chapter and verse for every lineament of
his portrait of Christ ; and that need not be denied.
But chapter-and-versicians are not always the most
faithful of followers : you do not begin to paint a tree
by counting its leaves. Something has escaped Mr.
Shaw's diligent penetration ; with a hundred traits
the character is not *there*. Let me take this for consideration :

Jesus saw no merit either in asceticism or martyrdom. In
contrast to John he was essentially a highly civilized, cultivated person. According to Luke, he pointed out the contrast himself, chaffing the Jews for complaining that John

must be possessed by the devil because he was a teetotaller and vegetarian, whilst, because Jesus was neither one nor the other, they reviled him as a gluttonous man and a winebibber, the friend of the officials and their mistresses. He told strait-laced disciples that they would have trouble enough from other people without making any for themselves, and that they should avoid martyrdom and enjoy themselves whilst they had the chance. . . . He is convivial, feasting with Roman officials and sinners. He is careless of his person, and is remonstrated with for not washing his hands before sitting down to table. The followers of John the Baptist, who fast, and who expect to find the Christians greater ascetics than themselves, are disappointed at finding that Jesus and his twelve friends do not fast, and Jesus tells them that they should rejoice in him instead of being melancholy. He is jocular, and tells them they will all have as much fasting as they want soon enough, whether they like it or not. He is not afraid of disease, and dines with a leper. A woman, apparently to protect him against infection, pours a costly unguent on his head, and is rebuked because what it cost might have been given to the poor. He pooh-poohs that low-spirited view, and says, as he said when he was reproached for not fasting, that the poor are always there to be helped, but that he is not there to be anointed always, implying that you should never lose a chance of being happy when there is so much misery in the world. He breaks the Sabbath ; is impatient of conventionality when it is uncomfortable or obstructive ; and outrages the feelings of the Jews by breaches of it. . . . He has no modest affectations, and claims to be greater than Solomon or Jonah. When reproached, as Bun-yan was, for resorting to the art of fiction when teaching in parables, he justifies himself on the ground that art is the only way in which the people can be taught. He is, in short, what we should call an artist and a Bohemian in his manner of life.

For every trait, says Mr. Shaw, I can give you chapter and verse. But let me ask this : to whom can

this Christ appeal, except to dialecticians of genius
like Mr. Shaw, and the lesser crowd of psychologists,
critics, reformers and professors of heterodoxy ? But,
Mr. Shaw will desperately repeat, I tell you these
characteristics are all in the Gospels. It need be
neither admitted nor denied ; for it is not what is put
in that is to be questioned but what is left out. What
Mr. Shaw has put in are the inessentials, the modern
personalia, the touches thought vivid ; and they are
put in as familiarly as possible, with a nimble hop-
skip-and-jump, not because he wants to be irreverent
or shocking, or disparaging, but because he is so sur-
prised that even the figure of Jesus Christ can be made
to respond to a method so—shall we say modern ?
And what, then, has he left out ? A little natural
reticence may make it hard for many people to say.
He has left out that profound spirituality which
changes men's lives ; he has left out the love which
overwhelms and humiliates and renews those that
apprehend it ; he has left out not only the divinity
which he takes for granted is a mere delusion, but the
humanity which is like a sun behind all the small points
of light within his narrow vision. One thing is plain to
every reader of the Gospels, that the character of Jesus,
in its purely human manifestation (which is all that Mr.
Shaw recognizes) is one of power and authority ; and Mr.
Shaw is alone in remaining unawed in that presence.
And one thing is plain in the nineteen centuries at
which he so lightly glances, that from Jesus has been

derived the power that has saved the civilized world from the grossness of uncivilized night. Power? this primary virtue, this origin of all virtue, is entirely wanting in Mr. Shaw's picture. Were Jesus in the likeness of this discomposed composition it would not be for His religion that Mr. Shaw would now be so singularly pleading. It is not (to end all this)—it is not such a figure as Mr. Shaw erects that has renewed the hope of the world and sweetened it with light.

Nothing could be more lucid than Mr. Shaw's characterization, nothing more meagre. Is any character quite so simple and plain as Mr. Shaw's portrait of the chief character of human history? I do not think that anything has more strongly impressed me in the character of Jesus than its unfathomable mystery, and I believe that is the commonest impression. Those to whom He is the most profoundly realized personality, by reason of love and renewal through Him, are the least assured in their contemplation of Him. His sayings are dark, they appear inconsistent, or they are so plain as to be bewildering ; what He does and what He says seem different in their meaning, yet with a complete personality (to put that no higher which many cannot put too high) you know there cannot be inconsistency save in seeming. . . . I must leave whatever else should be said to worthier hands.

And although I should like to follow Mr. Shaw in his argument as to the meaning of Christ's teaching concerning man's business in the world, I do not think this necessary. If his reading of the character is at fault, it is possible that his reading of the lessons is also wrong. Yet a writer of Mr. Shaw's brains cannot easily be wrong upon inessentials (as they are in the present case) as well as upon essentials. History is even now striding forward to realize many of the things which our author thinks must be realized if the world is to be endurable. Whether the teaching of Christ leads directly to "modern communism" or to an intensive individualism, may very well be left to Mr. Shaw and Mr. G. K. Chesterton. Here, in this brief postscript, I will only add two things; that Mr. Shaw has in this characterization—written, let it be repeated, with as much sincerity as may exist with so much self-consciousness—presented his own mind more clearly than anywhere else; and that he has only himself to thank if the prefacing of his study to a farce such as *Androcles and the Lion* be resented by people who do not easily associate the sacred personality with farce.

H. G. WELLS

I

MR. WELLS may be called an improviser, and the word will be the right word if we remember that to improvise is, at best, a preliminary to creation, and at worst, a token of inventiveness. All that I have said of Mr. Shaw in the last paper indicates that he too is a swift improviser ; and the difference between Mr. Wells and Mr. Shaw is this :—that Mr. Wells is a positive influence, and Mr. Shaw a negative influence. Mr. Shaw is active,—sharp and potent as frost or nitro-glycerine is sharp and potent ; but Mr. Wells is active as an architect or bricklayer is active, influential and capricious as water.

II

For all the nervous variety of his work, it is not difficult to trace the later Mr. Wells back to his earlier writing, and read in his first experiment as a popular author a prophecy of his development. He admits, as men will thoughtfully admit the most transparent things, an intense curiosity as dominant in his char-

acter; curiosity about natural laws, about physiological facts, social phenomena and much else that
concerns men. He scarcely needed Montaigne or Sir
Thomas Browne to teach him the sweet delights of
speculation, and the luxury of confession. Curiosity
so impatient and restless is not the finest of gifts for
a man who sets himself serious work in a short lifetime, but it is at any rate an excellent spur to serious
work. I doubt if men of large capacity are ever quite
so urgent, hasty or exuberant as some of our modern
leaders. I think a certain slowness, an apparent
lethargy, a reflectiveness so profound as to be almost
slumbrous, is characteristic of the wiser spirits; and
such nimbleness as is conspicuous in Mr. Shaw, Mr.
Wells and Mr. Chesterton is a hindrance in some directions as much as a help in others.

Mr. Wells has told us in more than one place of his
early days—eager, narrow, filled with longings and
bitter with sharp suppressions. Always there has
been this eagerness, this thirst for life and experiences.
You can trace in book after book a self-portraiture so
vivid and so unconscious as to be more than a little
naïve. This is his contribution to modern types. . . .
And with the type the environment : mean, disordered, ignorant, distracting, unhealthy, and withal
intensely vital. Mr. Wells has repudiated in no gentle
phrase the common notion that " genius will out " in
despite of the fell clutch of circumstance, and calls
this (*Mankind in the Making*) a stupid superstition;

but it is one which men possessed of genius seem pretty generally to hold. Nothing but his earlier environment would have made him what he has been made, and it is doubtful (if it be not impertinent to speak of another man's development, when one's own has been so treacherously obscure) whether any other Mr. Wells would have been so interesting. All that we can say with the slightest certainty is that his adolescent circumstances, un-ideal as they were, very plainly failed to obscure or even to retard his attainment of those difficult arts, the art of seeing and the art of expressing. Curiosity served him as admirably as any gift ever served a man : curiosity led to scientific studies and to a scientific trick of mind. It led to the adoption or unconscious formulation of scientific values and standards of life.

And so, when he turned his thoughts from the lecturer's to the author's desk, his scientific acquisitions were present riches. He brought a certain freshness of view, an unworn fantasy, which only a curious man whose curiosity had already purchased experience could command. *The Wonderful Visit, The Island of Doctor Moreau*—they are both perhaps trifles, but ingenious trifles. The former has the ingenuity of irresponsible fancy, the latter the ingenuity of extravagant horror. Only a fantastically clever man could have written the one ; only a profoundly curious man could have conceived the other ; only Mr. Wells could have written both.

This diversity of interests and activities has remained and extended. Fondness for the fantastic has become a passion for romance; fondness for the scientific has been transmuted into a passion for social regeneration. The story-teller has run step by step with the theorist; vast and vague imaginings have peopled planets and darkened space with wars of annihilation; the adventuring spirit of man has been dispatched upon ways undreamed of by other novelists; and, meanwhile, impatient plans have been devised for the birth, nurture and admonition of a finer race. Mr. Wells has never allowed any strength of conviction or any loyal consistency to drive out of his work the dæmon of speculation, the good dæmon haunting all those weightier activities which commonly entitle a man to be called a " serious " writer. One advantage of this is that he can turn from fiction with a dash of speculation, to speculation with a dash of fiction—*A Modern Utopia* for example—with but slight danger of losing his large attentive audience. But let it be remembered to his credit that he has ventured, as few popular authors venture, to experiment and experiment again, darting upon fresh lines with ever-renewed energy, and with a certain fine faith that good work of any kind is *not* inevitably suicidal work. The faith has justified the courage of the experiment, but the experiment remains courageous. It is so easy to repeat " what the public wants," and apparently—though by no means certainly—so difficult to disgust the public with what it wants and gets.   So we have in Mr. Wells's list of his writings an unusual variety of subject and method.   In his own precise classification he counts " romances," sociological or socialist essays, and many novels, besides abundant short stories.   Apart from all there stands one extraordinary book, half novel half tract, *The New Machiavelli.*   It is to the production of this that his many inventions move : a book meant to include romance, essay and novel, and sum up within its covers the author's view of that enormous " complex "—England in 1911.

It is significant that there is manifest, before this interweaving of form, a singular interweaving of motive.   In *The First Men in the Moon* he follows Jules Verne's fancy, with a much wiser scientific conception, and sees in the moon a possible colony for the terrestrial destitute.   *The Time Machine* presents the Thames Valley in 8,200 A.D., a distressingly gloomy picture of the spiritual enervation of the governing classes on the one hand, and the spiritual degradation of the servile classes on the other :—a forecast, pregnant with misgivings, of a possible result of continued material improvement and slow spiritual exhaustion.   *The Sleeper Awakes* is concerned with the same obstinate questionings, the same blank misgiving about the future of an industrial world.   Even that astonishing invention, *The Invisible Man*, a perfect short story save for the accident of its length, may be interpreted not quite fancifully as a warning against scientific investigation uncontrolled by an equal development of the moral sense—a sequel, almost, to *Dr. Moreau.* And such a light and strangely overpraised novel as *Kipps* has for its burden the illustration of the local muddle and the all but vain attempt at definition and withdrawal. So with later stories. In a word, even while Mr. Wells's fancy has been most riotous, his critical attitude has been preserved alive, and he has watched the real present fermenting in the unreal future, wit an undimming eagerness.

III

Mr. Wells is too eager a craftsman not to have touched sharply the alluring problems of m dern fiction, walking still around his Jericho although the walls fell long before he came. He naturally takes liberal views of the province of the novel, and will not hear of any arbitrary circumscription of subject or reproof of method. In *An Englishman Looks at the World* he writes :

> I suppose it is conceivable that a novel might exist which was purely a story of that kind [i.e. of real things] and nothing more. It might amuse you as one is amused by looking out of a window into a street, or listening to a piece of agreeable music, and that might be the limit of its effect. But almost always the novel is something more than that and produces more effect than that. The novel has almost inseparable moral consequences. It leaves impressions, not simply of things seen, but of acts judged and made attractive or unattractive.

H. G. Wells

And again :

I stick to my thesis that the complicated social organization of to-day cannot get along without the amount of mutual understanding and mutual explanation such a range of characterization in our novels implies. The success of civilization amounts ultimately to a success of sympathy and understanding. If people cannot be brought to an interest in one another greater than they feel to-day, to curiosities and criticisms far keener, and co-operations far subtler, than we have now : if class cannot be brought to measure itself against, and interchange experience and sympathy with class, and temperament with temperament, then we shall never struggle very far beyond the confused discomforts and uneasiness of to-day, and the changes and complications of human life will remain as they are now, very like the crumplings and separations and complications of an immense avalanche that is sliding down a hill. And in this tremendous work of human reconciliation and elucidation, it seems to me it is the novel that must attempt most and achieve most.

It is a fine aim but surely not a new one, for Mr. Wells himself names the novelist, Dickens, who has already used the same freedom for the same implicit ends. The novel, he warns us, not unconvincingly, is not a new sort of pulpit ; he does not mean for a moment that the novelist is going to set up as a teacher. The novel :

Is to be the social mediator, the vehicle of understanding . . . the criticism of laws and institutions and of social dogmas and ideas. . . . We are going to write . . . about the whole of human life. We are going to deal with political questions and religious questions and social questions . . . until a thousand pretences and ten-thousand impostures shrivel in the cold clear air of our elucidations. . . . Before we have done we will have all life within the scope of the novel.

The Moderns

Has Mr. Wells quite forgotten Tolstoi and Balzac ? Is " all life within the scope of the novel " such a new aim ? As a profession of faith, as a personal avowal, it is excellent, but as a war cry it is something obsolete. The whole attitude is, at this date, unduly assertive and noisy. He calls up spirits from the vasty deep merely for the satisfaction of dismissing them again. No one, in short, wants to interfere with the novelist and what he is pleased to call his art.

But the cry remains, I said, an excellent personal avowal : and you will understand at once the vitality and movement of Mr. Wells's high gifts, if you will but observe how surely his own work has developed from *Love and Mr. Lewisham*, through *Tono-Bungay* to the large and earnest scheme of *The New Machiavelli*. *Love and Mr. Lewisham* is a good average novel with flashes of inspiration. Youth is often so charming, how cramped soever in its activity ; and the slightly auto-biographic touches of charming youthfulness in this average novel tempt one to repeat the phrase, flashes of inspiration. The author himself does not think meanly of it, and he is an excellent judge : *Love and Mr. Lewisham*, he writes at a distance of some years, "is indeed one of my most carefully balanced books." Usually his books are singularly lacking in balance. For us, at the moment, its interest lies in the fact that the characters draw the magic of their youth across the dim background of social problems—dim indeed as yet ; but indisputably, palpitantly there. Perhaps

H. G. Wells

it is there because it was there in Dickens to whom Mr.
Wells is noticeably indebted, so far as this novel at
any rate is concerned.   And here too is an instance of
the weighing of the present with the future, the parents
with the child, and the implicit assertion of the child's
vastly greater importance.   The idea recurs in book
after book, with developments and accompaniments of
which we must speak in a moment.

Love and Mr. Lewisham, and the inferior *Kipps*, are
insignificant in comparison with *Tono-Bungay*.   In
this you have the same strong autobiographic elements,
the same student-of-science atmosphere, the same
poverty and repression ; but for the first time you have
in a clear explicit rendering what has only been vague
and implicit in the other novels—the social welter and
perplexity, the incapable dignified old-fashionedness,
of the old order that has no intention of yielding place
to the new.   Mr. Wells sees his characters not simply
in themselves or in relation to each other, but in relation also to the whole social framework.   The rendering of this last subtle and variable relation is his
peculiar contribution to English fiction.   Characteristic
are such passages as this :

> The ideas of democracy, of equality, and above all of pro-
> miscuous fraternity, have certainly never really entered
> into the English mind.   But what is coming into it ?   All this
> book, I hope, will bear a little on that.   Our people never
> formulates ; it keep words for jests and ironies.

The passage occurs in a description of Bladesover—

" a little working model of the whole world." He
stations the Quality and the Common Sort in their due
order, and seems as much amused as amazed at the
spectacle. But he is too sincerely concerned with the
novelist's craft to allow the social background to
become an insistent foreground. George Pondevero
with his uncle and aunt remain individual—the two
latter, indeed, being vivid characterizations. George
himself, narrator of the story, is the familiar faintly
autobiographic hero, weaker brother to Mr. Lewisham,
with the familiar scientific dabblings, and the familiar
sex-discovering curiosity. " Romance of Commerce "
is the author's phrase for the book, as though romantic
were the same as fantastic. The social manifestations
are, if explicit, still subdued. The story indeed is a
good story, but I imagine that if one looks at it a
second time it is not for the story but just for these
social impressions—the microcosmic Bladesover and the
hundred allusions to it ; George Pondevero's adolescence ; the unfailing curiosity of the world to them
that are young or keep young. Like a live butterfly
against the impenetrable glass of a specimen case, he
beats upon the walls of his existence, teased with the
obsession of sex. " I could see," he confesses in the
midst of a betrayal, " I could see no way of honour or
fine living before me at all. ' What am I to do with
life ? ' That was the question that besieged me. . . .
' Life is a thing that hurts, my dear.' " He finds
" salvation " in the idealization of science ; more pre-

H. G. Wells

cisely, in the invention of an aeroplane supported by the money pouring from a gullible public which his quack-mongering uncle has persuaded to buy Tono-Bungay. The curious use of so definite a word as salvation is not accidental. In *First and Last Things* Mr. Wells describes, in his own person, what he means by salvation, wrenching the term, with others, from the familiar connotations. And after this experience of salvation by aeroplane (the machine founders, by the by, while he is helping his volatile uncle to escape arrest for forgery) George looks back on his life :

A story of activity and urgency and sterility. I have called it *Tono-Bungay*, but I had far better have called it *Waste* : I have told of childless Marion, of my childless aunt, [and too of his childless mistress] of Beatrice wasted and wasteful and futile. What hope is there for a people whose women become fruitless ?

The gloom of his retrospect is shed over a rapid sketch of England—" England ! This is what I wanted to give in my book "—but stained at the last by a gleam of faith and hope. The faith and hope are expressed in this personal impression, this new " note."

It is a note of crumbling and confusion, of change and seemingly aimless swelling, of a bubbling up and medley of futile loves and sorrows. But through the confusion sounds another note. Through the confusion something drives, something that is at once human achievement and the most inhuman of all existing things. Something comes out of it. . . How can I express the values of a thing at once so essential and so

63

immaterial.   It is something that calls upon such men as I
with an irresistible appeal.

I have figured it in my last section by the symbol of my
destroyer, stark and swift, irrelevant to most human interests.
Sometimes I call this reality Science, sometimes I call it
Truth.   But it is something we draw by pain and effort out
of the heart of life, that we disentangle and make clear.   Other
men serve, it I know, in art, in literature, in social invention,
and see it in a thousand different figures, under a hundred
names.   I see it always as austerity, as beauty.   This thing
we make clear is the heart of life.   It is the one enduring thing.
Men and nations, epochs and civilizations pass, each making
its contribution.   I do not know what it is, this something,
except that it is supreme.   It is a something, a quality, an
element, one may find now in colours, now in forms, now in
sounds, now in thoughts.   It emerges from life with each
year one lives and feels, and generation by generation and age
by age, but the how and the why of it are all beyond the compass of my mind.

I will say nothing for the moment of the method of
the story, but in its aim and scope, its care for ideas,
its fulness of vigour, it is an honourable book.   There
are faults of taste, things that might have been spared,
digressions that might have been pruned—suggestions
of haste, touches of shabbiness.   It remains, nevertheless, conspicuously a novel of modern life.   I make
no stupid and superfluous comparison of the genius of
Dickens with the genius of Mr. Wells, but I cannot
refrain from noting that *Tono-Bungay* is as clearly
representative of the early bubbling twentieth century,
as any book of Dickens of the early nineteenth.   Here
is a novel, in short, in which the protagonists—as yet
dim and cloudy as the Polyphemus in Turner's picture

—are not love and honour, this and that woman,
passion and ambition, but the spirit of order and disorder, the frail spirit of the future and the giant
spirit of the past.

IV

I pass now to *The New Machiavelli,* Mr. Wells's
largest novel. He punctiliously explains why he has
given it this title, writing thus in the person of Remington, the central figure of the book :

A certain Niccolo chanced to fall out of politics at very
much the same age as I have reached [our author's "locutions,"
as he would say, are sometimes more convenient than scru-
pulous], and wrote a book to engage the restlessness of his
mind, very much as I have wanted to do. . . . I claim kindred
with him and set his name upon my title-page, in partial in-
timation of the matter of my story. He takes me with sympathy not only by reason of the dream he pursued and the
humanity of his politics, but by the mixture of his nature.
His vices come in, essential to my issues. He is dead and
gone, all his immediate correlations to party and faction have
faded to insignificance, leaving only on the one hand his broad
method and conceptions, and upon the other his intimate
living personality, exposed down to its salacious corners, as
the soul of no contemporary can ever be exposed. Of those
double strands it is that I have to write, of the subtle, protest-
ing, perplexing play of instinctive passion and desire against
too abstract a dream of statesmanship.

Thinking much of Machiavelli :

He becomes a symbol for me, and none the less because of

65

his animal humour, his queer indecent side, and because of
such lapses into utter meanness. . . . These flaws complete
him. They are my reason for preferring him as a symbol to
Plato.

The preference is more than a little odd. However,
following the author of *The Prince*, " the vision of the
strengthened and perfected State is protagonist in my
story." But he cannot view the world with Machiavelli's eyes. In the first place, the French Revolution
has altered absolutely the approach to such a question.
That is to say, the republican idea has usurped the
place of the monarchical. In the second place, says
Remington, we are discovering women.

It is this gradual discovery of sex as a thing collectively
portentous that I have to mingle with my statecraft if my
picture is to be true, which has turned me at length from a
treatise to the telling of my own story. In my life I have
paralleled very closely the slow realizations that are going on
in the world about me. I began life ignoring women : they
came to me at first perplexing and dishonouring : only very
slowly and very late in my life, and after misadventure, did I
gauge the power and beauty of the love of man and woman,
and learnt how it must needs frame a justifiable vision of the
ordered world. That last love of mine brought me to disaster,
because my career had been planned regardless of its possibility and value.

The ambitiousness of the scheme of the book is un-
deniable, and it may as well be plainly said that the
scaffolding is vaster by far than the building. And,
too, I cannot help questioning this use of Machiavelli's
name. The mantle of the Florentine surely extin-

guishes the ex-Fabian : and my misgiving became triumphant when I found that the acute appreciation of the book by Mr. J. L. Garvin in *The Observer* bore for heading *The New Rousseau*. No juster criticism has been passed on it. The nervous instability of Remington himself, the feverishness, the avidity for experiences rather than for experience, the stumbling enthusiasms, the furtive treacheries, the moral shabbiness (the word must be repeated)—all are indicated by this subtle change of title. . . . Once again Mr. Wells resorts to the suburbs of London, to science schools, to the old autobiographic touches, and never were they so deftly used. The whole book, be it said, throbs with the agitations of that part of life which chiefly engrosses Mr. Wells's reflections—adolescence. There is the period of sex-adolescence and the period of intellectual adolescence : the two periods are not wholly concurrent, and it is difficult to say which is the more changeful or the more acutely important in this account of Remington's development. Of his earlier years, when he was in his mother's hands, he writes :

I suppose I am a deeply religious man, as men of my quality go, but I hate more and more as I grow older the dark shadow of intolerance cast by religious organizations. All my life has been darkened by irrational intolerance, by arbitrary, irrational prohibitions and exclusions.

The claim to be a deeply religious man is a little

67

curious, and I think it can only be sustained by giving the term a laxer and wider significance than it is usually permitted to carry. I have noticed that many people of sceptical or agnostic tendencies have demurred at being deemed irreligious. I cannot understand why men—I mean intelligent men of decent life—should assiduously disclaim religious belief and repudiate all religious doctrines and sanctions, and yet be hurt if the term religious be denied them. Says Joubert, " Religion is neither a theology nor a theosophy ; it is more than all this : it is a discipline, a law, a yoke, an indissoluble engagement." Hard words, these. Perhaps it is that, as yet, an extra respectability, a social guarantee, still clings to the profession of faith, as a householder is supposed to be more respectable than a lodger. But this, I imagine, does not trouble Mr. Wells, who nevertheless here, as in the whole of *First and Last Things*, makes claims which ordinary people will think merely arbitrary and unsustainable.

" The broadening of human thought," says Remington, " is a slow and complex process. We do go on, we do get on. But when one thinks people are living and dying now, quarrelling and sulking, misled and misunderstanding, vaguely fearful, condemning, and thwarting one another in the close darkness of these narrow cults—O God, one wants a gale out of heaven, one wants a great wind from the sea."

Prohibitions and exclusions serve also to render " the secrecies of sex " dangerous as well as secret. " That strange combination of fanatical terrorism and

H. G. Wells

shyness that fenced me about with prohibitions . . .
caused me to grow up, I will not say blankly ignorant,
but with an ignorance blurred and dishonoured by
shame." It is important to note this and similar
remarks, since they point to the rocks in the sea where
Remington's " career " went down irrecoverably. I
will do no more than indicate briefly the precipitation
of that catastrophe. Remington's constant desire, as
a young man with an enlarging political reputation,
was :

> To leave England and the empire better than I found it,
> to organize and discipline, to build up a constructive and
> controlling State out of my world's confusions. We had, I
> saw, to suffuse education with public intention, to develop a
> new, better-living generation with a collectivist habit of
> thought, to link now chaotic activities, etc. etc.

The identity of Remington's aim with the aim expressed in those many books in which Mr. Wells speaks
avowedly for himself, will not escape the reader. In
his acquaintance with " the Baileys "—a mordant,
merciless, murderous caricature—Remington finds the
direction of his political energies ; is welcomed, en-
couraged, admired, married, followed. . . . I pause
on these words to remark that in spite of the infinite
labour of his creator, Remington remains, politically
at least, a passive figure, and only in his passions something like a man. His subjection to " the Baileys,"
however, is not complete or lasting, because he is
aware of a " profound antagonism of spirit " :

69

> With me, beauty is quite primary in life. I like truth, order and goodness, wholly because they are beautiful or lead straight to beautiful consequences. The Baileys either hadn't got that, or didn't see it.

The curious thing is that although Mr. Wells here and often elsewhere is so keenly insistent upon the thirst and necessity for beauty, no writer of his own rank—a high rank—conveys so slight an impression of beauty. Always is he crying out the beauty of order, of truth, of perfect adjustments : seldom does he catch a gleam of it. He repeats, you come to think, what he has heard, and proclaims that which he has never seen. . . . You might forget how little of beauty he captures, were it not for his frequent clamour for beauty. It is the advertisement that makes so plain and unmistakable the loss.

Remington's ship founders on the sexual rock. He is quite frank in recounting the story of his illicit loves, and explicit in enumerating them. Of the merely squalid casual lapse he writes :

> How ugly it is to recall : ugly and shameful now without qualification. Yet at the time there was something not altogether ugly in it, something that has vanished, some fine thing mortally ailing.

One simply notes, and passes on. Modern literature, says the author of *The Wheels of Chance*, is indecorous revelation : and surely decorum, one might add, a mere Slawkenbergian frump. Remington loves his

wife without being in harmony with her. His mind
is " kinetic " (to use Mr. Wells's favourite word), hers
static. But he loves Isabel too, and *is* in harmony
with her : and so, after secrecies exposed and remon-
strances defied—flight with Isabel and the end of his
public career !

The question raised is the question of Mr. Granville
Barker's *Waste* : whether private delinquencies, how
gross soever, should make social service impossible.
Remington chooses to find himself and lose the world
and Margaret ; and you are left with no doubt as to
the author's private judgment upon the world which
insists on this waste.

Is it wonderful that to us fretting here in exile this ostracism
should seem the cruellest as well as the most foolish waste of
necessary social elements ?

Remington chooses, and since his choice involves
the ruin of his political future, he conceives of himself
as the new Machiavelli, while we are at liberty to call
him the new Rousseau.

In tragic life, God wot,
No villain need be : passions spin the plot,
We are betrayed by what is false within.

The campaign of order against disorder is aban-
doned ; the projected Endowment of Motherhood goes
on the wind away ; that novel shibboleth, " Love and
Fine Thinking," dies into silence ; and the young
toryism of his latest affection is rent clean from his

The Moderns

consciousness in the sudden gust of passion, as was
Antony's resolution at Actium. . . . They are acting
badly, Remington owns, but feels nevertheless that
they are acting inevitably, and would so act again
given a new choice. Remington, in short, burns his
boats and then " unpacks his heart of words " because
he can't swim. It is not unbelievable that a man
should barter his political career for a triumphant
passion, or that he should rail at the world because
there is no way of securing the triumph of passion
save at the expense of his career ; but it is almost
incredible that a man of Remington's intelligence
should deliberately choose the thing he felt most burningly necessary, yet still shoot malediction at the world
for giving him the choice.

V

Let us now turn for a moment to the method used
by Mr. Wells in *Tono-Bungay* and *The New Machiavelli*. The novel, for him, is, as we have seen, a serious
—almost a horribly serious thing. He has written
short and long stories of various kinds and merits :
short stories that are but reported incidents, long
stories that are hardly more than overgrown short
stories. And he has written several books in a more
" serious " form, speculations and prophecies of the
social movement. To these we must turn anon : here

H. G. Wells

I only wish to say that *The New Machiavelli* marks the fusion of the two activities—the novelist's and the essayist's. It is true that it does not represent his only experiment in form, since *A Modern Utopia* is an attempt at finding a *via media*, avoiding the formalism of the essay and the exigencies of the novel. *A Modern Utopia* is, however, only a very poor story strangled by a dozen essays. You remember that it should be a story, and perceive that it is not. But no such haunting disabilities are to be found in *The New Machiavelli*. There are arid pages, indeed, pages heavy with political discussion ; sometimes the bones of the tract break through the skin of fiction. To change the metaphor, the author sweeps with a very new broom, and finds all manner of interesting things. He discusses, discusses perpetually—the classics as a subject for school study, the universities and their imperviousness to ideas, officialism, conservatism, party leaders, newspapers ; but the book for all that remains a vital story of warring desires. What, chiefly, makes its method remarkable is the sense of volubility which it conveys. It is as far as it can well be from the meticulous discursiveness of Sterne, whom Mr. Wells so justly and so vainly admires. The book is one enormous, insistent explanation. Certain events happen, certain passions wake and burn, certain circumstances form themselves crystal-wise ; and events, passions and circumstances, their interaction, development and consequences, are untiringly explained. Nothing is

73

thought lucid which is not explicit. You are conscious of the author's intense desire to make motive and action and circumstances clear and plain ; he protests and protests that this or that discursion is necessary, and that do what he will he cannot make things as clear as he would like to make them. There is an incessant surface busyness, a kind of minute topographical survey ; and the very restlessness of the survey often prevents your seeing that at most it is but a scratching of the surface. Mr. Wells, in fact— I hope this does not sound too harsh—appears to have fallen into a habit of thinking in words. Sentence seems to rise from sentence, explanation from explanation, rather than from any immediate thought. It is the snare of facility, how admirable and enviable soever such facility may appear. You think that your author has been at no pains to sift and select ; that of possible paths he has chosen all ; that the very rapidity of his phrase points to impulse without reflectiveness. Of the unwisdom of this there can be no question. The mind of the reader has its own unconscious economy, and simply and quietly discards what the author too hastily thrusts upon it.

Since *The New Machiavelli* Mr. Wells has written— how many books ? Panting Time toils after him in vain, and the most eager critic limps a little. All I can do is to give brief bird-like glances and pecks at the later novels that surge so tempestuously around that central work : *Ann Veronica, Marriage, The Pas-*

*sionate Friend, The Wife of Sir Isaac Harman, The
Research Magnificent*—I lose count of these repetitional,
voluble things, these large and so easy improvisations.
Only physical difficulties, one suspects, have prevented their multiplication. Art has very effectually
concealed itself in this sketchy shower. Not one of
these books lacks interest, or retains it beyond the last
page ; but meagre and familiar beneath the swift
colours you detect, if you look narrowly for a brief
moment, the *formula*. There is usually the brilliant,
perverse youth, the youthful infatuation, the following
youthful preoccupation with sex, the youthful scarce-
subordinate concern with social reform, " Empire "
and the rest ; usually the domestic tangle and the
crippling of social value ; usually the abrupt tragical
conclusion before youth's errancies are exhausted.
The concern with social reform may be limited in
direction—as in *The Wife of Sir Isaac Harman*, confined to " doing something " for waitresses ; or as in
Marriage, to passionate scientific research ; or as in
The Passionate Friend, it may gesticulate over all
human affairs. In either case, it flourishes very
pleasantly through the book, making it less fatiguing
than the purely sex novel, of which *Ann Veronica*
remains a too tedious example. *Ann Veronica* is a
sketch of mere eroticism, justifying a defiance of current moral standards, yet evading rather meanly the
logic of that defiance (if one understands rightly) by
the marriage of Ann and her lover. But these other

books show their author more agreeably. *The Research Magnificent* shows him amiably " ethicising," sweeping whole continents with his glass and whole people into a formula. " Life," he remarks, " nowadays consists of adventures among generalizations " ; and he does not anywhere suggest a criticism of *that* generalization. Neatly he sums up Amanda Benham as " an animated discursiveness," providing a phrase which conveniently leaps to one's fingers in surveying all these books. It is Benham himself who presses the Research Magnificent into the uttermost parts of the earth, and in the end discovers that man

> Takes conclusions ready made, or he makes them in a hurry. . . . The last devotion of which he is capable is that devotion of the mind which suffers partial performance, but insists upon exhaustive thought. He scamps his thought and finishes his performance.

Passages such as these, and Mr. Wells is acute and lavish enough to cast them freely, make my task easy. There is nothing even faintly unfamiliar in the views so copiously illustrated, although it must be said at once that it is largely through Mr. Wells that we have been made familiar with them :—as, let us say, the view of a " new aristocracy," formed of self-appointed aristocrats, coming to the rescue of blind civilization. In a word these books repeat, with how engaging and unapologetic a naïveté, the theme, the thoughts, the predicament, of *The New Machiavelli* ; and why in the world should not Mr. Wells (an admirer may well cry) go on repeating until the British Museum bursts ? What else is a writer to do, so intensely aware of his own personality, so frankly interested in himself, so candidly and honourably important to himself, so changeable and so remarkable to himself—what else should he do but expound and expound the one inexhaustible, entrancing theme ?

VI

To turn to those books of Mr. Wells's which I have not yet mentioned, *Anticipations, New Worlds for Old,* etc., is to be faced with perplexity. They, like the later novels, present him as a social theorist, reformer, prophet, as a man intensely concerned with the amelioration of the world. He is not an entirely new type of reformer, but he is a very modern and remarkable type. I wish it were easier to indicate his ideas and his advocacy of them ; and I can only fall back upon the clumsiest and crudest paraphrases. I am constrained to ask pardon of Mr. Wells even before asking the reader's. He is, as we have seen, consumed with a sense of the madness and disorder and perversity of the world. Not his the cry :

> Oh, it is nothing that a day is fair,
> If life cannot be sweet !
> If souls cannot be lovers and if care
> School not desire's feet !—

But certainly his the next stanza :

> —If always generations generations breed,
> And race gives place to race
> Sapped by inadequacy, doomed to bleed
> And, dying, pine for grace !

Faith in the future of the race, he perceives, too often covers the present lethargy of the race. He will leave nothing to chance : he would rather a little good made secure than a great good perchance. For sentiment, for pity in particular, he has small room. It is true that " Love and Fine Thinking " is the war-cry of *The New Machiavelli*, but of what he really means by it you do not gather the faintest hint. It is odd that, carefully emptied of sentiment as his social books are, he should in the best of them make use of the vaguest of sentimental appeals. But usually sentiment is shunned. Efficiency, economy, as expressions of the finest social order, are his aims.

Anticipations is a tentative survey of the present, and a forecast of the human community as he pictures it at about the end of this century. He observes that local and national administration is still based upon the conditions that prevailed before steam had simplified the problem of locomotion. To local and national administration, therefore, he devotes sharp criticism and indicates the sort of reorganization which the transforming twentieth century renders imperative. He judges that the habit of collective action will grow, and national distinctions lessen, while a language contest will increase ; and he appears to anticipate an extending liberty of thought by the side of a severer restriction of action. In a word, he moves towards the definite socialism of his later writing. In the looser sense of democracy he is anti-democratic. He does not anticipate that elected government of the modern sort will have any far-reaching designs, and suggests the jury system as a " trial " of parliamentary candidates. He will not admit that democratic government can fitly be responsible for public education. The final development of the domocratic system, he says, will be not the rule of the boss, trust, or newspaper, but simply the dictation of international rivalry. . . . Not very clear, you say, except in the distrust of democracy. Towards the end of the book he writes of a process at work :

> Whereby the great swollen, etc., mass of to-day must give birth at last to a naturally and informally organized class, an unprecedented sort of people, a New Republic dominating the world.

·That New Republic is to recur as the central theme of later books. He believes it will appear as a movement with distinct social and political aims, ignoring most of the existing political apparatus, or using it only incidentally. How the men of the New Republic—a sort of voluntary aristocracy—are to secure control of a nation while ignoring its administrative machinery, I confess I do not see.

The Moderns

From *Anticipations* to *Mankind in the Making* was a natural step. How are men made now, how shall we make the men of the New Republic—the subjects as well as the rulers ? Closely practical as *Mankind in the Making* is, it is less amusing but far more valuable than its predecessor. Restrictions and prohibitions are multiplied, and he suggests a severer scientific method of dealing with questions of birth and education. Compared with *Anticipations*, *Mankind in the Making* has an immense advantage in its superior definiteness. In the latter book, Mr. Wells judges collective human institutions solely according to their influence in securing wholesome, hopeful births, and their further influence towards a higher standard of life. The higher standard, of course, is the life of the New Republic—not in its perhaps remote predominance, but even in the tentativeness of its voluntary beginnings. He sets himself to answer the question, What will the New Republic do ?

At once a certain sanity, a welcome unextravagance of idea, becomes apparent. Eugenics, he says in effect, in a chapter on " The Problem of the Birth Supply," is all very well, but what favoured types are to be aimed at ? Here, obviously, is the prime and the ultimate difficulty. The breeder of cattle has a very simple ideal : " He breeds for beef, he breeds for calves and milk . . . towards that ideal he goes simply and directly." But the analogy breaks down if you apply the aims of the breeder of cattle to the breeder of men.

What, precisely, is to be aimed at ?   It is no longer a question of mere physical fitness, of strength alone, of beauty alone, of brains alone, of energy alone.   The physically sound may be mentally degenerate, the beautifully formed vicious, the resourceful type criminal, the energetic inhuman.   Much nonsense is talked about the fit and the unfit, culture and elimination ; and it is lucky that such a writer as Mr. Wells should point out that " our utmost practice here must be empirical."   That this is a reason for doing nothing and caring nothing is far from Mr. Wells's thought ; there is, if nothing else, clear and patient observation of types and influences.   But he is wise in tempering with a little honest doubt the enthusiasms of those who are apt to regard " good breeding " as a short way to a better race.   It may be a short way, only we must first try to discover what good breeding is.

When he passes from this problem to that of securing the best chance for every child born, he is on less contentious and perhaps less perplexing ground.   Here there is more room for immediate hope and confidence ; and though he does not deny himself the luxury of rather gloomy plans and summaries, he nevertheless recognizes something distinctly *better* in this generation's view of its opportunities and responsibilities, in comparison with the view of the last generation.   It is in dealing with questions of education that his writing grows sharp to acerbity, and his occasional impatience petulant.   I have already mentioned his preoccupation with adolescence :—here he pleads for more freedom, privacy and elasticity of study, as well as for a severer concentration. The pressing business of the school, he asserts, is to widen the range of inter-course ; and he anticipates the probable charge of vagueness by framing a course of education almost wholly literary, and sufficiently ambitious to make one desire it with an exceeding great desire. For he insists upon the teaching of English language, and the under-standing of English literature, in a more than perfunc-tory fashion. Of the liberation of ideas, the increased responsiveness and mobility of thought which such a training would purchase, there is small need to speak.

Upon another vital and ever-recurrent educational question, the illumination of the adolescent upon sexual matters, Mr. Wells speaks sensibly. I am frankly glad that while much that he has himself written upon sexual subjects seems to me detestable, his injunctions upon this delicate aspect of education are considerate and prudent. He perceives that it is almost an instinct of natural modesty to hide the fer-menting young apprehensions ; and that this instinct leads, not unnaturally or seldom, to furtiveness. He enrols himself on the side of the Puritans in the sup-pression of the public, provocative vulgarities with which the streets and hoardings are drenched ; yet at the same time he doubts if there is anything he would not regard as fit to publish . . . What then ?—He advises the fixing of a high minimum price for " adult " books. This, clearly, would simply mean that well-to-do young persons would find accessible what was inaccessible to the poorer; but even this inadequate precaution is not to be quite despised. And I mention this detail of the scheme for a new way of life not so much to point out its inadequacy, as the sincerity of Mr. Wells's attitude.

Assuming, then, the healthy desirable birth and the healthy liberal education—an education as liberal, in its measure, for the poor as for the rich—upon what lines will social regeneration proceed? Sane also in this, Mr. Wells avows the necessity of working through existing political forms and existing social formulæ, and making *them* the finest expression of what the New Republicans believe and hope. (He forsakes, it will be noted, his earlier position of "ignoring" the existing political apparatus.) To say that he does not look for revolution by violence but for revolution by stealth, is but to say that he is practical and far-seeing. His most impossibly revolutionary idea is the substitution of "election by Jury" for the present electoral system, to which allusion has already been made. Some years have passed since this suggestion was put forward, and it will be superfluous to say now that it is not because of its defects that it has been quietly ignored. Mr. Wells can hardly have expected that it would not be ignored, since to press such a proposal at the beginning of the twentieth century, and before the New Republicans are here, is very much like erecting a complete scaffolding before the building contract has been signed.

Nevertheless, he is here buoyantly hopeful. " At a thousand points," he writes in a disarming flash of confidence, " the New Republic already starts into being." I do not know that its " being " is less indeterminate now, than when he gave it his apostolic blessing a few years ago ; but I do not like to think of such a fine and sharp-edged enthusiasm failing of its due influence. Dubious as many statements in it may seem, baseless some of its hopes, unlikely some of its forecasts, *Mankind in the Making* is yet valuable for its practical spirit. " It is to youth that this book is finally addressed, to the adolescent, to the students . . . to those who being still plastic can understand the infinite plasticity of the world." He ends with an emphatic charge :

For the New Republican, as for his forerunner the Puritan, conscience and discipline must saturate life. He must be ruled by duties and a certain ritual in life. Every day and every week he must set aside time to read and to think, to commune with others and himself ; he must be as jealous of his health and strength as the Levites of old. Can we in this generation make but a few thousands of such men and women, men and women who are not afraid to live, men and women with a common faith and a common understanding, then, indeed, our work will be done.

I have dealt thus with the book because only in his distinction of detail is it possible to understand at all clearly what Mr. Wells really means and for what, effectively, he really counts. In a later essay, *New Worlds for Old*, he resumes the close consideration of his problem of establishing and developing the New Republic. I repeat that phrase for the reason that he understands by it something precise and distinctive. I am not sure that such a conception is not a pure necessity of his mind. He admits a love for putting things concretely and is indeed over-prone to conjure up visions of all-embracing institutionalism. *New Worlds for Old* is an explicit and confessed advocacy of socialism in a more definite form than previously foreshadowed. The author's passion for order, for economy, for collective thought and action, impels him to the candid assertion of his persuasion. He does not formulate any generally acceptable creed, and is at no pains to reconcile discrepant sections. He reiterates that socialism, as he views it, is a moral and intellectual process, and asserts that the whole purpose of the book is

> To insist upon *the mental quality of Socialism*, to maintain that it is a business of conventions about property and plans of reorganization, that is to say, of changes and expansions of the ideas of men . . . of their spirit of action and their habitual circles of ideas. Unless you can change men's minds you cannot effect Socialism.

Elsewhere he defines it as being ultimately a moral and intellectual synthesis of mankind (vagueness again, you note) ; and, as a primary necessity, " we must

ensure the continuity of the collective mind." Near
the end of the book he indicates its several lines of
advance as,

> *Firstly :* " The primary intellectual process, the elaboration,
> criticism, discussion, enrichment, and enlargement of the pro-
> ject of Socialism." In this he includes all science and litera-
> ture.
> *Secondly :* by propaganda—the publication of ideas, the
> irrigation of mankind by the new spirit of education.
> *And Thirdly :* by the actual changing of things in the direc-
> tion of the coming Socialistic State.

The book, in fact, is partly a challenge and partly a
defence of Socialism as understood by Mr. Wells's liberal
mind. To secure its triumph he calls upon a certain
quality which he terms Good Will ; he wants to saturate that Good Will with the ideas of liberal socialism.
He judges that the slow visible social revolution will
follow the slow visible revolution of ideas ; his own
mind is pregnant with ideas, and the delivery seems
sometimes premature. He regards the inevitable
revolution of ideas as inevitably socialistic. His socialism, indeed, is so wide and inclusive as to be either a
little vague or a little too comprehensive. He identi-
fies, for example, socialism with science ; " Secrecy,
subterfuge, and private gain : these are the enemies of
socialism and the adversaries of science." In his own
phrase, " socialism is a corner in ideas."

Is there not a certain exorbitancy in all this ? Mr.
Wells has only to claim whatever broadening of the

legislative spirit is apparent to-day as the fruits of
socialism, in order to prove the advance of socialism.
Yet it is probable that such books as Mr. Wells's play
no mean part in that leavening of ideas which makes
the current legislative activity possible. He is far
from being the prime spirit in the movement, but he is
a conspicuous one. He has but taken up the task and
followed the call, upon far different lines, which Ruskin
heard and took up. There is, I think, no acknowledg-
ment in Mr. Wells's social inventions of the work of his
predecessors ; he has made everything out of his own
capacious head. Yet it might be remembered, not
with a thought of diminishing his position, that if his
books are influential it is because others have laboured
and he has entered into their labours. He makes no
appeal to the inward, powerful and stupefied conscience of men, but it is this that Tolstoi and Ruskin
(nor they alone) have stirred. All Ruskin's despairing
passion for beauty, even Tolstoi's creative, Shakespearian splendour, sink into lesser importance in comparison with the moral and spiritual awakening which
they independently attempted. Did they not give a
conscience to Europe ? Few men have preached such
impossible things ; few men have inspired such noble
things.

Far different in conception, far humbler in idea, is
Mr. Wells. His is the scientist's mind, the scientific
conception of social order, the scientific detestation of
social disorder. He is concerned to redress the social

evils of the times, not because they are morally shameful but because they are economically shameful. Waste, for him, is worse than sin :—rather, the only sin is waste. All his pleas are a little low-spirited ; you remark the lack of generosity, the airless burrowings of his agile mind. He gives but what he has to give, and does not pretend that it is more ; it is for us to remember that there is an infinite more which Mr. Wells if he live to a hundred will never be able to give. And it is for us to remember too that he not only cannot give this larger, nimbler more, but seems never to betray a misgiving that there is a spiritual continent beyond the material shores of his neat island. Even the definiteness of his material conception of a New Republic has its antecedent in Ruskin, as his romantic fantasies of the future have their antecedents in William Morris and many another. You will find in *Fors Clavigera* whole passages which, but for the accident of their nobler prose, might have come from *A Modern Utopia*. Ruskin established his St. George's Company much as Mr. Wells has sought to establish his New Republic. Ruskin's was that idea of collective effort, of co-operation and subordination, of conscious common intelligence and purpose ; Ruskin's the conception of a voluntary aristocracy committed to the redemption and service of the unheeding world. The points of difference are as obvious and striking as the points of likeness. Ruskin's Company was to bear for distinction a natural humility of spirit,

H. G. Wells

to avoid the grossness of competition, to be subject to a personal Master, to be as a city set on a hill, and to observe precepts which, to be candid, are sometimes trivial and fussy. For none of these things will the New Republican care, and most of them he would regard —not without reason—as medieval and obscurantist.

When that New Republican is safely born and wisely educated, he will take part in a new world, a world which his creator has laboriously surveyed in *A Modern Utopia*. That book is as it were a map of the future, when Mr. Wells's ideas shall have fermented in men's consciousness. Incautiously he speaks of Theleme, and tempts you to remark that the inscription over the portal of the New Utopia will be, Do what you are told. He calls the book a mere story of personal adventures among Utopian philosophies ; but it is a very serious story of very purposeful adventures. There is little need to follow closely its scheme, for it shows only the expansion or crystallization of ideas already discovered in its predecessors. It presents those ideas concretely, without adding to them. The voluntary aristocracy of the New Republic becomes here the Samurai, with a code of curiously ascetic austerities. Another point to which it recurs is Mr. Wells's favourite scheme, the Endowment of Motherhood. The Modern Utopians will, it need scarcely be said, regard maternity as the most solemn function in the new economy— a function for which many are called but few chosen. As Mr. Wells's most ambitious sketch of this kind, it is a singularly dull book, and for the main part has little more than the childish interest of a box of bricks, which in various combinations show various pleasing pictures. Mr. Wells has shaken his theories together, and this brightly coloured, confused, ill-jointed picture is the result. . . . To change the metaphor, you are at times aware of the author's ideas as being unduly stretched to the measure of the Utopian scheme, and showing in consequence a little thin. " Unless," he avers, " you can change men's minds you cannot effect Socialism." Well, and if you change men's minds, if you even achieve the harder ask of re-sensitizing their consciences, is this New Utopia quite inevitable ? But Socialism, to repeat him again, is a corner in ideas ; and what could one say if Mr. Wells stepped impetuously forward at the millennium, and planted the Red Flag in the capital of the world by right of conquest ? Truly the Socialistic position, if Mr. Wells's elucidation is to be received, is but that of the old genial trickster, " Heads I win, tails you lose." It is only fair, nevertheless, to add that he has not remained quite stockishly constant to formal socialist movements. Equally imperative and easy has he found it to criticize with marked detachment what may be called the official socialist position, pointing out not simply its difficulties as he now apprehends them, but also the failure, as he apprehends that too, of the official socialist to realize them. The " pleasure " of all this, as we say jocularly of many pretty conflicts, is ours.

VII

Turn again to the most important of Mr. Wells's ideas—the most important, I mean, in their immediate intention and influence. What has here been said of his constructive work is, however inadequate, at least sufficient to show him as an earnest, ingenious man with the passion of a Futurist. He is as solicitous for to-morrow as Christian was for the Eternal Day. He builds great bases for futurity. Really, there is little of the fantastic in his more considered schemes. His plans for the coming generations are not, like so many others,

> Begotten by despair
> Upon impossibility,—

but the expression of an only half-reflecting hopefulness.

What of the relations of men and women to each other in the New Republic ? What relations does he regard with approval now ? He has the reputation of an " advanced " thinker, which is usually taken to imply the devastation of ordinary standards and common conduct. In these matters the revolution of ideas is supposed complete enough to shape itself as revolution of conduct ; but the revolution of conduct, he unfailingly insists, must have primary regard to the welfare of the child. " Because we criticise the old limitations, that does not bind us to the creed of unfettered liberty." In the New Republic marriage will be just such a matter of legal contract, with all manner of official investigation and registration, as the transfer of land in our present day. But that is, of course, merely the machinery of marriage. Mr. Wells surprisingly admits the marriage question to be complicated and difficult even in Utopia, remaining indeterminate between the proprietary and the companionship alternatives. Upon some points, however, he speaks definitely. One inviolable condition will be the chastity of the wife ; but he does not insist upon a reciprocal condition on the part of the husband, since that is not necessary to prevent inferior births. For economic reasons he prefers marriage of long to marriage of short duration : the family influence at its best is too valuable to lose. But beyond indicating such a preference he will not speak for the future, contemplating a wide range of companionship within and without the marriage code, according to individual choice. Since the modern Utopia is to be, before all things, synthetic and not special or exclusive, latitude and simplification will be inevitable. Mr. Wells seems not to fear that it will take more than a few decades of moral education to teach effectively the distinction of liberty from licence.

It will be seen that for once he shrinks from prophesying. I wonder a little if there has not been some timid conscious retrocession from the position held in *Anticipations*. There he conceived humorously that a man would have children because of his " scientific basis," which would teach him that the whole of life is a struggle to survive. That is merely instinct made conscious, though Mr. Wells appears not to notice this obvious fact. The same book contains his opinion that the newer culture will result in compromise in the question of private morals. But, he goes on :

> " This impending dissolution of the common standard of morals does not mean universal depravity. . . . It means that for one morality there will be many moralities."

The extension of such a rigid word as morality, until it includes its own contradictions, is typically Wellsean. There may easily be more than one morality, but an infinite number of moralities means none at all, since the mere term implies conformity. But a casual solecism is nothing to those who shrink not from social innovation, or, if you please, social renovation. *First and Last Things*, a later and more personal book, takes up the same idea of latitude. Its author is convinced that much greater facilities for divorce are necessary [1] —on the ground, e.g., of mutual consent; and finds **it** impossible to condemn those who already anticipate for their own reasons the recognition of that latitude. Condemnation from the creator of *Ann Veronica* would indeed come a little oddly. More oddly still from the author of *The New Machiavelli*, seeing how hot is

---

[1] In *An Englishman Looks at the World* (1914) he thinks that besides a wife being divorced from her husband, children might, on due grounds, be divorced from their parents.

the protest against the ostracism and political waste of Remington and Isabel. Like Mr. Shaw, he discovers women who want maternity without the intolerable concession of conjugal rights ; and such women have a right to exist in their own way. Well, they have it already ; what they have not, as yet, is the world's applause, and that, presumably, is the object of Mr. Wells's advocacy. . . . These things are avowed in his later period of definite socialism, but he is careful to remark (*New Worlds for Old*) that in such matters socialism does not decide. The disclaimer is airily made, but not so airily admissible. This is to be the result of the lifting of social problems to higher planes, the achievement of the collective wisdom of mankind. Amid the gradual and general increase of social tension, amid the subtly growing rigidity of social responsibilities, this the most significant of social contracts, the most profound of social intimacies, is to be left to individual innovation. What religious impositions may be endured by the people will not be forbidden ; but in any case the religious sanctions will have a merely secondary and decorative value. So long as healthy children are born—do what you will ; only remember that family life at its best is an excellent nursery.

There remains the yet more intimate and variable relation, the religious relation of the New Republican. It is one which Mr. Wells regards as at most of secondary importance, as indeed he needs must seeing that the

94

basis of his projected state is exclusively material.
One gathers that he assigns as small an importance
to religion for its own sake as to morality for its own
sake. He admits, however, a certain utilitarian value
in any religion, in any creed securely held ; and, one
may fairly conclude, in any quasi-religious vagaries, so
long as they are not flagrantly anti-social. Religion
will have (to repeat the phrase) a decorative value, as
Burne-Jones's semi-religious pictures have ; but it
will, beyond this, possess the value of a sound political
asset, as in the political activity of nonconformity.
" The New Republicans will have no positive definition
of God at all "—who has ?—" they will content themselves with denying the self-contradictory absurdities
of an obstinately anthropomorphic theology." Cum-
brous words : and they are followed with this farther
repudiation :—

> The same spacious faith that will render the idea of airing
> their egotisms in God's presence through prayer, or of any such
> quite personal intimacy, absurd, will render the idea of an
> invisible and punitive Deity ridiculous and incredible.

The faith that leads to this fatuous misapprehension
may be spacious but can hardly be deemed intelligent.
And the ignorance, be it observed, is not ignorance of
divinity, but of mere common aspiring infinite humanity. Airless burrowings indeed are Mr. Wells's thoughts
on religion. His view of it is so entirely external, so
wonderfully unilluminated, that one reads his words

with only less amusement than regret :—the disclosure, you think, is so gratuitous ! . . . Yet he cannot keep from prying into these " close corners of the brain," and as though aware of the externality of his view, must perforce erect his own untroubled temple of faith. He needs a whole book, *First and Last Things*, for the discovery of his personal relation to God, and all that I can clearly resolve from its vagueness is a gentle sentiment of reverence (on silent starry nights), a diffused sentiment of worship, a faith in the material and moral development of mankind, and a determination to work out his own salvation with neither fear nor trembling. . . . I am minded to recall the irony of these words, since the spiritual bewilderment of a man of high talent is sorrowful enough. And I will say no more save that, if *First and Last Things*—Mr. Wells's personal *Apologia*, *Imitation* and *Grace Abounding* in one volume—gave him any satisfaction in writing, it yields conspicuously little to us in reading. I am afraid the simple fact is, that the spiritual experience behind this book is thin and vague, the background arid and flat. There is a lack of spiritual impulse. Turn from his lucid brisk pages to the more perplexed *Holy War* of Bunyan, or *Grace Abounding*. The difference is in the quality of personality, in the human experience of each book. Mr. Wells is concerned to tell you of what he thinks, but has little to tell you of what he feels. He is busy with institutions (the Catholic Church, for instance), and perceives how valuable the spirit informing them may be to the State he dreams of. Only, looking externally, he regards that spirit as so much dead fuel.

VIII

One is a little uneasy with Mr. Wells's prophecies, of things remote as of things near, since the present war has afforded unexpected opportunities of testing his prescience. The satisfaction of the prophet who prophesies truly is only surpassed by the malicious satisfaction with which he is reminded of his failures. A paper dated 1911 in *An Englishman Looks at the World* is burdened with our author's dismallest apprehensions. He does not believe in our great lumping Dreadnoughts—vulnerable above, below and around— and would fain tuck them away and employ their crews on smaller weapons. He acutely foresees the elusiveness of the German fleet, but somewhat less acutely anticipates German submarines and things driving our battleships into secret shelter—on the west coast of Ireland, of all kindly places ! What is really wrong is the " complete arrest of the British imagination in naval and military matters." Is not this a little ungrateful from Mr. Wells, who has done his far from insignificant best to concentrate the national mind upon *domestic* concerns of the more prosaic order ? The British imagination, if it fail at all, might well fail from exhaustion in its attempts to visualize the many Utopias thrust before it by transcendental enthusiasts. So lately, again, as 1914, Mr. Wells, discussing *Will the Empire Live ?* in the same book, has " very grave doubts " concerning " the possibility of a unified organization of the Empire for military defence " ; and seems to find no solid ground upon which the colonies might stand with us and share our exasperation. . . . History has seldom been more prompt with her answer. He holds it " too usual " to regard Germany as the common enemy, and discovers in her an energy and humility— to clamber above us in the scale of civilization. For science, philosophy, good plays and an understanding of " the contemporary European mind," you are to study German ; for the English, art and thought and literature and the rest are nothing. Mr. Wells, you detect, has a tendency to scold. Yet in another essay of 1914 he sees Germany :

In the likeness of a boxer with a mailed fist as big as and rather heavier than its body, and I am convinced that when the moment comes for that mailed fist to be lifted, the whole disproportionate system will topple over.

History has seldom been more sardonic with her chuckle.

Let me not pursue these changing shadows. Why should a prophet be expected to be more than pictur- esque, supplementing by new dreams the exhausted old dreams ? Yet in looking at Mr. Wells's perusal

of the post-war complexities it is well to remember
the difficulties which even his sagacious mind has
experienced in the deluding task of prognostication.
Let no man reproach him if he is wrong, but rather
wait eagerly (nor long) for renewed anticipations.

These post-war problems, are sketched—I had
almost said studied—in a book published in the middle
of 1916 with the title, *What is Coming!* Here Mr.
Wells is proud to have anticipated by a year Sir Percy
Scott's doubts of the decisive value of battleships;
and his book comes punctually with the battleship's
vindication in the Jutland action. But this is merely
a spot in the sun. Let us even ever so briefly look
at the future in its light. Near the end of 1916 universal lassitude will make straight the path of peace.
There will be a "practical bankruptcy of western
civilization"; yet out of evil comes good. Simply
because Germany can't be "crushed" in any crude
sense, the Allies must preserve their league long after
the war is ended; the very threat will bind together
the several powers now held by common danger,
quashing their international rivalry and giving the
world a blessed breathing-space. For forty years this
alliance for Germany's isolation must endure, and
then shall we live happily with the Germans ever
after. Mr. Wells looks for the destruction of the
Hohenzollern dynasty and the founding of a modern
repetition of the third French republic.—Pity that
puddings don't come by calling flour! He steps gaily

on to his old ground in a chapter on *The War and Women*, and finds that "in every way the war is accelerating the emancipation of women from sexual specialization." He foresees the dissolution of the harsh lines drawn between married and unmarried mothers. The "essential link" between people that marry will be—not the home ; and with that he all unknowingly raises misgivings. What sort of people, one asks, does Mr. Wells dream among ? Surely he knows (for has he not lamented it ?) that the English people of whom he is so vehemently critical are not at the mercy of ideas—least of all of ideas spurted at them by contemptuous intellectuals ? Is it not a complaint we are used to hearing, that Germany is amenable to ideas, but we deaf and stony ?—Quite odd, too, is our author's notion that Germany, under the economic pressure of the Allies, will not desire a very great increase in her population for a while. As if the poor restricted their families because they are poor, or the rich multiplied theirs because they are rich ! If anybody happens to know why the large families of the poor are large, certainly nobody knows why the small families of the rest are small.

Mr. Wells, to end this catechism, does not move but gyrate. There are many things in which he is obviously right, and it is ungrateful to begin to enumerate those in which he as obviously is not. He ends with an admirably candid and true word : "We want patience—and silence."

H. G. Wells

IX

Mr. Wells remains a prominent and interesting figure in the ranks of modern writers. Few have charmed so skilfully or so successfully, few have made a wider appeal to the mass of readers eager to follow if someone will but lead. He has a constant impulse to move on. Even his passion for the future owes something to his nervous impatience with the present—with the present because it is present as well as because it is disordered. So you come to note in his work much activity but little power, haste without advance, and (for the ultimate truth) curiosity without reflectiveness. . . . Quarrelsome fairies, I think, were at his birth, and one gave him a tiny precious cup of romance, and one of splendid discontent, and one of unrest like the unrest of water, and one an all but empty cup of beauty, and one a brimming beaker of curiosity. Alert, agile, nervously responsive, there seems to be nothing he has not heard, and but little that he has experienced. All his busyness is as the scratching of a worn hard road. Up and down the road go the feet of men hurrying in confusion on divers errands, picking their way among sharp flints, holes, quagmires and universal dust. A child goes plodding up the hill of futurity, and he calls out some direction which the child does not hear or does not understand ; and so unheeding passes out of sight. But Mr. Wells remains with his back to the sun, serious, sincere, and infinitely explanatory.

THOMAS HARDY

I

M R. HARDY is at once unique and typical among modern English writers. He is unique in the steady, unconceding pursuit of his own thought, of his own method ; unique in his grave philosophical view of life; unique in the sombre sincerity which he has employed upon the discovery of human character and relations. Yet he is typical too : typically English (if a phrase which suggests everything in general suggests anything in particular), home-centring, earth-loving ; in the pure sense of the word, he is a typically popular writer. You may perhaps find in his novels analogies with or even certain literal characteristics of French literature ; but you will find, too, that all his notable qualities are self-developed. He has an English pride in England, for his ears have for years and years been haunted with echoes of the heroic period of the Napoleonic wars ; and his few utterances since the present war began do but testify to his established pride. He does not escape the charge of coarseness—as few men of real independence can. Nature, or that outward aspect of life which we so refer to, has taught him to overlook niceness as a virtue. He can be called a pessimist by them that know only men who shut their eyes to hope, and men who shut their eyes to facts ; but he has looked too long and closely at life to be brought into any such simple category. He is so interesting and important a figure because in him, I think, a pure force speaks anew, the force of native unsophisticated character. He is, in the subtler meaning of the phrase, a " natural " writer.

To take Mr. Hardy's novels one by one would be small economy, since his work is curiously unequal. *Desperate Remedies*, the first, is a very poor novel, yet is followed after a year by such a good-humoured, excellent thing (in the mode of George Eliot's master-piece, *Silas Marner*) as *Under the Greenwood Tree*, and after two years by *A Pair of Blue Eyes*, which ranks near the finest. That again is elbowed by *Far from the Madding Crowd*, and so on with a rough alternation of good and indifferent, right down to 1892, when the memorable *Tess of the D'Urbervilles* is followed by the immemorable *Well-Beloved.* So I purpose dealing pretty much at random with the best of the novels, if the liberty be pardoned, approaching the author's characteristics almost exclusively in their finer evidences.

Yet it may be as well to make a slightly indirect approach. Leaving apart the more obviously inferior novels, let us look at one a little below the best, at

Thomas Hardy

The Trumpet Major. There are things here that are in Mr. Hardy's finest manner, and the whole book is intimately linked to the time to which he has given so much thought—the Napoleonic period. To this book, indeed, he traces the genesis of *The Dynasts.* Those spacious stirring days of strife and expectancy afford some of the author's best opportunities, and in the subordinate features of this book you may easily notice how he has profited by them. That sense of unseen watchers, for instance, which he so often suggests, of watchers human or purely spiritual, appears in such a sentence as this :

> [When the troops arrived and encamped] Though nobody seemed to be looking on but the few at the window and in the village street, there were, as a matter of fact, many eyes converging upon that military arrival in its high and conspicuous position, not to mention the glances of birds and other wild creatures. . . . Apparently unconscious and careless of what all the world was doing elsewhere, they remained picturesquely engrossed in the business of making themselves a habitation on the isolated spot which they had chosen.

The unsuspected watchers—they come into book after book. Again, you have here many examples of that curious and striking precision of description, by which he seems to endeavour not so much to give you his own impression, as to give all the materials, and nothing short of all, with which you are yourself to build an instantly vital impression. It is curious and striking that Mr. Hardy should stand thus apart

from the common tradition of impressionism, and
rely upon the close rendering of details, and the justice
of the reader's comprehension, for the impression he
necessarily seeks to communicate. And this habit—
need I say ?—implies a much more careful and vivid
intelligence in the author than is found in writers who
simply describe, and a much more difficult task than
that of the brilliant " impressionist," who is thought
to succeed in proportion to the vivacity rather than
the truth of the impression created. Now it is, I think,
because of Mr. Hardy's determination to give you the
exact essentials of an impression—no more, and certainly no less—that sometimes he seems a scientific
before an imaginative writer. He describes, I mean,
with his eyes too close to the subject, and is apt to give
you the facts separately, in a mere list, instead of in
their mutual relation. Intent upon saying just what
he sees, he inclines to say it with a certain stiffness,
using words as though they were literally weighed, as
dead things, not as living.

The Trumpet Major exhibits both the excellence and
the defect of Mr. Hardy's scrupulous method. Here
are three brief extracts which will speak for themselves,
and I need only say that while the third has perhaps
an intention in its oddity, it shows how easily the
method slips into oddity :

She could hear the frequent shuffling and tossing of the
horses tied to the pickets ; and in the other direction, the miles-

long voice of the sea, whispering a louder note at those points of its length where hampered in its ebb and flow by some jutting promontory or group of boulders.

.   .   .   .   .

The rain decreased, and the lovers went on. John looked after them as they strolled, aqua-tinted by the weak moon and mist.

.   .   .   .   .

The bow was just over her forehead, or, more precisely, at the point where the organ of comparison merges in that of benevolence, according to the phrenological theory of Gall.

There is one other passage which I must give, for its sheer wonderfulness. Of the " Victory " passing at sea Ann Garland says :

She is twisting round in a curious way, and her sails sink in like old cheeks, and she shivers like a leaf upon a tree.[1]

This is the more remarkable as it comes unexpectedly and not quite appropriately from the girl's lips.

But admitting these advantages of subject and treatment, why is it that *The Trumpet Major* is not among Mr. Hardy's best novels ? Well, there are certain clear evidences of inadequacy which might be noticed. With a pleasant variety of character and

---

[1] I need not point out how surely this echoes those Elizabethan and Jacobean poets whom Mr. Hardy is fond of quoting. He is perhaps too " literary " a novelist for some. He quotes the classics, refers often to Sophocles, and of modern poets loves to heighten his pages with fragments of Shakespeare, Donne, Crashaw, Shelley and Swinburne.

incident, there is but a very mild interest attaching to
the love affairs of the Trumpet Major, his brother,
their rival and Ann Garland. The *level* of the story
is low. It is, of course, easy for a tragedy to rise to
cloudy heights of passion and woe ; but it is not impossible for comedy to rise also, to passion if not to
cloudiness. The emotional activity of this book is
slight, and as to the intellectual activity, this may be
judged by a single prominent feature. I refer to the
strangely free use of coincidence. I admit at once
that life shows abundant and amazing coincidences ;
but I doubt if a novelist does wisely to resort frequently
to coincidence in the arrangement of his plot. Let it
be remembered that a novel is a highly artificial and
conventional thing, and yet, at least in Mr. Hardy's
hands, aims at *presenting life.* The more natural,
then, and the more inevitable the action appears,
the more happy the disguise of the fact that, after all,
the novel is but a contrivance, a conventional illusion.
Now in actual life, coincidences often point to human
arrangement, and sometimes are traceable to arrangement ; and even when most obviously fortuitous,
suggest to the mind a possible cunning stage arrangement by unseen hands. It is the vanity of our hearts,
perhaps, that prompts us to think coincidences more
than coincidences :—vanity, supported by those instances where they have actually proved more than
coincidences ; and at any rate, the fancy is far from
unusual. If, then, the artist, in his careful simulation

of history, makes frequent calls upon a convenient fortuitousness, is he not himself providing evidence against himself—evidence that the artifice of fiction is but an artifice ? If coincidences really make life itself seem artificial, how can they but make the simulation of life more intensely artificial ? The novelist is free to eliminate at least the obviously artificial from his fiction, in order that he may suggest that his pages are indeed pages fairly selected from life.

The Trumpet Major teems with these too-lucky meetings, these too-convenient arrangements. The whole courtship of Ann by the braggart Festus Derriman depends upon a series of almost amusing coincidences ; and when Ann escapes from his persecutions, riding wonderfully upon his affrighted charger, it is her own true lover of all people who catches her as she falls. A " special Providence " seems to be detailed for duty in the case of Festus, and another in the case of Matilda Johnson, each neatly assisting the other ; so that when Matilda utters her petulant " How I hate them ! " Festus is fetched within hearing distance and answering " How I hate them too ! " contrives with her Bob Loveday's destruction.

It would hardly be difficult to parallel these with instances from the other lesser novels of this writer. I have called this dependence upon coincidence (I hope not offensively) a sign of inadequacy. It means that the intellectual as well as the emotional activity is faint ; and this is the more remarkable because we have heard a good deal—said with perfect justice—of the *art* of this author. A certain sluggishness seems at times to overcome him. Possessed of his subject, he writes with a sure power and imagination which is beyond the impertinence of praise. In his best work, he is kept at this high pitch almost from the first page to the last : the chief mark of his mastery of form is the equal felicity of every chapter of his finest novels. Much depends, and necessarily depends, upon his choice of subject :—hence, possibly, the fact already mentioned, that all the best work is not the latest, nor all the lesser the earliest. But even apart from choice of subject, there seems to be a strange variability in the power of its development. The invention becomes poor, coincidence rife, and through pure indifference the story moves hastily rather than swiftly and surely. And looking back over such a novel, and remembering the really unique achievement of the author, you think that he has written perfunctorily because his interest has been perfunctory.

In another and finer novel, *A Pair of Blue Eyes*, the signs of this are seen, but are far less frequent and plain. They are, too, mostly different. *A Pair of Blue Eyes* is as painful as *Romeo and Juliet*. Sorrow speaks there, mere, unreasonable, unrestrainable. Few histories could be simpler or more natural. The woman's love for the lesser man gives way to her love for the greater man :—but lesser and greater man are equal in love for her. Innocence harassed by the dis-

loyalty of love's growth—there is the tragedy of the
book. It is the earliest of Mr. Hardy's greater works,
and only in its details falls short of the greatest.   Coincidence and the widow Jethway are unnaturally intimate, but apart from this the chief flaw of *The Trumpet
Major* does not appear here.   What does appear is an
occasional somewhat singular note of externality, as
though Mr. Hardy were not writing a novel, but an
essay upon a novel :

> It is difficult to frame rules which shall apply to both sexes,
> and Elfride, an undeveloped girl, must, perhaps, hardly be
> laden with the moral responsibilities which attach to a man
> in like circumstances.   The charm of woman, too, lies partly
> in her subtleness in matters of love.

More conspicuous is the intrusion of this note upon
one of the noblest imaginative pieces in all the novels
—the chapter describing Knight's peril, hanging over
the nameless cliff, and his salvation by Elfride.   As
he hangs, and strains to hang there a little longer, and
almost unconsciously notices, with a geologist's eye,
the imbedded reliquaries of many unhistoried centuries,

> Time closed up like a fan before him.   He saw himself at
> one extremity of the years, face to face with the beginning
> and all the intermediate centuries simultaneously.   Fierce
> men, clothed in the hide of beasts, and carrying, for defence
> and attack, huge clubs and pointed spears, rose from the
> rock, like the phantoms before the doomed Macbeth.   They

lived in hollows, woods, and mud huts—perhaps in caves of the neighbouring rocks. Behind them stood an earlier band. No man was there.

But then, as he reads and wonders, and wonders too, how much longer he can endure, you are disconcerted by such a passage as this:

Knight had over-estimated the strength of his hands. They were getting weak already. "She will never come again; she has been gone ten minutes," he said to himself.

This mistake arose from the unusual compression of his experiences just now: she had really been gone but three.

"As many more minutes will be my end," he thought.

Next came another instance of the incapacity of the mind to make comparisons at such times.

"This is a summer afternoon," he said, "and there can never have been such a heavy and cold rain on a summer day in my life before."

He was again mistaken. The rain was quite ordinary in quantity; the air in temperature. It was, as is usual, the menacing attitude in which they approached him that magnified their powers.

This is a clear but not a solitary instance of the careful man of science snatching the pen a moment from the imaginative writer, in order to insert his irrelevantly precise correction. You might fancy there had been a moment's interruption in the conception of the scene, an interruption fatal to its completion. Things that would pass unnoticed in a gayer book show like a starved child's bones in such a tragical history as *A Pair of Blue Eyes*. It requires but a

small thing to disturb the mood of the book because
the mind, oppressed with such sharp natural sorrow,
readily takes any chance of escape from its too-sore
pressure.

The accumulation of sorrow is less weighty in *Far
from the Madding Crowd*, and there is brightness on the
last page. But it is not simply because it is a happier
that it is a finer novel, but because you must look hard
to find any uncertainty, confusion or weakness of
invention. I am not sure whether, of all his novels,
this is not the one to which Mr. Hardy's readers will
most often turn ; for though in intensity and profundity others may surpass it, this book has an amenity
even in its grief which is gracious and welcome. I
think this comes not from any intentional softening of
touch, but simply from the steadfastness of such a
character as Gabriel Oak. Upon the perplexed and
foiled passion of Bathsheba, Troy and Boldwood
Gabriel casts a fixed and calm light, the light of honesty
and wise passiveness. He is as reassuring as an irrefragable proposition in philosophy, and it is to be
remarked that both Bathsheba and Boldwood rely
upon him as upon something sure and selfless as
Fate.

" Love is a possible strength in an actual weakness,"
says Mr. Hardy. It is the virtue of this book to display it. Love vehement and errant in Bathsheba,
light and false in Troy, ruinous in Boldwood and in
Gabriel earnest and intent, but subordinate to moral

independence—you have in their histories the ex-
tremes of possible strength and actual weakness.
There is description as fine and as powerful as prose
can very well compass—of a storm rivalling the fury
of that which accompanies the inner tumult of *Richard
Feverel.* One small citation must be made here, in
token of Mr. Hardy's extraordinary clearness of vision
and statement :

> The light had a sinister aspect. A heated breeze from the
> south slowly fanned the summits of lofty objects, and in the
> sky dashes of buoyant cloud were sailing in a course at right
> angles to that of another stratum, neither of them in the
> direction of the breeze below. The moon, as seen through
> these films, had a lurid metallic look. The fields were sallow
> with the impure light, and all were tinged in monochrome, as
> if beheld through stained glass. The same evening the sheep
> had trailed homeward head to tail, the behaviour of the rooks
> had been confused, and the horses had moved with timidity
> and caution.

But the storm, let it be said in passing, is not described for its own sake : nothing ever is in Mr. Hardy's
work ; he is never superfluous. It is described in its
relation to human activities and made, for all its
grandeur and fury, a little less than the human activity
which is busily thwarting it. . . . And if this book
seem less impressive than, say, *Tess,* it is because it is
easier to heap up painful impressions of pure tragedy
than the more various impressions of a less unhappy
story. . . . One other thing might be said of *Far
from the Madding Crowd,* namely, that you can think

of the children of Gabriel and Bathsheba with a far
more confident hope than of the possible children of
many a nerve-racked pair in modern fiction. Of fire
and earth equally is Bathsheba made, with nothing
of a type or formula clinging to her ; and I cannot
think of another of the women of these novels who
shows so fine and natural a virtue—weakness so human
and strength no less human ; and Gabriel is the meet
masculine of her instinctive feminine.

II

I pass to those novels, *The Return of the Native*,
The Woodlanders, *Tess of the D'Urbervilles*, and *Jude
the Obscure* which, beyond the rest, have given Mr.
Hardy his salient position among English novelists.
The two former stand apart from the two latter ; or,
more correctly, *Tess* and *Jude the Obscure* stand apart
from all others of their author's work. It is in *The
Woodlanders* that Mr. Hardy first shows his tendency
to become occupied partly with a thesis and partly
with character, and no longer purely with character.
In the preface he avows his interest in the thesis :

In the present novel, as in one or two more of this series
which involve the question of matrimonial divergence, the
immortal puzzle—given the man and woman, how to find a
basis for their sexual relation—is left where it stood.

It is, of course, the indirect rather than the direct

answer that is significant :—hence the opportunity
and the responsibility of the novelist, who can display
dramatically and with vital warmth what were else
no more than a distant proposition. I am afraid
that Mr. Hardy's art suffers a little from the introduction of a formal thesis into his conceptions. His
preoccupation is usually with the graver issues of life,
and the very intensity of his human sympathies prevents the formalization of his work. It may not be
always spontaneous, but it is always sincere. Yet
are you conscious that character and incident in *Tess*
and *Jude* are not wholly free from the pressure of the
thesis.

The thesis is absent from *The Return of the Native*,
but this book has certain features in common with
The Woodlanders. In each case there is, distinct in
the background, that singular and passionate Presence
—the woodland tree, the bare heath—which is more
enduring and almost more personal than the human
persons of the drama. Put it as a minor advantage
that *The Return of the Native* has no such failures
in portraiture as Fitzpiers and Mrs. Charmond ;[1] but
it must reckon as a major advantage that, for all its
sorrow, it is not embittered with such an amazing betrayal as that of poor Grace to the repentant sensualist,
her husband. Elsewhere Mr. Hardy may be gloomy

[1] It is a failure hardly so much with the individual characters in this book, as with the social class here and in other
books which seems to chill the ardour of his thought.

and depressing, but not, I think, merely cynical in the main and ultimate development of his story. It is, presumably, one of many stealthy stabs at the persistence of the common view of marriage—at its intended indissolubility ; and here the theory spoils the novel. But the theory is more than the novel ?—No : the novel has an imaginative life of its own ; it lives on in our imagination, peoples with its characters the kingdom of the mind, and is real to us beyond many theories. . . . So *The Return of the Native,* untouched by this defect, is a finer novel than *The Woodlanders.* And because its idea is wholly implicit in the character and action, and not expressed in a theory to which action and character are subordinated, it is finer even as a contribution to the study of social life. Mr. Hardy sees that merely to apprehend the moral vagrancy of Wildeve and the moth-like splendid futility of Eustacia, is to understand something more of the mystery and richness of life :—to know, in short, that in character rather than in circumstance is all the drama of life, whether tragedy or comedy, surely unfolded.

But in *Tess of the D'Urbervilles* and *Jude the Obscure* the " criticism of life " is sharper and more intent. It is a criticism directed not simply upon human responsibility but upon the extra-human aspect of life. There is, their author perceives, a universal untowardness in human relations and social exactions, in the rigidities which forbid happiness, and punish almost equally observance and infraction. And beyond these he sees a gloomy, unapproachable spirit sinister—cold, ironic, unquestionable. The burden of *Jude* is, The letter killeth ; and of *Tess*, the grim malignity which is faintly hinted at in such an aside as this :

> Nature does not often say " See ! " to her poor creatures at a time when seeing can lead to happy doing ; or reply " Here ! " to a body's cry of " Where ? " till the hide-and-seek has become an irksome outworn game.

In *Tess* is displayed the motion of the spirit sinister, Fate ; in *Jude*, the annulling omnipotence of custom. Both features appear in each book, as complementary ; but one dominates each. To this dominance is attributable whatever defect or excess a student of life or a student of the novel might venture to point out.

I have said—and obvious though it be, can hardly say it too often—that Mr. Hardy's novels, and these in particular, are conceived in the profoundest human sympathies. And the very keenness of his apprehension seems to lead to acerbity, excess—even to touches of cruelty. Marty South, in *The Woodlanders*, endures the bitterness of unheeded love from beginning to end of the book, nor ever hints at the bitterness or the splendour of her love until the final paragraph, which leaves her murmuring a simple and august elegy over the else-forgotten grave of Giles Winterborne. This is right and true enough. Her heroic sorrow arises purely from the love of a girl for one she knows intimately, and knows to be cold to her, but wasted fire to another. But neither from *Tess* nor *Jude* is this simple and direct impression received. You are teased ever and anon with an appearance of contrivance. *Tess* is a study in unrelieved sorrow ; *Jude* a study in unmitigated horror. More precisely might it be said, of *Tess*, that it is a study in unrelieved sorrow springing from injustice :—the injustice of a man betraying a girl ; of another—his own fault forgiven—denying forgiveness to her ; the injustice of the fell clutch of circumstance upon her faithfullest aspiration ; the injustice of forgiveness arriving too late. And over all there hangs, cloud-like chill, the injustice of Fate, the " President of the Immortals," who tosses her into criminal infamy when, as Mr. Hardy says, " he had ended his sport with Tess." Injustice is the sorrowfullest thing on earth, and, beyond earth, the most malignant. Mr. Hardy intensifies sorrow with malignity ; and it is at this point that one hesitates to follow him. Life falls awry, is hard for many, distresses and discourages, is almost without gentle mitigation . . . yes, but seldom freezes ! But *Tess of the D'Urbervilles* freezes.

It is with trepidation that a mere critic pries into the remoter questions of art, when the artist is Mr. Hardy ; yet questions worm themselves persistently between the neat stones of one's affirmations. Does not Mr. Hardy (to put the question boldly) load the dice against Tess ? On sorrow's head are sorrows accumulated to a degree which is, unhappily, not quite beyond human experience, but is yet so extreme an experience as to make it perilous to draw any general conclusions. Accident plays too large a part. The letter in which Tess discloses the ache of her past is, by accident, unseen by Angel Clare ; by accident she overhears a conversation concerning Angel which prevents her approaching his parents ; by accident the loathsome Alec D'Urberville, her former lover, sees her again ; by accident her penitent husband only discovers her after her return in sheer hopelessness to Alec. In tragedy, the lower depth is sounded when, to one who might be simply oneself, there come large irremediable sorrows, as natural and direct as they are unavoidable and cureless. The more simply typical is the character and the history, the more immediate and unquestionable is the appeal to our central emotions. In *Tess* I cannot help thinking that the unusual is substituted for the typical, the strange for the unquestionable ; and that, nevertheless, the attitude—tacit and overt— of the author, is one which only a general or at least very frequent experience as disastrously unhappy as Tess's could support.

What of this attitude ? Mr. Hardy sees *Tess* (and of course not Tess alone but equally, it follows, those linked with her) as the sport of the gods ; and this depressing suggestion is emphasized by the casual utterances, the " asides," of the book. One has already been cited ; and there are others, not frequent

but bitter. His reflections upon Tess's woe-presaging
fall, even, have less of sorrow than of sardonic hopelessness ; he imagines her guardian angel to be like the
god jeered at by the " ironical Tishbite," drawn afar
on other business than hers. The same spirit even
animates some of the action. Alec's conversion is not
very credible, and his relapse does not make it more
credible. . . . Or rather, you do not think whether
either incident is credible, but feel that each has the
painful sourness of a gibe. The idea that Tess's sum-
less griefs are but the jests of the Immortals stings
her creator into sombre resentment. Yet why utter
that resentment ? The belief that there is a purpose
of wisdom in the most inscrutable of sad happenings,
is a consoling and humane belief, even though not
demonstrably sure. The belief that there is nothing
of will or purpose in them may be depressing, but
is not insupportable. But the belief that there is a
malignant purpose, an intention and effect of irony ;
the *deliberate* undramatic proposition (in a passage
quoted in the preface to *Tess*) that :

> As flies to wanton boys are we to the gods ;
> They kill us for their sport——

this, I must say, seems not merely dismaying, but
disabling. Holding this view as Mr. Hardy does,
it is inconceivable that he should write a book to pro-
mulgate it ; yet he has written it.

But the interests of truth demand it ? Not so !
Grant that this view is truth, and since you had no
voice in the acceptance of life upon these terms, you are
at liberty to make the sole available retort upon the
maleficent dark Will—that is, by returning the unsought gift. I call the view disabling because I can
see no way but this left if one sincerely accepts it.
Even pleasure given by the gods in cold sport were
an indignity ; but sorrow and injustice arising out of
the ironic mirth of the unquestioned powers freeze
the roots of life. And just as there is no candid reason
for preaching the strict doctrine of nihilism, or for a
strict nihilist preaching any doctrine at all ; so the
perception that the course of life is determined by
ironic sport, should of itself forbid the announcement
of that perception. If the rule is ironic, let the irony
be overcome by that ever-sufficient retort to subtle
ironists—unconsciousness. Irony unadmitted is irony
defeated ; but irony perceived and acquiesced in, is
the bitterest recognition which humanity can concede.

And—need one add ?—th e tacit impeachment of the
cold Immortals is hardly just. The tragedy arises,
so far as it does follow naturally, from the flaw of character. Tess, like Elfride and others of Mr. Hardy's
women, has a childish love of concealment ; Angel has
a morbid, ideal fastidiousness, an aversion from the
mere facts of life. Here is sufficient matter for a
tragedy of old unhappy far-off things, things far-off
that would be forgotten if they were not concealed.

Thomas Hardy

The attack in *Tess* upon the ironical Immortals (if it indeed be an attack and not a mournful tribute) becomes in *Jude the Obscure* an attack upon chilling, immense custom. No superhuman tyranny now, but the vast tyranny of convention is the enemy. I don't know a more dismal book. Zola's novels are usually depressing, since they point to a waste of immense industry; but this book of Mr. Hardy's is far more depressing, since it is the outpouring of a singular genius. So incomparably higher and finer is Mr. Hardy's achievement than Zola's, that one's depression is incomparably greater.

Jude is a grey November book. Damp winds whistle through its pages, tree-boughs are snapped, fog settles upon the town and rain upon the country. Now and again there is an almost ostentatious coarseness, an insistent directness of speech; but to this no one can decently object. A bare, undelightful, angular book, it is yet intensely interesting. Jude's ways are continually being snared, and he is an easy prey; but it must be observed that he sets many of the snares for himself. The tragedy of the book, like the tragedy of *Tess*, is inherent in the characters of Sue and Jude. She is the modern " type "—the girl whose education has fitted her to challenge the world, but whose character is too merely feminine to permit her to endure the trial. Jude, the slow-moving masculine principle (one is strongly tempted to talk in abstract terms of this novel) is, if less striking, hardly less convincing.

The depressing influence of the book comes not so much from the characters or action, as from the gathering conviction, gained in reading, that Jude and Sue and Arabella and the hapless children are, in Swift's phrase, not so much born into the world as damned into the world. Swift, indeed, might have been grimly pleased with *Jude the Obscure* in the wreck of his own genius.

I said that this novel is a study in unmitigated horror. You have before you more than once the question whether the marriage-vow may not be more honoured in the breach than in the observance ; how far physical aversion is to be condoned—applications of the text, "The letter killeth but the spirit giveth life." But all the uneasy trouble of the book is forgotten in the face of the acute and gnawing horror of one scene. For a few years Jude and Sue had lived peacefully together, though without the courage to marry. Then, when trouble leers at them, and Sue confesses to Jude's eldest child—bred in a moral quagmire and named "little Father Time"—that she will soon have another baby though their difficulties are already severe, then comes the catastrophe. Father Time and the two smaller children are found hanged, and the death of the poor infant suicides is explained by the scrawl they have left :

"*Done because we are too menny.*"
The boy's face expressed the whole tale of their situation. On that little shape had converged all the inauspiciousness and shadow which had darkened the first union of Jude, and

all the accidents, mistakes, fears, errors of the last. He was their nodal point, their focus, their expression in a single term. For the rashness of those parents he had groaned, for their ill-assortment he had quaked, and for the misfortunes of these he had died.

As the miserable parents look at the three small corpses, there comes in from the neighbouring college organ, " Truly God is loving unto Israel."

After the physical, the moral horror. Sue is self-persuaded that her real husband is the man who divorced her, and that Jude's real wife is the lewd woman he had divorced. So, her clouded mind leading her to covet the anodynes of religion, they part, Sue to re-marry, for pure self-abnegation, into her old state of physical aversion, and Jude to be recaptured by Arabella, and die of drink and damnation.

Whatever is, is wrong, you might sigh, shutting the book. *Tess of the D'Urbervilles* is a grievous thing, but has the relief of scenes that recall the sweet Theocritean note. From *Jude the Obscure*, relief is strangely withheld. Jude, as he walks meditating upon his studies and prospects in the church, is trapped by Arabella ; Sue's husband, for acting as his conscience directs and giving her freedom again, is persecuted ; Jude himself, dying with the curses of Job upon his lips, is assailed with the jubilant " hurrahs " of victorious crews. Every sour has its mocking sweet, every ascent its downfall. Obedience to convention is found immoral, defiance miserable ; nothing's sweet under the sun—and Jude is not thirty when he dies.

III

When, in 1898, Mr. Hardy issued *Wessex Poems* it was found to have an interest beyond its interest as verse. His first novel was published in 1871, his first valuable one (*A Pair of Blue Eyes*) in 1873. But in his first volume of verse are found poems precisely dated as long ago as 1865. You have only to turn the pages to notice that in the main this book is a verse rendering of the sombre themes of the novels. Some of the poems are ostensibly personal, but the author's warning is to be remembered :—

The pieces are in a large degree dramatic or personative in conception ; and this even where they are not obviously so.

The verses in the first part of the book belong to the latter class. Here Mr. Hardy presents, without dramatic medium, the view of life which he constantly presents through that medium. The sonnet called *Hap* contains the profession that an ire unmerited could be borne if one knew it to be designed. But the " Doomsters " are purblind and all is unshaped, unpurposed. As melancholy is the last piece in the book, where the regret is uttered that the heart shrinks not as shrinks the flesh.

But Time, to make me grieve,
Part steals, lets part abide ;
And shakes this fragile frame at eve
With throbbings of noontide.

This melancholy breathes out from some of the most beautiful of the verses. Love, its aspirations and falseness ; Time's swiftness ; the crassness of " Casualty " ; the severing sea, laws of men, mode's decree ; memory's treachery ; desire unbearable and sense too strong :—of these he writes, sometimes to slow music, and sometimes to a tune so gay as to be more intolerable than the saddest. Upon these dark, close-bosoming things he broods with an intensity which wrings almost their last explicit sadness from sad words, and leaves a fruitless melancholy abiding like a shadow on the soul. In the novels this impression is perhaps equally strong and direct, but balanced by those interludes in the story's development which are as necessary as they are welcome. But here in the solemn poems you have the naked uncompanioned body of sorrow. *At an Inn*, for example, is complete in itself, complete in its grief, with no mitigation of its sharpness such as even a short story might contrive. Lyrical poetry is, of course, open to exaggeration by reason of its very truthfulness. It records moods so narrowly and intensely, with such exclusive sharp veracity, that its influence is sometimes out of proportion to the mood's duration. In prose, gravity of matter is often expressed by gaiety of manner ; but in verse, gravity of matter usually seeks a yet farther and stranger gravity of speech, deepening the instant effect until the heart fails from mere soreness. Had the whole of *Wessex Poems* been occupied with such untempered speech, it would have been much less to us than it is and would, indeed, have failed of its appeal. But this is just avoided—if indeed quite avoided—by the dramatic pieces, of which some are meant to remind us of characters or scenes in the novels. *Valenciennes*, for instance, is a song by Corp'l Tullidge, of *The Trumpet Major*:

> They bore my wownded frame to camp,
> And shut my gapen skull, and washed en cleän,
> And jined en wi' a zilver clamp
> Thik night at Valencieën. . . .
>
> I never hear the zummer hums
> O' bees ; and don' know when the cuckoo comes ;
> But night and day I hear the bombs
> We threw at Valencieën. . . .

Others, again, present the tragical histories of which Mr. Hardy feels all the force and—may one say it ?— but little of the sad exaltation. He seems but faintly aware of the renewal which thrusts bulb-like even through the heavy earth of misfortune and grief. Grief he finds eternal and unlessening ; or if lessening, then so much the worse as full of mockery. Irony is an unnatural gift. No man is born with it, no man endures it easily ; it is almost like a curse of second sight, giving you the illusion of sight, but nothing of its comfort. The humane nobility of this poet's genius has taught him how general and moving sorrow is, how tragical the simplest lives. Upon this pure apprehension of sorrow his intellect has been busy, and the very generality of sorrow has sometimes in these poems overwhelmed him. Nearly all the pieces in *Wessex Poems* are concerned with obscure lives, and nearly all the lives are stricken, acquainted with grief. And if the grief by chance be too lightly gone, its transience itself is a farther grief. One poem he calls *Neutral Tones,* and is merciless to press the utmost hopelessness into the four chill stanzas, of which the last two are :

> The smile on your mouth was the deadest thing
> Alive enough to have strength to die ;
> And a grin of bitterness swept thereby
> Like an ominous bird a-wing. . . .
>
> Since then, keen lessons that love deceives,
> And wrings with wrong, have shaped to me
> Your face, and the God-curst sun, and a tree,
> And a pond edged with grayish leaves.

My Cicely describes the degradation of early love, and describes it as Time's too-mocking repartee to Love's re-expression. Of another, he has written a poem, *Her Immortality,* in which the dead loved woman restrains her lover from suicide :

> A Shade but in its mindful ones
> Has immortality ;

> By living, me you keep alive,
> By dying you slay me.

The pitiful remonstrance avails, yet even in her immortality, thus purchased, there is nothing of comfort :

> But grows my grief. When I surcease,
> Through whom alone lives she,
> Ceases my Love, her words, her ways,
> Never again to be !

Ivy clasping trees is for Mr. Hardy a symbol of ineffectuality ; astronomy a sad scanning of Nescience ; nature herself (in a poem with a snapped key for significant head-piece) he overhears asking :

> Or come we of an Automaton
> Unconscious of our pains ? . . .
> Or are we live remains
> Of Godhead dying downwards, brain and eye now gone ?

> Or is it that some high Plan betides,
> As yet not understood,
> Of Evil stormed by Good,
> We the Forlorn Hope over which Achievement strides ?

But nothing answers ; " Earth's old glooms and pains are still the same."

So might one go through piece after piece, finding the same steady sadness, with only a grimmer irony for relief. It happens with some writers that experience changes their minds, or deepens the spiritual channels through which their energies move. Time works : but without wandering into impertinence, it may be remarked here that it is not Time that has worked this shadow of sorrow into Mr. Hardy's verse. His attitude is to be regarded as the sincere native attitude of his mind ; and there is something strangely impressive in the almost inexorable rigidity of that attitude. . . . *Almost* inexorable rigidity, I say, because, happily, the passing of years has, as may be discerned, relieved the gloom a little. Certainly, the poems collected into the later volumes, though not themselves all of later date, " take the reader forward, even if not far, rather than backward."

Poems of the Past and Present gain from the extension of their interest to subjects hardly old enough to be historic. There is a number of songs and ballads upon the South African War, or rather upon that general human aspect of war which is more easily capable of treatment in poetry. *The Dead Drummer* expresses in a large universal way the unmournful death of Drummer Hodge. The sonnet *Embarcation* ends with the wise throbbing couplet :

Wives, sisters, parents, wave white hands and smile
As if they knew not that they weep the while.

And there is a delightful ringing, nimbling rhymeful *Song of the Soldier's Wives*, none the less gay for being not far from tears.

But then Mr. Hardy the ironeist must needs muffle the singer and write *A Wife in London*, of which the

first stanza (*The Tragedy*) tells of her receiving a cable-
gram of her husband's death, and the second (*The
Irony*) of her receiving the next day a letter from " his
hand, whom the worm now knows," written in the
dear anticipation of return and re-union. Now this is
actual enough, but in its presentment here too raw,
and too obviously raw. Indeed, one might say that
in this unhappy sequence of false good upon ill news,
there is nothing even of irony—nothing but dark
sorrow. True irony would demand—would it not ?—
the impact of the sharp ill upon the comfortable good
news ; but for a woman already sea-deep in woe,
ironic contrast is lost. There is here, in fact, a suggestion almost of violence, as if Mr. Hardy, impatient with
the rose-red, flung himself impetuously upon the
thorny dark hedge of sorrow, with a bitter satisfaction in the sharp stabbings.

This, however, is almost the only poem in his second
volume in which the sardonic and bitter humour of the
first appears. The book is a more human book. The
first shows indeed no lack of human interest, but
there it is shadowed by an eager bitterness, an unre-
mitting questioning, which leaves you hardly free
to think of the human situation in itself and pure of the
author's predilections. *Poems of the Past and Present*
has a less confined, a less obstinate note. There are
dark things here too, journeyings in " vaults of pain."
Her Immortality, mentioned a moment ago, can be
matched here with *His Immortality*, which describes

Thomas Hardy

the gradual loss of " a dead man's finer part "—his immortality—as those in whom it shone themselves die. It is followed by the lament of lately-dead men, not yet quite forgotten but grieving in their graves because forgotten they too will soon be, " our future second death " :

> But what has been will be—
> First memory, then oblivion's turbid sea ;
> Like men foregone shall we merge into those
> Whose story no one knows.
>
> For which of us could hope
> To show in life that world-awakening scope
> Granted the few whose memory none lets die,
> But all men magnify ?

Even here the humour is gentler, though not less grave. . . . What chiefly distinguishes the work from its predecessor is the note of *The Darkling Thrush*, or the note of *To Lizbie Brown*. The first especially, together with the precision and vividness which Mr. Hardy's prose commonly, and his verse often display, has a lyrical buoyancy that is purely delightful :

> An aged thrush, frail, gaunt, and small,
>   In blast-beruffled plume,
> Had chosen thus to fling his soul
>   Upon the growing gloom.
>
> So little cause for carollings
>   Of such ecstatic sound
> Was written on terrestrial things
>   Afar or nigh around,

133

That I could think there trembled through
His happy good-night air
Some blessed Hope, whereof he knew
And I was unaware.

Tess's Lament, echoing as it does the most tragical
of woeful stories, has yet a merciful amenity—more
memorable, indeed, than any dolorous excess might be.
The unperturbed note of *To Lizbie Brown* is found more
often in the third volume of poems, *Time's Laughing
Stocks*.   To take in full one brief musical song, in token
for many, let us note this :

To Carrey Clavel

You turn your back, you turn your back,
  And never your face to me,
Alone you take your homeward track,
  And scorn my company.

What will you do when Charley's seen
  Dewbeating down this way ?
—You'll turn back as now, you mean ?
  Nay, Carrey Clavel, nay !

You'll see none's looking ; put your lip
  Up like a tulip, ˄o ;
And he will coll you, bend, and sip :
  Yes, Carrey, yes ; I know !

" Love Lyrics " and " A Set of Country Songs " are
the titles under which Mr. Hardy has grouped the
gentler and lovelier of his songs.   Some of the " Love
Lyrics " are as various, spontaneous, careless as Browning's :—like his, too, their metrical cunning.
  The *Country Songs* are introduced by a poem which

puts into words the attitude of most men who see
nothing clearly as they would.

> Let me enjoy the earth no less
> Because the all-enacting Might
> That fashioned forth its loveliness
> Had other aims than my delight.

This would sound a little odd, I think, amid the
careful melancholy of *Wessex Poems*. Some of the
songs are like rhymed versions of the felicitous rural
scenes in which the novels abound, and they gain from
the nimble trip of the rhyme. Such an incident is *The
Homecoming* with its eloquent refrain :

Gruffly growled the wind on Toller downland broad and bare,
And lonesome was the house, and dark ; and few came
there.——

and its rustic funny roughness. One of these *Country
Songs* seems to me to have fallen unluckily into its
place here—*The Husband's View*, a poem of which the
unreal cynicism is only made possible by the provision
of an impossible coincidence. Of this, however, more
than enough. . . . Mr. Hardy's all but finest things
in lyrical poetry appear in the opening pages of *Time's
Laughing Stocks*. *A Tramp-woman's Tragedy*, for example, is a pregnant and profoundly unhappy story of
mortal ill ; a story developed without emphasis or
superfluousness, bitterness or moral. The metre used
is a favourite one with Mr. Hardy, as indeed it might
well be with any poet lucky enough to use it once.
These two stanzas with which the poem ends will

reveal the drift of the matter and the excellence of the form :

> And in the night as I lay weak,
>   As I lay weak,
> The leaves a-falling on my cheek,
>   The red moon low declined—
> The ghost of him I'd die to kiss
> Rose up and said : " Ah, tell me this !
> Was the child mine, or was it his ?
>   Speak, that I rest may find ! "
>
> O doubt not but I told him then,
>   I told him then,
> That I had kept me from all men
>   Since we joined lips and swore.
> Whereat he smiled, and thinned away
> As the wind stirred to call up day . . .
> —'Tis past ! And here alone I stray
>   Haunting the Western Moor.

Unlike this moving poem, *A Sunday Morning Tragedy* gains nothing from its form, which only makes the stark treatment seem more stark, the pain more pitilessly painful. Need it be said that the sincerity and simplicity of both poems are as manifest as they are essential ; and neither poem has a hint of the bitter distaste which at times appears not only in the author's regard of particular lives, but of life itself.

Merely singular as the view may appear, I am afraid I must say that the last volume of verse, *Satires of Circumstance*, disappoints more than it delights. Perversity seems to have written many of the pieces, and perversity alone, unhelped by music or any grace

or subtlety, perversity expressively crude, has written
the fifteen poems specially bearing the book's title.
With an artist of so definite an individuality as Mr.
Hardy's work reveals, and so small a natural ease, a
failure of mood involves a failure of felicity ; the failure
itself thus witnessing by its prominence to the general
sincerity and strength.   There are I hesitate to count
how many poems in this book revolving on the old
theme of deceived husband and desired lover.   Not
Congreve in his lightness is more persistent in devotion
to this theme, than is Mr. Hardy in his sombre relish
of it.   The very sharpness of the verse, the bare pro-
tuberances, the general gauntness, make the theme—
the constant theme of deceit and desire—the more
powerful but also the more paralysing.   *The New-
comer's Wife* is typical :

> He paused on the sill of a door ajar
> That screened a lively liquor bar,
> For the name had reached him through the door
> Of her he had married the week before.

He hears men speaking of his wife being in luck at
last, and himself pitied that he doesn't know her :

> Nor dreams how many a love-campaign
> She had enjoyed before his reign !

> That night there was the splash of a fall
> Over the slimy harbour-wall :
> They searched, and at the deepest place
> Found him with crabs upon his face.

I do not think the statement that an unknown man, married to a woman of whom we know nothing but the fact of her frailty, has drowned himself on hearing what she is, is inevitably brought by rhyme any nearer to poetry than it is by prose. . . . Often the lyrical impulse is not strong enough to bear so heavy an irony, and the ironeist is a poor poet if he is not much more than an ironeist. One may say these things with less reluctance because Mr. Hardy has included in this book poems not less bare and direct yet splendidly and plainly *poems*, which it would be delicious to quote if quotation were possible.

Let us interrupt here this rapid glance over Mr. Hardy's shorter poems, to ask what impression remains ? Of the first book, to take each alone, a sadness almost disabling ; of the second, a sadness less vexed and bitter, with gleams of delight even amid the darker sighful branches ; of the third, a yet more liberal and flexible attitude in the face of subjects hardly less grave ; and of the fourth a somewhat curious return to the harshness of the earliest poems. Take them together, and you will recognize with astonishment the full endowment of this novelist who has been so long a poet unknown. Whatever high station he may ultimately hold among English poets, he will hold it equally by reason of his pure lyrical gift touching an immense number of themes, and by reason of the moral earnestness of his work, as notable in this as Wordsworth's own. That is to say, he has laid the surest foundations of enduringness. Like Wordsworth, he has avoided the merely pretty, the merely easy, and sought in the lives of obscure men some features of the eternal. Take from these poems their occasional slyness, and you have much that Wordsworth might have written in moods of misgiving. Each poet has that sense of the meaning and value of common lives, which we are apt to think an exclusive characteristic of our own day ; and while the diversity of their treatment of common lives is very plain, the frequent identity of their sense of tragedy in common life—of its intense emotional activity—is no less obvious.

Consider, for a moment, the question of form, and you will notice the independence as well as the vitality of Mr. Hardy's work. I have already spoken of the early date of many of his lyrics ; and when it is remembered that they were written in the years that gave us *Atalanta in Calydon, Thyrsis, The Prince's Progress, Poems and Ballads*, Morris's narratives in verse, *The Ring and the Book*, and the *Poems* of Dante Rossetti, you will marvel that this poet's work is so entirely free of traces of their influence. If his early sonnets, for instance, echo any poet, it is Shakespeare or Drayton ; and of other strict forms of verse you will find scarce any that is familiar save the triolet which moves somewhat unexpectedly and stiffly in his pages. With extreme metrical inventiveness, you will note often an extreme inflexibility. The verse moves slowly and heavily ; but then you find that it is not unnatural or uncharming. As a single line may hold echoes in its mere sound of the very sense it is meant to convey; so whole poems of Mr. Hardy's in their grave stiff movement echo most surely the gnomic thought that cries in his heart for utterance. Dissonances fall into their place in the general music, and seem in a scarce explicable way to increase the harmony of the many poems into a harmony of one clear noble poem. Take a single stanza, and a child can point out its stumbling lumbering movement; take the poems as a whole, and it needs a critic of far wider and bolder abilities than mine to show adequately how in page after page idea and verse " a correspondent breathing seem to keep."

There is more than this to be said. Mr. Hardy has studied closely the effect of verse-forms upon poetry, and has experimented untiringly. Most conspicuous is his sense of the loveliness of rhyme, and I think this must be due to his prolonged rural associations. Every reader of the novels will have noticed the author's fondness for bell-music, the frequency of his allusion to it; and as frequent is his reference to village music of " viol and bow." It is a native fondness. Now this shows itself constantly in his verse. Whatever slowness we discover in it is assuredly not the result of metrical incompetence. I think he is as finely dowered as any poet of our time. Music reigns in his verse: his poetry is, in the strictest sense, written to music. Rhyme is bells for him, and

the cunning of chiming bells, their sweetness and
gravity, their joyful or sorrowful significance, is part
of his clearest effect. Among the later poems this is
yet plainer than among the earlier. There are a score
of proofs in *Time's Laughing Stocks*, some of which
have already been used in quotation above. Sometimes the rhyme is as lovely as the loveliest—as
Christina Rossetti's, even ; but if any other poet be
remembered in turning these pages, it is William
Barnes.

Of Mr. Hardy's love for Barnes—a love shared by so
different a poet as Coventry Patmore—many evidences
have been given. Did Barnes make him a poet ? A
poet he must needs have been, but I wonder whether
the direction of his work into this purely lyrical channel
is not due to his fellow Wessex poet. I wish Barnes
were better known ; he is not a great poet, but I
think of him as Prince Henry thought of his intellectual
master, Falstaff : I could better spare many a better
poet. Barnes's simplicity, his truthfulness, his *love*
(to say in one large word what might be missed in
twenty small ones), are expressed in verse of delicate
intricacy, so full of music as to seem at its best like
an echoing belfry jealous of every escaping note. Now
Mr. Hardy's themes are usually graver, often more
tragical than Barnes's ; but Mr. Hardy is like Barnes
in his aspiration to music. Wordsworth and Barnes,
with theirs alone is his lyrical work comparable ; with
an earnestness matching Wordsworth's, a music clear

The Moderns

as Barnes's, he has brooded upon matters of strange power and abiding significance. And as the severe sadness of his first poems lightens with the extraordinary gleams of the later, you recognize the development as being not only from the smaller to the larger view, but also from the lesser to the greater accomplishment. Constant return to the three earlier books of verse does but deepen the conviction that it is as a poet, far more surely than as a novelist, that Mr. Hardy's genius finds its most natural and essential expression. The praise that an imaginative writer of our own race might chiefly covet falls securely upon him—he is an English poet.

This conviction is but strengthened by considering *The Dynasts*. *The Dynasts* is Mr. Hardy's largest work, by reason at any rate of its subject. It is devoted to that huge historical complexity, the Napoleonic wars. The background of so many novels and poems becomes here the real matter of the drama.

As for its size, it forms three volumes, with nineteen acts. The subject is vast, the arena in which it is developed no smaller than all Europe, and its importance—even for us who can look at it in historical perspective—still immense. It is a drama of Napoleon *contra mundum,* or of Napoleon against Pitt, against Nelson, against Kutūzov, against Russian snows, against the inscrutable "Immanent Will" before which Pities and Ironies together are bowed. Napoleon is like a torch brandished over a bewildered hemisphere, and plunged hissing into indiscoverable night.

Let us note what Mr. Hardy himself says. He calls this work merely " a panoramic show," and reminds you " that in devising this chronicle-piece no attempt has been made to create that completely organic structure of action, and closely webbed development of character and motive, which are demanded in a drama strictly self-contained. . . . The subject is familiar to all; and foreknowledge is assumed to fill in the curves required to combine the whole gaunt framework into an artistic unity." It will be apparent, then, that such a play is only suitable for mental performance, as its author himself acknowledges; yet by a defiance of probability it was actually presented in a not wholly inadequate or unintelligible form, and with delicious success, a while ago.

Whether it be legitimate to use the liberties of the drama and at the same time disclaim the intention by which those liberties are commonly justified, is an old and fruitless discussion. I do not propose to flog this dead controversy anew, and will only point out that the adoption of the dramatic method here has made for an excellent economy. Lacking such economy, this immense conception would have needed an intolerably detailed unfolding. And farther, it must be remembered that the author, while assuming certain liberties proper to actual drama, has imposed on himself certain difficult restrictions, which point to a resolution almost as severe as that of the " scientific " historical writer :

> Whenever any evidence of the words really spoken or written by the characters in their various situations was attainable, as close a paraphrase has been aimed at as was compatible with the form chosen. And in all cases outside oral tradition, accessible scenery, and existing relics, my indebtedness for detail to the abundant pages of the historian, the biographer, and the journalist, English and foreign, has been, of course, continuous.

Another preliminary is that the action is enlarged and assisted by Phantom Intelligences—" contrivances of the fancy merely." Chief of these Spirits are, the Spirit of the Years, of the Pities, of Rumour, and (it is precisely characteristic of the author) Spirits Sinister and Ironic ; each Spirit with its own chorus. They have a " Fore Scene "—the Overworld—for their first manifestation, and they appear frequently throughout the panorama, in fulfilment of their double office. That office is, on the one hand, to give summary intelligence of the action and its obscurer causes and effects, and on the other, to convey a supra-terrestrial impression of human events.

> Their doctrines are but tentative, and advanced with little eye to a systematized philosophy warranted to lift " the burthen of the mystery " of this unintelligible world. The chief thing hoped for them is that they and their utterances may have dramatic plausibility enough to procure for them, in the words of Coleridge, " that willing suspension of disbelief for the moment which constitutes poetic faith."

But there is yet another Spirit—the ultimate, the absolute Spirit, the " Immanent Will "—into whose central darkness or sightless light are gathered all the threads of action. Mr. Hardy really means God but shrinks from so naming the " First or Fundamental Energy " ; and he speaks curiously of the abandonment of the masculine pronoun in allusion to " It," as the necessary consequence of the " long abandonment by thinkers of the anthropomorphic conception of the same." Upon this point we need not raise an endless dispute. Let us rather glance at the activity of these great Intelligences and their hints of the Immanent Will.

To the question of the Shade of the Earth the Spirit of the Years replies that the Immanent Will " works unconsciously,"

> ——Like a knitter drowsed,
> Whose fingers play in skilled unmindfulness.

The Prime Mover is a Puppet Master, and these Intelligences watch the twitchings curiously, even excitedly, from the precincts of the Overworld.

It is in this conception that the range and activity of the poet's imagination are displayed. Clear-eyed in immensity he looks from the Overworld :

The nether sky opens, and Europe is disclosed as a prone and emaciated figure, the Alps shaping like a backbone, and the branching mountain-chains like ribs, the peninsular plateau of Spain forming a head. Broad and lengthy lowlands stretch from the north of France across Russia like a grey-green garment hemmed by the Ural mountains and the glistening Arctic Ocean.

The point of view then sinks downwards through space, and draws near to the surface of the perturbed countries, where the peoples, distressed by events which they did not cause, are seen writhing, crawling, heaving, and vibrating in their various cities and nationalities.

I have already spoken, in dealing with the novels, of Mr. Hardy's wonderful range of vision, but nowhere are such clear evidences of it to be seen as in this drama. On the wings of an eagle he rises with the imagination and large intelligence of a poet, and reports his vision in such a sharp view as this, where Europe is minified to a prone emaciated figure. From such a height must you look with him upon the distressful confusion of this many-peopled continent. Or sometimes these Spirits mix with men, and as they withdraw from the crowd :

The confused tongues of the assembly waste away into distance, till they are heard but as the ripples of the sea from a high cliff, the scene becoming small and indistinct therewith. This passes into silence, and the whole disappears.

This quotation reminds me of the oldest feature of the Phantoms' activity—their tricksy intervention in human affairs. They love to masquerade among the maskers, to assume recognizable shapes, to drop incredible news into a man's ears and then vanish before he can interrogate them. But the wisest of the Phantoms is the Spirit of the Years, the interpreting spirit, the spirit of Wisdom, colder than the Pities, purer than the Ironies. It is by means, chiefly, of the Spirit of the Years that the author's apprehension of the Immanent Will is shown:

> The purposive, unmotived, dominant Thing
> Which sways in brooding dark their wayfaring.

Whether viewed simply as drama, or simply as philosophy, *The Dynasts* is of profoundest importance. Look at it by the light of these frequent flashes of apprehension. The Spirit of the Pities laments:

> ——the intolerable antilogy
> Of making figments feel——

But the older spirit of Wisdom does not lament, but looks. At the start of the disastrous invasion of Russia by Napoleon and his docile armies, the previsioning Pities see returning from the campaign only a docile leader and " a chattering flock, bleached skeletons." Why doth he go ? they ask:

SPIRIT OF THE YEARS. I'll show you why.
The unnatural light before seen usurps that of the sun, bringing into view, like breezes made visible, the films or brain-tissues of the Immanent Will, that pervade all things, ramifying through the whole army, Napoleon included, and moving them to Its inexplicable artistries.

NAPOLEON (*with sudden despondency*). That which has
    worked will work !—Since Lodi Bridge
The force I then felt move me moves me on
Whether I will or no ; and oftentimes
Against my better mind . . . Why am I here ?
—By laws imposed on me inexorably !
History makes use of me to weave her web

> To her long while aforetime-figured mesh
> And contemplated charactery : no more.

At another time watching the bloody desolation of Borodino, this absolute Spirit is discerned as :

> A Will that wills above the will of each,
> Yet but the will of all conjunctively.

At Waterloo, when " the see-saw sways," and the slaughter seems as indecisive as endless, the Spirit of the Years sees :

> That shaken and unshaken are alike
> But demonstrations from the Back of Things—

and discloses the innermost truth of all this loud conflict :

> A transparency as in earlier scenes again pervades the spectacle, and the ubiquitous urging of the Immanent Will becomes visualized. The web connecting all the apparently separate shapes includes Wellington in its tissue with the rest, and shows him, like them, as acting while discovering his intention to act. By the lurid light the faces of every row, square, group, and column of men, French and English, wear the expression of that of people in a dream.

And when Waterloo is won and lost, all that is seen by this clear-viewing Spirit is men driven to demonry by the " Immanent Unrecking " that works as one possessed ; while the Ironic Spirits declare its aim to be only

> ——to alter evermore
> Things from what they were before.

But not in this profound satiric despondency,

mocking at its own hopelessness and therefore more bitter than blasphemy, not so does *The Dynasts* end. There is an After Scene, in the Overworld, where the assembled Intelligences of this drama judge, not dispassionately, of the dark actions which have agitated these cruel confusions of the time. The Spirit of the Pities would fain repudiate the conception of an eternally " Inadvertent Mind " :—shall blankness be for aye ?   The Chorus of the Pities sing " a final hope," a Great and Good Will :

> Who had'st not shaped such souls as we
> If tender mercy lacked in Thee !

But the Chorus of the Years knows only of Loveless and Hateless, and asks why the " All-mover " urges life on, " Apprehending not how fare the sentient subjects of Its scheme."

With the Pities, however, the last word lies :

> But—a stirring thrills the air
> Like to sounds of joyance there
>   That the rages
>   Of the ages
> Shall be cancelled, and deliverance offered from the darts that
>   were,
> Consciousness the Will informing, till It fashion all things fair !

This ending is significant.

One does not look to the dramatic interpretation of history for a strict and consistent philosophy of life. This brief summary of the Overworld conception of our Underworld shows inconsistencies, but shows also, and very plainly, the general tendency of the author's shaping thought. And it is, I think, to be counted as something valuable that Mr. Hardy, whose attitude before the door of the Enigma of life has elsewhere been dismaying rather than encouraging, should here, when he speaks more at length, speak more hopefully. He deems lightly of these abstractions, " intended to be taken for what they may be worth." Their chief worth is that they hold steady candles to illume the darkness out of which this grave and powerful poet has striven to resolve something fixed and intelligible.

Leave this, and think of the plainer large virtues of this great conception. Perhaps it is true, to repeat the old phrase, that *The Dynasts* is history read by light-ning flashes. I have already shown that it is more than a flat recital of historical events. It is more, even, than a wonderfully selected, vivid, cinemato-graphic series of historical moments. For one thing humanity is dominant. Napoleon is very real, and is regarded as a real person, instead of an heroic or in-famous myth. Wellington, again, even he lives and moves through these memorable scenes, though in the light of a chilly, stiff admiration which is all that Mr. Hardy can feel for him. And so with all the other proudly named and nameless ones, sweeping busily by in the intense incandescence of Mr. Hardy's imagina-tion. Statesman and peasant alike are bathed in that glow :—nay for the peasant the author preserves a sympathy that is more tender and noble. I like the

kindness of the occasional footnote in which Mr. Hardy
has securely set the else-forgotten names of certain
Wessex soldiers of these long wars. It is this sympathetic grasp of the obscure life, this gentle and firm
regard of all that is natively faithful and enduring, that
marks his work with clearest character. Then, too, he
has succeeded in presenting with admirable verisimilitude some of the most difficult aspects of his subject.
Only in Tolstoi's *War and Peace* will you find a comparable attempt in imaginative literature to render the
moral and material disastrousness of Napoleon's
Russian campaign. Is there a finer account than Mr.
Hardy's of the heroic confusion of Waterloo, of Ney's
fruitless charge after charge, of the wave-like uncertainty of that loud Sabbath, than Mr. Hardy has
compressed into his few throbbing pages? Is there a
nobler echo of the pathos of Nelson's loss than that
which Mr. Hardy redoubles across the years? I
know that of strict dramatic development there seems
little, and that you may read page after page without
discovering that you are reading anything but a rather
abrupt, too-succinct abstract of that great time of
European strife. But remove a little : lift your eyes a
thought higher, follow the vaster orbit of the poet's
vision, and you will see that there is indeed a general
and natural dramatic development and opposition
slowly resolving into a clashing of kings against peoples,
rights against right, force against ideas, yesterday
against to-morrow. In drama, it has been said, divinity

is always present ; in such a large human drama as this, divinity moves as inevitably as man himself, with motions that you may plainly perceive, though with an intention you may not even nearly conjecture.

But not until that more tragical drama which opened in August 1914 had caused us to reflect a little, could the full significance of *The Dynasts* be gauged. Of the countless poems which the present war has provoked Mr. Hardy's *Song of the Soldiers* is the finest :

> What of the faith and fire within us
>> Men who march away
>> Ere the barn-cocks say
>> Night is growing grey,
> To hazards whence no tears can win us ;
> What of the faith and fire within us
>> Men who march away ? . . .
>
> In our hearts of hearts believing
>> Victory crowns t' e just,
>> And that braggarts must
>> Surely bite the dust,
> March we to the field ungrieving,
> In our hearts of hearts believing
>> Victory crowns the just.
>
> Hence the faith and fire within us
>> Men who march away
>> Ere th 'barn-cocks say
>> Night is growing grey,
> To hazards whence no tears can win us ;
> Hence the faith and fire within us
>> Men who march away.

But it is only a repeated expression of that intense, proud Englishism which is conspicuous in so much of this poet's work. The English quality of his landscape, as clearly marked as in Gray, Wordsworth, Arnold, Tennyson, is one of his chief virtues. The delight in English scenes and characters, in English humours and stupidities, in ancient unmoving rusticities, tells how finely native is the brain that has seen and felt and imaginatively re-created these things. *The Dynasts*, for all its continental vastness and metaphysical reach, is not too large to hold some of these intimately English things. There is that noble English air :

In the wild October night-time when the wind raved round the
    land,
And the Back-sea met the Front-sea, and our doors were
    blocked with sand,
And we heard the drub of Dead-man's Bay, where bones of
    thousands are,
We knew not what the day had done for us at Trafalgar,
        Had done,
        Had done,
      For us at Trafalgar !

And such humour as this :—

And you've come to see the sight, like the King and myself ? Well, one fool makes many. What a mampus o' folk it is here to-day. And what a time we do live in, between wars and wassailings, the ghost o' Boney and King George in flesh and blood ! . . . Everybody was fairly gallied this week when the King went out yachting, meaning to be back for the theatre ; and the time passed, and it got dark, and the play couldn't begin, and eight or nine o'clock came, and never a sign of him. I don't know when 'a did land, but 'twas said by all that it was a foolhardy pleasure to take.

FOURTH SPECTATOR. He's a very obstinate and comical

old gentleman, and by all account 'a wouldn't make port when asked to.

SECOND SPECTATOR. Lard, Lard, if 'a were nabbed, it wouldn't make a deal of difference! We should have nobody to zing to, and play single-stick to, and grin at through horse-collars, that's true. And nobody to sign our few documents. But we should rub along some way, goodnow.

But beyond all this *The Dynasts* holds passages which greet one now with a new ironic value :

> Five hundred thousand active men in arms
> Shall strike, supported by Britannic aid
> In vessels, men and money subsidies,
> To free North Germany and Hanover
> From trampling foes ; deliver Switzerland,
> Unbind the galled republic of the Dutch,
> Rethrone in Piedmont the Sardinian King,
> Make Naples sword-proof.

Or note this of Berlin, when Napoleon is approaching and a lady of the Court cries through her tears :

> The kingdom late of Prussia, can it be
> That thus it disappears ? a patriot-cry,
> A battle, bravery, ruin ; and no more ?

And now, too, when the figure of the Kaiser is so continually thrust before us, and the soberest sees it as best but tragicomic, it is with fresher interest that we turn back a moment to Napoleon in *The Dynasts*. In all that astonishing rise and fall Mr. Hardy sees nothing trivial or comic, but only the errancy of genius uncontrolled ; and there is a pure tragic note in the last scene when Napoleon, entering listlessly the

Wood of Bossu, is " stung by spectral questionings,"
knowing he has lived too long for his own greatness :

> I came too late in time
> To assume the prophet or the demi-god,
> A part past playing now.

The present time illuminates the phrase afresh.
" The Spirit of the Years," accosting Napoleon as he
broods, reminds him that his glory was that of the
Dresden days, when wellnigh every monarch bent
before him :

> Saving always England's—
> Rightly dost say " wellnigh." Not England's,—she
> Whose tough, enisled, self-centred, kindless craft,
> Has tracked me, springed me, thumbed me by the throat,
> And made herself the means of mangling me !

The Dynasts is a rare if it be not a unique instance of
a great creative work conceived in or touched by an
ironic spirit. Time has tragically deepened the irony,
and the nations of our alliance may ask if indeed the
fall of the Napoleonic system is but the forecast of the
fall of that darker military evil against which civilized
Europe has risen in desperate revolt.

IV

Mr. Hardy seems to me at times to be an Elizabethan
re-born, as Mr. Doughty is. Some of his characters
have the large simplicity and directness—whether well
or ill intending—and also the fantasticality, which we,

who have grown in subtlety, observe in looking back
at the great age. The singularity of certain scenes—
the scarlet reddleman dicing with Damon at midnight
by the light of gathered glow-worms, with piles of old
guineas at their sides; Troy imprisoning Bathsheba
within a swift dazzle of sword-strokes, as he shows her
the trick of his flashing weapon at dusk in the fern-
hollow; Stephen and Henry and Elfride meeting in
the tomb of the family into which she is doomed to
marry, the tomb she will so soon share; Tess and Angel,
after the murder of her enemy, groping at night around
the ancientry of Stonehenge;—this singularity alone
would serve to remind one of Webster and Tourneur,
of that delight in bold and energetic things which they
and others of their company sustain even when most
sombre in aim and effect. Another reminder of the
Elizabethans is seen in the coincidence of singular
power and careless technique. It has already been
suggested that Mr. Hardy is far from being an ideal
artist. There is a weakness of invention—how many
secret marriages or secret attempts at marriage will
you not find in the Wessex novels! The development
of the story is often uneasy, and resolved into a mere
series of episodes. To put it briefly, the intellectual
movement is sometimes slower than the moral or the
spiritual. . . . But the singular power is over most
though not all of his works. I once referred to Mr.
Hardy, from the secure shelter of an anonymous article,
as an English Turgénev. I think that is wrong. For

one thing, he lacks Turgénev's fine sense of form ; for another he yields to an excess of grief or horror ; he has a melancholy more enduring than the melancholy of the Russian master ; and he lacks that crowning beauty of Turgénev's noblest work—its lingering sweetness, like music hanging upon the ear after the last noise of a sunset storm.   He is, of course, like Turgénev in giving you the sense of " how interesting, how absorbingly wonderful, life is ! " rather than the mere sense of " how interesting so and so is ! "   But Mr. Hardy is more truly to be compared with Dostoieffsky, or with that English novelist of whom Dostoieffsky, even, reminds us, Emily Brontë.   There are authentic reverberations of the spiritual disquietude of *Wuthering Heights* in *The Mayor of Casterbridge*, *Tess* and *Jude the Obscure*. . . .   But let all these comparisons be taken simply as indirect suggestions of the true power and value of Mr. Hardy's contribution to imaginative literature, even of the uniqueness of which I spoke a moment ago.   Concede as much as you will, there remains clear token of the distinctive value of his work —its imaginative intensity, and its moral intensity.

When Mr. Hardy describes, does he describe an outward, detached thing ; or does he not rather look in his own heart, as though only *there* was the visible world contained, and describe natural appearances and natural influences with the same grave passion as another man might devote to the apprehension of his own soul ?   In his heart are stored those impressive

finely etched scenes, as truly imaginative as Wordsworth's. Thus a storm is felt as though it were the
death of a friend ; a heath becomes a mood, and trees
are to be counted amongst the persons of his drama.
Whatever visible phenomena are touched upon have,
you become persuaded, chiefly a passionate subjective
life.

Of the moral intensity of Mr. Hardy's prose and
verse I have already said, I fear, too much, or too much
that is impertinent. He touches life and it bleeds ; and
he touches it again with a quivering, aching earnestness that for pure pity laughs and mocks. Had he
published nothing since *Jude the Obscure*, we should
have murmured indeed at the exhaustion of all colour
and grace, all courage of life, even from his later work.
We should have seen in him an example of that spiritual
dismay in the midst of material advance which is
far from rare in the literature of the last twenty years.
Life's a hard thing, he seems to say, because of iron
convention ; an unjoyful, raptureless thing, because
of unfulfilled aims everywhere apparent ; worst of all,
a vain mocking thing, because the sport of ironic
Immortals. But Mr. Hardy's work does not end thus ;
both in his lyrical and dramatic verse a finer hopefulness, a firmer assurance, has lightened the later darkness.

Unique as he is in power, his restrictions are remarkable. Not his to take " all life as his province " ; nor
is it his to attempt it. The recognition is rarer than

the power, even. The bare bones of life are seen in his work, as in Wordsworth's and Crabbe's, of life at its simplest and most elemental ; and when he turns to the more complex social regions, he is moving about in worlds not realized. He is (you might say in a hasty effort to get near the truth) all that Meredith is not. Reading Mr. Hardy, you think of Meredith as, in reading Wordsworth, you might think of Shelley. Swiftness and slowness, restlessness and sluggishness, the mercurial and the saturnine—the opposing qualities are sharply revealed in the two novelists. Wit set many snares for Meredith, but humour often saves Mr. Hardy when philosophy and science have done their worst to make him dull. His attitude is an essentially modern one—sombre, intent, unshrinking ; confronting life steadily and a little bitterly ; an attitude from which life is seen as a tragical thing and (half for pity's sake) turned to irony. Life makes each a poet : Meredith a poet with a vehement faith built upon somewhat uncertain foundations ; Mr. Hardy a poet with a steady disavowal of faith, justified by a not quite fair presentment of character and circumstance. They are both typical of our swift much-considering days, when questions are more often and more easily asked than answered.

MAURICE MAETERLINCK

I

IN one of his later writings, *Mary Magdalene*, Maeterlinck raises questions which need a little space for answering. The subject of this play prevented its production in England, at any rate until lately ; and thus English readers have been debarred from judging the little drama precisely as the author conceived it. But apart from this there is, for some, the point of the admissibility of dramatic treatment of themes which they regard as uniquely sacred. Many people—and of them many not avowedly religious—demur at the dramatic presentation of such a theme as this of *Mary Magdalene*, because they conceive in the death of Christ a significance more solemn and awful than clings to other deaths, or to the mere idea of death. Death itself, without this unique personal reference, is profoundly sacred, and indeed much might be said for prohibiting death-scenes (and others of scarcely less solemnity) from theatrical presentation. But no such exclusion would be tolerable in England, where amazing liberties are shadowed by more amazing prohibitions. And for myself, though I hold by the uniqueness of that scene which is the second subject of Maeterlinck's play, I cannot join in the objection to its dramatization merely on the ground of its unique sacredness.

Let me say why this is. I think that the crucifixion of Christ appeals always in a dramatic way to those who regard most devoutly its exclusive sacredness. Love always has a swift and powerful dramatic tendency ; and some men whose religious love has been at once profound and transfiguring, have seen the atonement as a constant, moving tragedy of sacrifice in which they themselves, with the egoism of supreme humility, have taken a privileged if supernumerary part. Around the central figure they see ranged all the world, in a vast cirque of multitudinous human experience, and themselves present, foremost in the crowd acclaiming or reviling. Except with themselves dramatically present, except in the light of this pious egoism, they do not and could not realize His life and death. . . . I speak of people who, turning sometimes late in life from muddy ways of life, have brought to their religion a motley experience but an inviolate love. They have been often poor people, upon whom the great revelation has fallen blindingly ; and when their spiritual perception has returned, it has been to discover a new world more intensely real, more overwhelmingly urgent, than the insistent plain world around them. Whatever shrewdness, whatever intellectual veracity, whatever inward loyalty of love lingered in them before this revelation came so blindingly—and the reader

may perhaps believe that poor unlearned people are
not always empty of shrewdness, veracity and love—
has been perpetually renewed and increased, as lamps
are renewed with oil ; and this shrewdness, veracity and
love have unfolded before their spiritual vision the constant drama of the life of Christ and His disciples.
They conceive these things, I say, dramatically : else
never at all ; and how better to conceive them I cannot
think. Admit that their theology is weak, their doctrine sharp and crude ; but their apprehension of the
spiritual truth within the doctrine, of the supreme
Personality of which the doctrine presents scientifically
a separate aspect, is amazing and irrefragable. I have
heard them unfolding the miracles of Christ as they
saw them ; and never till then did I know how intense
was the dramatic instinct of the soul, nor how inseparable it was from pure devoutness. I remember, for
instance, their sharp visualization of the miracle of
the impotent man let down through the roof of the
house where Jesus sat :—how keen was their enjoyment
of the crowd's protest against this forcible, clamorous
intrusion ; how jealously they, the bearers of the
impotent man's bed, wrenched wider the opening in
the roof so that he might be cunningly lowered to the
Lord ; how instinctively *right* was their swift identification of themselves with the timorous, mistrustful yet
eager sufferer. *They* were the crowd that rambled
round the house ; *they* the bearers that bore the impotent man on his bed ; *they* the people within the house,

astonished at the tumult on the roof ; *they* the impotent man let down into the divine presence, and healed, and turning adoring away. For theirs was the release from the apathy, the isolation which the outer world had set as a seal on their hearts. . . . And as with this, so with another and another of those throbbing human incidents in the divine life. These people, I repeat, were not fools ; they had, with the vigorous shrewdness of the adult mind (necessarily occupied with unending problems of bread and shelter), the simplicity of the child's mind, which is always dramatic. And I am sure that the dramatic scene constantly present to them—of sublime tragedy with frequent relief of delightfully instinctive comedy[1]—had a vividness, an essential reality, beyond the reality of Shakespeare or Synge, Webster or Tolstoi, Molière or Dostoieffsky. Equally sure am I that except thus, and except with the imaginative identification of themselves with every person of the drama save Jesus Himself, they could never have apprehended the profounder truth within every incident and every word.

Will this long digression be pardoned ? Yet it is not purely a digression, since it serves for the criticism of *Mary Magdalene*. *Mary Magdalene* is in many ways a simple and beautiful play. It is occupied less than any other of its author's works with the evocation

[1] The comedic relief which these devout people perceived in blind Bartimaeus (for instance) calling down to the Lord from his tree, was always naïve and delightful.

of a childish simulation of fear or mystery. It is straightforward, and not so seemingly "refined" as those others. There is a natural characterization seen faintly in Mary Magdalene herself, more sharply in Silanus and Nicodemus. But Maeterlinck sometimes forgets not to be Maeterlinck of European reputation ; and then he drops such an undramatic Maeterlinckian phrase as : " We stand here face to face, with our two madnesses, *which are more powerful than ourselves.*" Equally intrusive upon the mood of the play is the speech of Silanus,—a kind of Renan or polite Panurge, a typical reasonable amiable man,— though it gives in the compass of a single page a finer specimen of Maeterlinck's reflectiveness than may easily be found in his work : a specimen ending justly with, "Whether the dead sleep or wake, I will not give them a thought unless they teach me to make a better use of my life." . . . On the whole the play is remarkably simple, quiet, self-contained. No passion breaks through its peaceful waters, no violent life mars its beautiful immobility. Echoes float over it—as of Sterne—in the pages where Silanus reproves Longinus, with words of his own devising, for grief over a child lost,—irresistibly recalling, even by its entire extraneousness, the famous scene where Mr. Shandy consoles himself for the loss of his son. But this is easily forgotten when the third act is reached, in the house of Joseph of Arimathea. There is discovered a gathering of those whom Christ has healed, the named and nameless of the miracles of the gospels. Maeterlinck handles crowds impressively, conveying a rather curious sense of personal ineffectuality and thwarted intelligences. Three people in his hands become a crowd, and a crowd is reduced to three people. In this third act the healed and restored ones, prizing life the more since it is, by the Lord's mercy, richer now and larger, shrink fearfully away at the threat of danger, as nimble with disloyal fear as lately with grateful joy. It is Maeterlinck's old well-handled theme. There only remain uninfected Martha, Joseph of Arimathea and Mary Magdalene. In Mary Magdalene's hands is lodged all the energy of the scene ; and she upbraids the rest because they will not rescue Jesus by force. Verus, her lover, in turn upbraids her because she refuses to save Him but by force, and persists in refusal when his alternative is too plain to be put by. Sharply dramatic is the moment when Verus tells the timorous crowd that not only Christ but themselves also are betrayed by Magdalene ; and the crowd's fury against her is only diverted by the passing in the street of Christ and His captors on the way to Calvary.

The subject, you will notice, is a difficult one, and it is treated mainly with careful reverence ; though I imagine that objection may be felt at the jealous suggestions of Verus concerning the relations of Mary Magdalene to Christ. This Maeterlinck would doubtless explain as a simple dramatic necessity : and I cannot conceive of another explanation, or a worse. But this apart, the treatment is unobjectionable. Why then, is it that the play offends ?

Here we return to the larger view. The reason is that Maeterlinck sees the whole theme externally. That true and exciting dramatic treatment of the theme by common people springs from intense personal conviction. Probably such people, given the literary trick, would shrink horrified from the traffic of the stage with this for attraction, simply because of the intensity of their conviction ; but lacking that intensity of conviction the literary trick, however finely cultivated and richly associated with other gifts, will probably fail of its appeal. Farther : the subject is one of universal familiarity, but I do not see that it is of universal dramatic permissibility. Whether we of to-day like it or not, the Christian idea has penetrated so profoundly the whole of our life—conscious and unconscious, individual and collective—that its main and intimate truths are as general and as sacred as the very principle of life hiding in our veins. And beyond this, these main and intimate truths are regarded by a large body of people in different countries, speaking various tongues, of various position and ability, as uniquely sacred, to repeat the phrase. There is, then, a reason, founded deeper than reason, for approaching the life of Christ with reluctance when it is to be considered for a purpose so public, so general and—largely—so crassly unimaginative and unilluminated as theatrical representation. Maeterlinck has treated his subject with care but not with the reverence of discipleship. His attitude has at best a kind of retrospective politeness : careful, precise, cold. You look in vain for any hint of passion, warmth, or even intimate understanding. It is true that the outward and visible signs are there, but not the inward, invisible emotion. Christ's entrance is decorated with " an incomparable silence," amid which " there rises, absolute sovereign of space and the hour, a wonderful voice, soft and all powerful, intoxicated with ardour," etc., etc. . . . In such a tone and with far more of human ecstasy does Meredith describe the voice of Emilia heard at evening in the pine wood. Even from a purely dramatic point of view the impression is unfortunate, since it goes to confirm that deeper impression of externality—most fatal of all impressions for a dramatist.

There is another unfortunate thing of which I must speak, namely, that the play appears after all but a contribution to the literature of the courtesan, to which French books (and the literary Maeterlinck seems purely French) have paid so inordinate an homage. No doubt there is a certain very obvious contrast between Magdalene the courtesan in the first act, and Magdalene the devotee in the third ; but then, the suggestions of Verus in the third act remind you only too surely of her position in the first. And so you wonder if, after all, the interest of the author—discreet and inoffensive in itself—has not been first and last in the courtesan ; and that again adds to the subtle feeling of distaste that grows throughout the play. Moreover, the conversion of Magdalene does not bring its own indispensable evidence and conviction of veracity ; relying upon your familiarity with the redeemed woman, the dramatist asks you to take on trust her redemption from the woman he shows her to have been. This, of course affects the distinctness of Mary Magdalene as a character of the play. There is a similar lack of conviction in the conversion of Bellafrond in Dekker's famous play ; but there the lack is less conspicuous by reason of the energy of Dekker's portrayal and the natural vigour of the whole work. Maeterlinck is content with the contrast, and thus simply emphasizes his apparent preoccupation. He ends with the parting of Verus and Magdalene, who has dismissed her sometime lover, " without anger, simply, in a voice from another life, full of peace, full of divine clarity and certainty." Magdalene " remains motionless, as though in ecstasy, and all illumined with the light of the departing torches."

Just such an attitude, just such a light, do I remember having seen in an exquisitely coloured photograph of the willing martyr in *The Sign of the Cross,* a play produced in London some years ago and still re-visiting provincial towns.

In *Joyzelle* Maeterlinck embraced the advantages and the disadvantages of familiar characters and familiar situations. Excellent opportunities are presented to the dramatist in many ancient stories, and the

Arthurian cycle has been prolific of dramatic or poetic interpretation. Translated by Mr. de Mattos, *Joyzelle* makes a wide appeal in English as an essay in philosophic drama. The obvious quip may well be spared, even though its justice be almost irresistible. So far as this play fails, it fails mainly because it provokes comparisons which are as unsustainable as inevitable, and as inevitable as absurd. Maeterlinck has taken Prospero from *The Tempest* and renamed him Merlin ; Ariel becomes Arielle ; Miranda becomes Joyzelle, and Ferdinand Lancéor. The only point of difference is that the beloved child is Lancéor, not Joyzelle. It is not at all difficult to see that Merlin is not the Merlin of Morte D'Arthur, and to forget that Mallory ever named him. But the scheme of *Joyzelle* makes it quite impossible to forget the scheme of *The Tempest.* Merlin, lord of his island, has brought together by his art and Arielle's aid Lancéor and Joyzelle, Lancéor not knowing that Merlin is his father ; and Merlin is presented as persecuting them, at once stimulating and befouling their love, and behaving as a Caliban-possessed Prospero might. Just as Shakespeare reveals Prospero artfully provoking and thwarting the love of Ferdinand and Miranda, but doing this for no indiscoverable reason ; so Maeterlinck presents Merlin overlording the love of Lancéor and Joyzelle, but for a reason which remains unintelligible until the end of the play is near. And as Prospero employs poor Ariel upon his lofty and childishly benignant purposes, and resorts to magic for his ends ; so Merlin engages his tearful Arielle and uses such gorgeous magicry as we in England usually reserve for the great scene in pantomime. Flowers grow huge and oppressively lovely, a wild megalomania possesses the enchanted garden ; and Arielle, assuming human shape, lures Lancéor with her naked beauty among the magic growth. Froward and omnipotent master of these spells, Merlin demands that Joyzelle shall desert Lancéor ; and Joyzelle, no wiser than the reader concerning the cause of this atrocious enmity, says she never, never will. By further magic stratagem Lancéor is brought to the brink of death, and Joyzelle is asked to save him by yielding herself to the decrepit desire of Merlin the Mysterious. She yields :—need it be said, not without maidenly shrinking and acute reflections upon justice and destiny ? . . . But no ! She will anticipate compliance by violence, and is arrested in an attempt to stab Merlin, lying seemingly asleep. Then is the way clear for those last act explanations to the astonished lovers which were the fashion—and indeed the necessity—of every play fifty years ago.

And what of the explanation ? That is given by Maeterlinck the philosopher to Maeterlinck the dramatist, to do what he can with it. Merlin's art has unfolded to him the malignity of destiny towards his son and Joyzelle ; this and that sore trial must be endured, this and that sharp or abhorrent proof of love required. His wisdom, aware of the dangers besieging the delicacy of young love in a harsh world, resolves upon anticipating what cannot be averted ; and so he assumes the part of the dark angel, tempting and proving and controlling, and adroitly whipping off the mask in the last scene. It is destiny that demands this, destiny that permits this evasion of the doom of the years to come, great and profound destiny that is subdued to this ingenious trick. It is destiny, too, that yields Merlin prescience of his ultimate humiliation by Vivianne, without permitting him to plagiarize his own doom.

Is it unpardonable to treat such a thing thus lightly ? If Maeterlinck wished to suggest an attitude towards destiny, an interpretation of destiny, he has surely loaded his laborious fantasy with heavy gear ; and if, on the other hand, the whole thing is but a fantasy, then the philosophical suggestion is profoundly unfortunate. The vague and curious relation of Arielle to Merlin forbids your acceptance of the play as merely fantastic ;—Arielle has been interpreted by one of Maeterlinck's eulogists as Merlin's subliminal consciousness, by which obscure previsionary power he is able to thwart destiny. . . . Maeterlinck is obsessed here with the idea of destiny and has thrust it into the speech even of his passion-vaunting lovers. It is perfectly true that destiny is the ultimate mystery of many of the classic dramas which Maeterlinck is fond of meditating upon ; but in them it is a power quiet and almost secret, just in proportion to its profound immanence. It hides in the heart of Antigone and Oedipus, Hippolytus and Phaedra, quiet as light, subtle as water. Whether Maeterlinck is right in reverting to a conception which, noble and lofty once, is not therefore equally lofty and noble always, is an inevitable question. To ignore all that immense liberation of thought, all that enrichment of life and purpose, all that extension of ideas, all that increase of perspective, which century following century has slowly purchased, is both inexplicable and sad. It is precisely against this exclusion that Maeterlinck the essayist animadverts so often and so strongly.

Monna Vanna preceded *Joyzelle* by a single year and an enormous superiority. Of all Maeterlinck's plays it is the one which would best appear on the stage, and the one we have had the least chance of seeing publicly performed in England, thanks to the nice care of the censor. Unlike his other dramas, *Monna Vanna* really moves, and breaks into a dramatic action as plain and natural as the action of wave against rock. The story, of heroic self-sacrifice, insane incredulity and savagery —the story, in short, of poor Lady Godiva lifted to a more dramatic level—is sufficiently well known to English readers to need no recital here. It is developed with admirable clearness and directness.—And is it not odd, then, that a play so good as *Monna Vanna* should have been followed so soon by one so weakly conceived as *Joyzelle*? *Monna Vanna* has a firmer hold upon earth than *Joyzelle* and is less strenuously

" philosophical " ; in the former Maeterlinck is content to let what philosophy there is appear where it properly should, namely, in the action of the play ; but *Joyzelle* is tediously distended by a great deal of curious quasi-mystical fancy. . . . There is one situation in *Monna Vanna*, that of the visit of Vanna to Prinzivalle, which calls for a singular care and delicacy in the author ; and the call is well and truly met save for one lapse. Unluckily, this is the more conspicuous since the author carefully avoids the obvious reflections upon her unique adventure and the sacrifice of modesty and more for the sake of starved Pisa ; but you are not given reason to doubt her sense of the vast sacrifice except in this brief passage. Mantle-clad only, she stands in Prinzivalle's tent ; and the Florentine general, remarking that the night will be cold, suddenly asks if she has weapons or poison concealed. " I have only my sandals and mantle," she answers ; " search me if you are afraid." There would be no need to pause on this were *Monna Vanna* not so finely and surely a play, as its author's other dramatic experiments sometimes fail to be. Nor would there be any need to question the fitness of the rather Platoish dialogue upon love, a dialogue which, in the acute circumstances of her visit, appears a little unconvincing. . . . One must hesitate to suggest a choice of subject different from an author's own choice ; yet is it possible to regret sincerely that Maeterlinck has not more often used his peculiar power in dramatic essays of such a plain human type as *Monna Vanna.*

I do not think it necessary to speak in detail of *Aglavaine and Selysette, Sister Beatrice* and *Ardiane and Barbe Bleue.* They do little beyond witness to the somewhat surprising versatility of their author ; they have no secure place in the development of his work, and no very bold merits of their own. *Sister Beatrice,* it must be owned, bears touches and hints of a passion rare in this calm poet ; but even in this it fails in comparison with the lyrical energy of John Davidson's *Ballad of a Nun,* dealing with the same ancient theme. *Aglavaine and Selysette* is in the manner of *Pelleas and Melisanda,* and has been so finely praised that I shrink from avowing a defective appreciation. In truth, it is a play too full of tears and kisses ; and tears falling unceasingly through five acts, kisses exchanged untiringly between two women, tears and kisses endlessly extolled and poeticized—I speak only for myself when I say that they become oppressive, and leave on the play a damp, melancholy, " missish " effect. Professor Mackail speaks with admiration of the play's construction, but the very instance he quotes as conclusive (that is, the exact repetition of a scene and a situation) points to a construction too easily neat. One should not look here for the compact, tense form of Ibsen ; it is, in fact, a virtue as strikingly foreign in *Aglavaine and Selysette,* as a patch of Elizabethan splendid rhetoric would be amid the delicate uncertainties of the dialogue. In this play, again, there is an instance of the ruthless and slightly callous exploitation of a small child's innocence and fear, which appears in the earlier plays. Maeterlinck seems not to see that an effective contrast can be too easily obtained, or to fear that the recurrence of a device in play after play is apt to emphasize any casual hints of artificiality. . . . *Ardiane and Barbe Bleue* gives another of these sharp reminders of the circular motion of Maeterlinck's mind. The most conspicuous thing in it, the disclosure of the six rooms full of dazzling jewels, is a parallel of the sumptuous description of showering flowers in *Sister Beatrice*, where the nuns are about to whip the offending Eve out of the Virgin, and find their lashes turn to miraculous blossoms.

II

Thus we reach the plays of Maeterlinck's earliest period, and they demand an attention more close and sympathetic than is evoked by any other of this poet's work. A quarter of a century has passed since *La Princesse Maleine* was published—a play that takes us back to the time when Maeterlinck was immersed in the study of our own Elizabethans. That he should even have made translations of Ford's raw and painful masterpiece, *'Tis Pity She's a Whore*, is only momentarily remarkable. True there does not seem to be very much of the wild energy of those splendid sombre playwrights of Shakespeare's period—Webster,

Turner, Dekker, Ford, etc.—in the hesitating fragility
of Maeterlinck's work. But you come to see in the
Belgian poet something of the same acute sensibility
to horror, the same intense preoccupation with terrible
and mournful things ; only, in the English originals
you will find an impetus and violent swiftness which
are wholly absent from Maeterlinck's plays. In *La
Princesse Maleine* Professor Mackail, himself one of the
first of English critics to appreciate Maeterlinck's work,
is unable to find anything more than " the morbid
overstrain, the piling of horror upon horror till the
final effect, instead of the tragic calm, is a kind of
exhausted stupor," which reveals itself to him in Ford
and Webster. With admirable confidence in his powers,
however, Maeterlinck disengaged himself from these
too-heavy shackles :—he could no more have expressed his soul in the Elizabethan medium than he
could " dance equipped from head to foot in iron
mail." . . . The play known to English readers as *The
Sightless* is characteristic of his strange personal talent.
It deals with horror, with the horror of blind men and
women suddenly left forlorn in a forest of extraordinary gloom. The priest has brought them from the
asylum and dies as he sits by, while they, the blind
men and women, not knowing where he is or that he
can no longer help them, accuse him of callousness
and grow afraid as children in the chilly dark. The
only external action of the play is the effort of the dog
who comes to lead them to their dead priest, and the

searching of the priest's body by the blind men for the fled signs of life.

Never has Maeterlinck achieved anything more difficult or more disturbing. The drama is a characteristically stationary one, of a quietness so acute as to be a positive, a sentient thing, rather than the mere negation of sound. Out of the gloom of the forest rise the brief querulous voices of the blind—themselves neither living nor dead, but awfully companioned by death, in the person of the cold priest, and by life in the person of the mad blind woman's child. Their voices are like tiny ineffectual sparks in that unhallowed darkness. The play is sustained unfalteringly at a tension the most delicate, by means the most simple. The short reiterated sentences have a poignancy for the reader which, when spoken, they have not for the poor blind ones, but which they will have for them too when these come to know what the reader suspects, and repeat to themselves all they have said and heard. The young blind woman says : " Il me semble que je sens le clair de lune sur mes mains." They smell flowers on the wind, and the sixth blind man goes to pick them for her, crushing them as he moves. " J'entends que vous brisez des tiges vertes ! Arretez-vous ! arretez-vous ! " she cries ; " Il me semble que j'ai vu ces fleurs autrefois "—and plaits them in her hair, while the oldest blind man says, " J'entends le bruit de vos cheveux."

This curious tenuity of sense is surely conveyed to the reader from beginning to end of the piece. In-

178

finitely remote do the sightless seem as you look
through the faint cloudy moonlight in which Maeterlinck steeps them. He misses no means of sharpening
this distant and poignant effect, using even a kind of
sombre irony; as when, of the fifth man who is deaf,
the third says, " Il faut avouer que les sourds sont bien
malheureux ! " Sounds heard by the forlorn blind
ones are charged with new mystery. " J'entends que
vous vous penchez vers moi," says the third; and the
first answers, " J'entends encore un autre bruit. . . ."
But the oldest blind woman thinks it is the mad
woman rubbing her eyes. The wind rises; and in the
midst of the noise, of which they each only distinguish
a part, the sound of footsteps breaks their echoing
reverie. " Je crois'que ce n'est pas le pas d'un homme ! "
and they find the dog has come back to take them to
the dead priest. Why did he die ? they ask. He lost
courage when they grumbled, says one; he died in
fetching water for the mad woman, says another.
Afraid, they sit by the dead man in the chill air, clasping hands. Snow falls, touching them like cold ghosts ;
they wonder what it is and, shivering, listen to the
mad woman's child wailing. They hear footsteps and
lift the child that he may see for them; and so they
all fall silent and the child cries more sorely.

Even if one shrinks from the introduction of the
child, the only seeing creature, into this scene, the
rare power and restraint of the play make it a remarkable thing. It is almost intolerable in its sharpness,

if you think long of the child. But this sense abides scarcely a moment, for its permanence could only be secured if the characters were human. Maeterlinck has not used men and women but merely voices ; and that in spite of this the play should stir so profoundly amid our deeper pity and terror, is its highest praise.

The Seven Princesses is stated by an English translator, Mr. William Metcalfe, to be a remarkable instance of hypnotism by iteration. I can believe that it is, and only add that hypnotism is notoriously uncertain in its action. I do not think that a hypnotic literature would be very admirable, or that Maeterlinck's reputation is well secured by a play which depends for its appeal on any sort of hypnotic influence, cunningly contrived by repetition or revolution. *The Sightless*, a far finer play, is to be read with the whole intelligence as well as with the whole emotions ; but to read *The Seven Princesses* with the whole intelligence would be disastrous.

But in *Pelleas* the full intelligence of the reader may stir in response to the intelligence of the poet. First you perceive this play to be a thing of beauty, next that the beauty is mostly pictorial, and then that it is sometimes truly dramatic. It is fantastic where Golaud finds Melisanda, in the second scene,[1] by a forest spring ; pictorial when she is brought to the typical

---

[1] Really the first of the play, as the first scene is, so far as I can perceive, quite unrelated, except for a faintly conceivable purpose of contrast.

Maeterlinckian castle in the typical gloom-enfolded
forest, and nurses an idle unease much as Mariana does
in Tennyson's lovelier verse ; dramatic when the love of
Pelleas and Melisanda is discovered, and Pelleas is attacked by Golaud, and when Melisanda, prematurely
bringing forth a son to the avenging Golaud, dies as
he sobs by her bed.   It is a slightly more human play
than *The Sightless*, but shows the same way of reitera-
tion, the same fondness for darkness, with but casual
gleams of extraordinary light.   Here as in the earlier
play a child is used for seeing ; and few things could
be more painfully effective than the scene of Golaud,
hungry with anger and jealousy, lifting little Yniold
to the window, that he may look in upon Pelleas and
Melisanda sitting silent in a sad ecstasy of nervous
love.   Here for the first time the poet masters the
secret of the active dramatic moment. . . . But there
is no more need to point to the haunting pre-Raphaeli-
tish beauty of this play, than to the beauty of *The
Defence of Guenevere* by the poet who was prompt to
recognize the quality of Maeterlinck's play.   One scene
in particular recalls that poem of Morris's—

> Rapunzel, Rapunzel,
> Let down your hair—

almost too emphatically. What, however, I would speak
of is the early indication of that attitude towards life
which is now so famously Maeterlinckian. Golaud
is brought home wounded. " I was hunting quietly in
the forest. My horse bolted all of a sudden, for no

reason. . . . I had just counted the twelve strokes of noon. At the twelfth stroke, he suddenly took fright and ran like one blind and mad, against a tree." Here is already an allusion to the unaccountableness of events which Maeterlinck afterwards sweeps into his theory of destiny, and weaves into whatever he happens to be writing.

And there is a touch of symbolism slightly too emphatic when little Yniold, trying to lift a stone, finds it " heavier than all the world, heavier than all that has happened." Symbolism which is obvious and conscious inevitably gives a suggestion of unreality, and Maeterlinck does not always avoid the suggestion. . . . These things, however, it would be too exacting to reckon faults ; they are merely features which assert themselves a little too sharply, and remind you of their reappearance in other works where they have a less felicitous neighbourhood. *Pelleas and Melisanda* remains perhaps the most beautiful of Maeterlinck's writings—not beautiful as urgent, beating life is, but with the arrested half-remote beauty of a picture by Rossetti.

Not beautiful as life is. . . . Is it not, after all, foolish to speak of human life in touching this play ? Is the beauty really human at all ? I feel a great hesitation in treating *Pelleas* as a human thing ; but if it be indeed more than a filmy fantasy of moonlight loves, what shall be said ? What shall be said of the moral enervation, the wispy listlessness of will, that betrays every character here (and many in other plays) as strengthless, strawlike and meaningless for men who see meaning and courage in life and grief and love ?

Turn now to *Three Little Dramas for Marionettes*, comprising *Alladine and Palamides, The Death of Tintagiles* and *Interior*. The first is a mere echo of *Pelleas and Melisanda*, an echo which has lost even the faint humanity of that play and simply goes reverberating among the idle chambers of the mind. It is such a brief little play as this that points to the distinction between Maeterlinck's real but fragile genius and the harder, larger, incorruptible genius of the greater writers. The first, a man of fine and high talent, repeats himself often and seldom to advantage ; the others never merely repeat themselves but speak anew out of a lively plenteousness. *The Death of Tintagiles* is once more an echo—a thin voice quivering out of the careful darkness which Maeterlinck evokes so faithfully. He plays cunningly upon the theme of a child's fear and the malignity of the unknown ; a theme used with such astonishing and overwhelming effect by the supremely subtle artist of *The Turn of the Screw*. But Mr. Henry James has developed his extraordinarily cruel and extraordinarily pitiful study within the range of human contact, and so justified the else unforgiveable acuteness of horror. Maeterlinck, on the other hand, has seemingly renounced the human contact, the human note ; and his play becomes an essay in abstract and dehumanized horror.

But look, then, at *Interior*, and you will at a glance
note how that tiny drama is saved from being no more
than an essay in dehumanized fear, and saved precisely
by the just-perceptible human sense that creeps ting-
lingly upon all that is said and done. *Interior* is a play
where the silences are sombre beyond the words, and
a mist rises slowly over the raw tragic sorrow that
knocks unheard at the door of the house. The situation—that of a group of poor folk halting outside a
house with news of overwhelming loss, and daring not
to enter—is one which the slow-moving, intense spirit
of the poet is peculiarly capable of realizing. There is
profound mournfulness in the group which he conjures
there, a mournfulness which is yet (you feel) but the
shadow of the more abiding sorrow which shall be
theirs who in the house sit on unguessing. Emissaries
of all the world's untowardness, the peasants hesitate,
half-warily, half-nervously, with their news like a
sword in their hands. . . . In their reluctance, and the
unconsciousness of the bereaved, lies that faint hint of
warm humanity which keeps the play sweet and vital
even in its sombre tremulousness.

III

I have gone thus backward through Maeterlinck's
plays, from the late to the early, because the early are
the best of all his inventions, and because I could not
be pleased to follow the best with the reluctant de-

preciation occurring here and there in what is said of
the others. Is it cruel to say of an earnest and thoughtful
writer, after years of work, that his earliest work is his
best ? I am afraid that all that Maeterlinck has purchased with the years' experience, all the purchase of
his care and patience, has not taught him any truer
mode of expression nor any better thing to express,
than is seen in those two or three plays of which it is
difficult to speak without quick admiration. And
indeed, why attempt to moderate one's admiration of
admirable things ? . . . But there remains one play
of which I have said nothing yet, since it seems hardly
in the line of Maeterlinck's normal development,
though it is so attractive a thing as *The Blue Bird.*

Did Maeterlinck ever dream of the popularity which
The Blue Bird was to win—and win not only in England ? Here alone scores of editions have been exhausted, while the theatre presented the delicious
pageant year after year to growing audiences. In
Russia, one is told, *The Blue Bird* has had a fascination
utterly dwarfing its fascination for the English mind.
To few men is it given to achieve this superb conquest
of alien peoples, and to fewer still to achieve it almost
equally in such different mediums as the essay and the
play. The curious fancifulness which is busy in earlier
plays and essays upon more serious and melancholy
missions, is here employed upon the etherealization of
the child's instinct for simple happiness. Or more
strictly, partly upon the etherealization and partly

(pardon the clumsy phrases) upon the moralization of that simple instinct. It is a charming pageant that Maeterlinck marshals, after the manner of that pageant which Lamb rehearsed in his *New Year's Coming of Age*. Just such a pageant would Longfellow have tried to set out, had his instinct for the theatre been more acute. Prevented from seeing it on the stage, I can yet understand without the least dubiety how excellently it must needs hold the stage ; and the theatre apart, more clearly still can I see how the constant sentiment of kindliness explicit in it must needs recommend it to all those who respond—as who does not !—to this ready stimulus in life and letters. It is inevitable that the parable should here and there show much as does a boy in a suit too short in sleeves and legs ; but this only serves to remind the reader of the difficulty of the author's task. Were the play a fraction less unpretentious or less sincerely meant for wise entertainment, some of it would appear ludicrous ;— as, for instance, " The Kingdom of the Future," a singular excrescence, or the added " Palace of Happiness," too undisguised a sermon. . . . But to speak thus is to choke *The Blue Bird* with the most indigestible pellets of criticism ; and the answer to all such quibbles is the enormous general popularity of the play. I have only one regret,—that Maeterlinck should have imputed to the Cat such incredible perfidy as Tylette's. It is not fairly done. I believe Maeterlinck has already been reproached for this injustice ;

but I could not face my own delicate, ferocious, faithful Persian Sappho, whose eyes are purest green, nor her enormous, mild, lithe son, Topaz, whose eyes are golden, without adding a solemn protest. They are beside me here, each of them strange, secret, and self-intent, yet with the unfailing loyalty of years in their look. Sappho has a more inveterate affection, Topaz a more invincible courtesy, than any one I know ; and strangers as they are to me, even after years, they are as incapable of treachery as of honesty. Never would they brush harshly against a child, even a child teasing them. At worst they would growl, and if that were unavailing, remove or endure with dignity. And they are but typical of their kind—the subtle, docile, inexplicable and ferocious creatures, whose whole life is a lesson in self-sufficiency and self-restraint. Maeterlinck has erred strangely, through an unhappy prejudice, in assigning to the Cat the sole infamy of his bright fantasy.

IV

Maeterlinck's first volume of essays, *The Treasure of the Humble*, followed happily upon his finest plays, and expressed directly the attitude of which he had given dramatic representation. One essay in particular, *The Tragical in Daily Life*, may be taken as his apologia for the " static " theatre, an apologia which no other writer could have made so justly and properly.

Other essays, though they bear such titles as *Silence*, *The Predestined* and *The Invisible Goodness*, are really no more than chapters upon aspects of the unapparent life which Maeterlinck is always trying to discern and explain. The ideas recur again and again, not only in various places in *The Treasure of the Humble* but also in later books, where they are given a fuller and more elaborate treatment. *The Buried Temple*, for instance, contains his later and ampler reflections upon the mystery to which he is constantly and, you might think, almost affectionately returning, the mystery of "destiny." It will be convenient, therefore, to study his attitude upon this urgently important subject as avowed in that book, rather than more fragmentarily in the first. Indeed, under this aspect of his philosophy (if I may so formally describe the engaging unpretentiousness of his speculations) may be grouped almost all Maeterlinck's doctrines of the unseen world. When he speaks, so quietly, slowly, beautifully, of the eloquence of silence, and the weakness of words, of the transparency of character, of the visible signs upon those "predestined" to early or violent death, of the soul's seclusion from personal contact and defilement, of the significance of unnoted things, of the superior spirituality of women, of the unreality of real things, of the shadowiness surrounding the tiny disk of light in which we move like marionettes, of the necessity of seeking God (for God hides), of the general superiority in importance, mysteriousness and beauty of the unseen over the seen :—when he speaks of these, he speaks of things which we have all more or less carefully pondered, with nothing or little of discrepancy in our thought. Some of them, indeed, you remember have been more arrestingly presented in the plays, where the more personal form of drama has always the effect of making the spectator an actor too, unseen but responsive.

It is this book, with its references to Emerson, Swedenborg, and Plotinus, which induced Mr. Walkley to describe Maeterlinck too as a mystic. For my own part, I cannot rid myself of the ungrateful habit of wondering what image we should have formed of an artist's work if we had but the first fruits of his genius. What should we have made of Shakespeare without the witness of his later and maturer plays ; of Milton with only the early lyrics ; of Wordsworth with nothing after *Lyrical Ballads* ? Nay, what do we make of Keats ? And what should we reckon of Maeterlinck, had he not so happily ,been spared to Europe in the decline of other writers of large influence ?

Well, we should hardly have guessed at any rate how earnestly he would have developed the hortatory exercise of his singular genius. Even from *The Treasure of the Humble* we should probably have failed to forecast his sedulous preoccupation with elusive things, or to foresee how the idea of destiny, and the problems wavering around it, would lure him into the shadowy uncertainties of his later essays. Doubtless we should

have regarded this first collection of essays by a playwright as a kind of casual, parallel exercise, and should
even have deplored the diversion of his interest from
dramatic to essay writing. We should have surely
been astonished had we been told that long before the
present year opened a new vista of ardours and per-
plexities, Maurice Maeterlinck would be regarded as a
seer, an evangelist, [more amiable than Mr. Shaw,
more persuasive than Ruskin, more agreeable than
Nietzsche, and in every way more acceptable than
Tolstoi. Let us see how this is.

The difficulty of dealing closely with Maeterlinck's
essays in practical philosophy is shown, as clearly as
anywhere, in *The Buried Temple.* The book contains
a long essay on *The Mystery of Justice,* and another
on *The Evolution of Mystery,* besides two shorter
papers. In all of them there is a faint gentle warmth,
or at least an *appearance* of fire. Two things, in fact,
are conspicuous : the tepidity of the sentiment, and
the extreme slowness of the thought. You can hear,
in Swinburne's phrase, the slow " shrieking hinges
spin." Behind all these essays you are aware of an
amiable sincere personality, whose delight it is to
reflect upon mysterious things. He walks round and
round his rock-like mysteries, in a far more pacific spirit
than that in which the magnificent Childe Roland to
the dark tower came. I spoke of Mr. Wells walking
round his Jericho long after the walls had fallen ;
Maeterlinck perambulates not with the hope of seeing

the obdurate battlements collapse suddenly as music falls, but merely for the sake of exercise. . . . Easily does he sink into solemnity : you can detect the deliberate clerical tremor in his voice when he talks of grave things, and the tremor is impressive. In this book he speaks of subtle things, and is not himself subtle but elusive, not profound but vague, not penetrating but full of conjecture. He is a swimmer in that stream of tendency which makes for righteousness. Righteousness, justice—the strenuous words are on every page of the first two essays ; his aim is as definitely ethical as the aim of the English Positivists.

Look a little closely, however, and you will find nothing positive in Maeterlinck's attitude towards these abstract problems. He speaks for those who do not believe in a unique, all-powerful Judge, but who believe none the less in the existence of Justice. When we observe, he says, disaster pursuing crime, we nearly all end in submission to " the justice of things " ; and he makes easy play with those who regard others' misfortunes as retributory, but their own as inexplicable mistakes. In a social scheme so inordinately unequal as that of yesterday and to-day, there is of course wide ground for pleasant discussion ; and well and truly does Maeterlinck urge—in his familiar reiterative way —that most of the social ills (poverty, for example) are not at all the result of any mysterious unexplaining doom of the beyond, but are the mere consequence of our own indifference and unfair social organization.

Obvious as this is, it is wise to clear away the mental lumber which it exposes, when considering what manifestations are observable of a secret mystic justice. He remarks that a mystery rarely disappears, but only shifts its ground ; and you think this profound until you discover that all that is meant by it is that we re-name our mysteries. " What was once called ' the gods ' we now term ' life.' The same quantity of mystery will ever enwrap the world." With a pleasant frugal fancy he pursues the shifting lodgment of the mystery of justice, finding its ultimate abode in the heart of man. This is really one of the few definite thoughts upon which one can take hold, and it yields Maeterlinck a welcome opportunity of impressing as a new thing the precept of a personal justice which is really very old. He goes on : " We are punished because our entire moral being . . . is incapable of living and acting except in justice." And while a humble intellect will find itself at home in justice, the errant man of genius will find everything strange to him ; and ready to his hand is the downfall of Napoleon.

Necessarily the discussion extends to the indifference of Nature, and he suggests that so far from Nature being unjust, there is some identity between justice and logic. The words hardly help us here, since one would never dream of questioning the identity. More precisely he discovers that the injustice of Nature ends by becoming justice for the race. It is, in fact, but the vastness of the curve that takes it out of sight. He returns with emphasis in closing to the assertion of the abidingness of an invisible and incorruptible justice in the heart of man, and appears to bring its existence as proof of its existence. Justice he declares to be the great mystery of man, and discovers it at the centre of our love of truth. He discovers too that it is pity, kindness, generosity, heroism, love, these being all the justice of a far-descrying man. . . . But this essay is hardly to be taken alone. *The Evolution of Mystery* is partly complementary. Surprisingly Maeterlinck seeks to diminish rather than enlarge the domain of mystery. He cuts, like Hotspur's Trent, " A huge half-moon, a monstrous cantle out," and rejects the idea of a mysterious fatality which appears, for example, in the classic drama. In the intimate weakness of personal character does he seek the cause of catastrophe, repudiating supernatural interventions which do not satisfy us to-day. He recapitulates those endless " why's " which always set us agog for explanations ; and finds that it is only the fervent believer who will still see in these vital discrepancies between merit and happiness the finger of divine intervention. But Maeterlinck suspects that perfect knowledge of all the circumstances—immediate and remotely contributory—of a tragedy how complex and cruel soever, would make such a tragedy not only less extraordinary but perfectly natural and almost inevitable. Knowledge so intimate and searching is impossible, and so

Maeterlinck takes on trust the unverifiable explanation of a mystery rather than the mystery itself. This credulous scepticism is essentially Maeterlinckian. He is, in fact, afraid of being compelled to make some reluctant admission of God. The poet, he concedes, is inclined to personify fatality and justice, but it is not the incomprehensible that crushes us : rather the thought of a possible Power over us, the Immanent Will of Mr. Hardy's *Dynasts*. " What we dread is the presence of a God. . . . it is always a God whom we fear." But he questions whether we are thus brought nearer the truth, and leaves you in doubt of his own station in the advance.

From *The Evolution of Mystery* it is well to pass to *Luck*, the final essay in *The Buried Temple*. Here is indeed a subject ready for the characteristic Maeterlinckian suggestion : What is luck, or Fate, and on what lines does it act ? It is one of extraordinary fascination, and he has felt the fascination with extraordinary intensity. Who has not pondered on the unaccountable awryness of events ? Which of us could not match the oddities instanced by Maeterlinck with yet more surprising oddities from his own human experience ! It is just this incalculable element, this amazing chanciness, which turns the dullness of life into a fable of the Arabian Nights. By what goblin trick is it, one might ask, following Maeterlinck, that of a virtuous family which I discovered the other day, the only member escaping extreme misfortune should be

an unvirtuous daughter ? What tricksy spirit was it
that, as De Quincey maliciously points out, punctually
removed by death or disease the occupants of those
posts which were just what Wordsworth successively
needed as his parental responsibilities increased ?—
Why Wordsworth, who of all men might best endure
privations without his peculiar genius being hindered
in its amazing development ?

I wish Maeterlinck could have given more clearly
his answer to the questions he raises : I am afraid of
misrepresenting his opinions. But at any rate he cries
clearly enough : Let us not look to the gods, nor to
the illimitable laws of the universe, for an explanation.
" Until the gods shall have clearly explained themselves, there is nothing that they can explain for us."
There is one possible mine of explanations in which he
omits on this occasion to dig : the finer and remote
circumstances which he mentions in *The Evolution of
Mystery*. Since we must not look to the gods, he
imagines that in ourselves is hidden the key of the
mystery. Beneath our conscious existence there hides
a profounder unconscious existence, wherein must be
sought the meaning of luck. To this invisible consciousness he devotes a page or two of glowing rhetoric ; but rhetoric, however profusely tropical, does
not help very greatly. Leaving rhetoric, this unconsciousness is asserted to be variably active in men ;
and from its varible activity is deduced Maeterlinck's
explanation.

It is this : that from the recesses of eternal laws an event, happy or unhappy, arises and blocks our way. It is an event which has come but for itself and pays no heed to us ; we approach *it*, and growing perhaps sensitive to its influence, flee it or confront it. Maeterlinck supposes a ship doomed (years ago) to wreck— a ship which is to carry say fifty passengers. These fifty have intended to sail, but it will happen that when the ship starts ignorantly on her last voyage, only twenty of them will actually sail with her. " For months past, perhaps for years, a mysterious selection has been at work " ; and to the activity of this uncon- sciousness is due the escape of thirty : *but their place will be taken by thirty others whose unconsciousness has not been so vigilant.*

It is, of course, a purely diabolical explanation. Always with great disasters to ships, trains and so on, one hears of men who have miraculously changed their minds, or have been almost violently prevented from embarking. That the ascertainable proportion of such apparent interpositions should be as thirty to fifty, is, I fear, somewhat questionable. And besides, the real point of objection is here : that while the explanation might be defendable if only twenty sailed in the end in the ship which Maeterlinck assumes to have been doomed years before, the full toll of fifty lives is still exacted, and you can never discover how far the selective principle has operated. The ex- planation can only be defended by infinite investigation of particular cases ; but more than half the evidence is destroyed in those who have been lost.

Maeterlinck is fond of insisting on natural laws, and has a peculiar affection for the law of gravitation. The word misleads him, and he forgets that laws do not *exist* except as assumptions—or as deductions which human experience makes from observed phenomena. An apple falls to the ground once : that does not demonstrate a law ; it falls a hundred times : that suggests a law ; or a million times—and that is held to prove an immutable law. Might not our essayist have seen it to be not less easily imaginable that God acts individually than that He acts generally ? that the apple falls each time in obedience to a specific and direct motion of an almighty mind ? that the world may wake one morning and find that the " law " of gravitation has failed—with serious and exciting effects upon one's body and blood ? that the hairs of our head *are* numbered ? Might he not have urged with his familiar persuasiveness that it were no greater miracle for omnipotence to work in one way than in another ? Might he not have pleaded with us not to shut our ideas of God within finite conceptions of laws and necessities, but to recognize a mystic potency determining individually every act and influence ? Might he not, with no more ingenuity than he has brought to its contriving,—might he not have dismissed this theory of the working of unconsciousness with his never quite contemptuous smile ? . . . Vain the speculation! Deep-hid in this unconsciousness, as our author pierces it, sits "luck," sinister, inexplicable, illimitable, and in its influence inhuman. One should fly from the unlucky; "ill-luck is a contagious disease: and one unconsciousness will often infect another." Questions of logic apart, one might be pardoned for resenting a philosophy thus inhuman. A theory that makes for separation and flight can only be rejected. . . . Yet even here Maeterlinck's logic fails, since he wonders, of men whose star is of pernicious power,—" Ought we unhesitatingly to fly from such men? . . . Yes, doubtless if their misfortune arise from an imprudent and unduly hazardous spirit, a heedless, quarrelsome, mischief-making, utopian, or clouded mind."

The chief difficulty in considering Maeterlinck's views in this book is that he is seldom precise. His subjects are of unusual interest, with applications burningly intense for perplexed human beings. But the very dimness of the subject renders precision of language the more desirable. Discipline of thought, discipline of speech—they are essential even to a light novel: they are of palmary importance in studies such as these, when author and reader alike are perforce humbly moving about in worlds not realized.

Turn to another book. *In Wisdom and Destiny* Maeterlinck devotes 353 pages to reflections dealing ostensibly with these grave themes, but resolving themselves into Notes for a Manual of Happiness. He is concerned to stimulate and console, and has a religious care for sufferers. If we say that the quest of happiness, too carefully pursued, seems a little weak and childish, it is not meant that Maeterlinck does not utter many true and simple things that are worth remembering. Only, a preoccupation with happiness is like a preoccupation with billiards—pleasant but slightly unworthy. One need not take an unduly solemn view of man's responsibilities, in asserting that personal happiness is such a private and capricious thing that it is best to take it as it comes, and if it comes, and to care not a jot when it goes. What is most conspicuously missing in Maeterlinck's entire conception of life is spontaneousness, instinct. He is always trying to cage the bird, and most earnest when it is most difficult to distinguish the bird from its shadow. He sometimes refers with admiration to the life and words of Christ, and does not notice how little Christ speaks of happiness. He thinks all men can learn happiness, and finds that to be happy is only to have freed one's soul from the unrest of happiness. I confess such a sentence leaves one wondering, and when I also read this :—" Happiness rarely is absent ; it is we that know not of its presence "—wonder becomes bewilderment.

Maeterlinck sits in the secure privacy of his own mind and spins his crepuscular web, in which are snared little fragile beings, the mind's ephemeridæ. You marvel at the length of the web, and you marvel yet more at its tenuity. It floats on the air, swaying dreamily like a dream within a dream. Tenuous and unseizable indeed is the thought of these many pages. Maeterlinck himself has divined an excellent rule— " in the life of thought it is our unvarying duty to pursue our thought right to the end "—yet has seldom observed it. The floating gossamer breaks, and leaves you with a sense of forlorn inconclusiveness. Is it not strange, then, that these books should yet be fondly read by earnest and devout people ? There are women whose interest in life is pious rather than passionate, and who place *The Treasure of the Humble, Wisdom and Destiny* and *The Buried Temple* by the side of Ruskin and *The Christian Year.* Maeterlinck may be indefinite and inconclusive, but for them he seems to hold one of the keys of the unknown. Why is this ?

It is a question I have often asked myself and I can only pretend to give my own answer. The reason is to be found in several circumstances. Firstly Maeterlinck is a doubter, and shows nevertheless practical piety. Never were more pernicious lines penned by a poet than those of Tennyson :

> There lives more faith in honest doubt
> Believe me than in half the creeds.

Doubt more or less honest and honesty more or less doubtful have snared many. To doubt yet not to repudiate is still the sign of a fine intelligence, unfettered yet not unfaithful. And when honest doubt grapples to itself Marcus Aurelius, Emerson, and all the pieties of the saints divorced from their imperious claims, it becomes an admirable thing, "standing tiptoe upon a little hill." Then, too, Maeterlinck is certainly stimulating. He insists upon the cardinal virtues, and simply because of the repudiation of Authority they seem more important and urgent. It is indeed true that to deny Authority as usually admitted is to appear—however quietly and unconsciously—as the primary promulgator of the edicts which you are but repeating. Nor is this all : besides the cardinal truths, Maeterlinck speaks of things that are less common and are of mystical growth, remote and subtle things—of destiny, chance, wisdom, love ; and he makes these so flatteringly easy and apprehensible that honest doubters are everywhere pleased. Add that he is never exacting, laborious or severely logical, that his style is slow but elaborately metaphysical, and I think you have a fairly complete explanation of Maeterlinck's popularity among devout and uncritical people.

Yet there is more than this, there is that which pervades all the rest, the hypnotism which is created by circular motion. It has been claimed (as we have observed) for one of the plays as a merit ; it is just as conspicuous in the essays. That the intellectual quality of the essays is on the whole inferior counts for nothing against the gentle hypnotism of this unfailing flow of soft words and pleasant images, that turn round and round and round. His speech has no " masculine persuasive force." The very order of the sentences is mechanical and soporific : statement, extension, qualification, again and again repeated. . . . This extract from *Wisdom and Destiny*, competently translated by Mr. Alfred Sutro, shows more than one trick of Maeterlinck's system :

> Wisdom is the lamp of love, and love is the oil of the lamp. Love, sinking deeper, grows wiser ; and wisdom that springs up aloft comes ever the nearer to love. If you love, you must needs become wise ; be wise, and you surely shall love. Nor can any one love with the veritable love but his love must make him the better ; and to grow better is but to grow wiser. . . . Love is the food of wisdom ; wisdom the food of love ; a circle of light within which those who love clasp the hands of those who are wise.

I suppose no one will read this without a certain brief sympathetic quickening ; and I suppose no one will read it with the least care and not notice the deliberate attempt to mesmerize, by the ingenious repetition and confusion of vague impressive words, the intellectual judgment of the reader. The passage could be paralleled by a hundred others.

And what, then, is the cause of this general inadequacy ? A lack of moral earnestness ?—no : —a lack of intellectual or spiritual vigour ?—yes. It is not simply that sharpness and precision are wanting : it is that force and liveliness are wanting. The human experience behind these essays seems small, the spiritual experience languid ; and no cunning rhetoric or stiff amplitude of ornate similes will disguise the frail vitality of the inspiration or the undisciplined weakness of the control. Now and again he speaks with unusual directness : " Complaints of injustice grow less frequent as the brain and heart expand." But even a brief incandescence is rare. Commonly you have but the sense of thought slow and docile and steady as oxen in Provençal wains.

There is one essay in a later volume, *The Double Garden*, that must be looked at as almost the only noteworthy one in a book containing little but magazine reprints of slight value or charm. In *The Leaf of Olive* is given, as the title suggests, the reason for the faith that is in Maeterlinck when he looks out on the world. " Though *we* no longer count, the humanity of which we form a part is acquiring the importance of which we are being stripped." This is the compensation offered for " the decrease of religious feeling," and for the fact that reason no longer sees any supernatural interest in doing good. Assuredly the social sense, the sense of humanity, is a growing and precious thing, and its visible influence in England upon the common life, upon political action, letters and art, is significant. But it is curious that Maeterlinck's survey of his time should lead him to this assumption [1]

---

[1] It is not a formal assertion but a passing dictum, a summary as of accepted fact. It gains of course in value from the casual manner of its appearance. A similar airiness characterizes a similar assumption with which a long essay upon *Immortality* (*Life and Flowers*) is opened.

of the " decrease of religious feeling." He pictures the emergence of man during the last few centuries from the great religious period ; he sees religion as a gloomy threatening background. . . . Here as elsewhere there is a stealthy antagonism towards Christianity ; and as you become aware of this, you see how much of Maeterlinck's prose work, especially *Wisdom and Destiny*, is stultified by the sedulous evasion of those suggestions which naturally arise when " destiny " is confronted with the affirmations of religion. Many of these questions which he raises so lightly and passes from so evasively would, perhaps, never be raised at all if a close consideration were given to the New Testament ; indeed, even the Old Testament, and the book of Job alone, would overwhelm the slightly querulous " posers " in which *Wisdom and Destiny* strangely abounds. It is curious to observe how discreetly and carefully Maeterlinck ignores all that is set up in the Bible as illumination of the darkness of this world. He does not examine, or denounce, or discard : he simply ignores. Speculation upon destiny is, indeed, a luxury which he can seldom deny himself ; and as has been seen, it is a subject of a constant reference even in those plays where we might least expect it. . . . Destiny becomes an ambiguous queen to whom this poet swings monotonously his incense and chants his slow unvarying tributes. He seems deliberately to prefer the vague to the precise, and simply because of the definiteness of " revealed " religion, will have none

of it. It is sufficient for the moment to note this preference as explaining the singular difficulty one has in
reading these essays, and the greater difficulty in ascer-
taining from them anything beyond a baseless cheer-
fulness and a cloudy kindliness.

Of all Maeterlinck's prose writings *The Life of the Bee*
is chiefly delightful. Primarily it is a book of observation and inevitably engrossing. The author has done
here what he has attempted nowhere else :—the faithful description of things seen closely during a score of
years. To leave the monotonous essays upon fate
and turn to the fresh, careful record of bee-keeping is
a happy experience. Maeterlinck has the advantage
of a curiosity widespread and acute and restlessly
scientific ; and though he has used the opportunity
for the renewed unfolding of his favourite theme, he
has yet written a book which has the fascination for
the unlearned of a novel of Balzac. Balzac, one fancies,
would have rejoiced in the scrupulous relation of detail
which Maeterlinck has here unwontedly condescended
upon ; and yet more, perhaps, in the free embroidery
of speculation. The facility of theory, the fancifulness,
the glow everywhere apparent in the vast work of the
French master of illusion, are observable also in this
little book of the Belgian poet. Like the more passionate kindred studies of that greater naturalist,
Henri Fabre, *The Life of the Bee* is written by the
poet rather than by the essayist. The poet's is that
delighted sense of interest and wonder and, more surely,

the delighted intentness upon natural phenomena. Regard the book as a poem, and surrender yourself to its lure, and you with the bees are feeding on—

Golden honey from a golden hive.

But from meticulous observation Maeterlinck passes to the comparison of the bee polity with the human polity, and is impressed with the bee's superiority at many points. Unfortunately, he is not content with this comparison. He must needs peer into the obscurity of the bee's instinct and, finding little help in that, falls back upon the unimaginable omniscience of destiny, named here the spirit of the hive. And thus he comes to affirm the most uncertain things, and speaks of the day when, as " the spirit of the hive has ordained, a certain part of the population will go forth *selected in accordance with sure and immovable laws,* and make way for hopes that as yet are formless." What those laws are, and the evidence of their sureness and immutability, you are never told. There is pure assumption here, as there is pure fancy elsewhere. But note how impressive a plain statement can be made to appear, when it is founded upon these pillars of cloud ! . . . For gauging the moral greatness of a race, he writes, we have but one standard—the dignity and permanence of their ideal, and their abnegation in pursuing it ; and he asks where we may encounter an ideal more disinterested or sublime, an abnegation more heroic, than the bee's. Yet he himself has indi-

cated elsewhere the immense difference in value of the
bee's civilization and man's.   The bees have developed
towards the merging of the individual in the common
life ; but is that ideal tolerable for man ?   Were our
problem of life so simple as, despite Maeterlinck's
magic mist, we still perceive the bee's problem to be,
we too might move rapidly on to the absorption of the
individual life into the indistinguishable many.   But
it is precisely because man's development is towards a
greater complexity, and because his powers are of such
infinitely various direction, that the very imperfection
of human organization is more wonderful than the
perfection of the bee organization.   Looked at thus
simply, the whole of Maeterlinck's elaborate analogue
is seen to be unreal and unconsidered.   Freely may
we admit the marvellousness of the hive and its inhabitants ; but we are not to forget that human evolution
can by its nature show no such general and uniform
movement.   What is it that instantly vitiates Maeterlinck's comparison of the perfection of the bee polity
with the violent imperfection of the human polity, but
this one immense difference : that man's eternal quest
is the reconciliation of individual development with
the development of the race ! While we remain
acutely conscious of this profound cleavage, and aware
nevertheless of that hunger for light and air which is
characteristic of both individual and common life to-
day, we need not be ashamed even at the sight of those
self-forgetting, self-murdering colonies of bees which

Maeterlinck admires with an eye too fascinated to be quite clear.

It is easy to forget what is perfectly obvious, but if this be timely remembered, the whole book falls then into a more natural proportion, and offers its observation for quick enjoyment, and its speculation for slow oblivion. Briefly, *The Life of the Bee* may be termed a semi-scientific essay of extreme interest, curiously enhanced with a lavish sentimentalism that grows more lavish as it grows more purely unreal.

In 1913 Mr. de Mattos produced for English readers his excellent translation of Maeterlinck's thoughts on death, survival, immortality and infinity, bearing the title, *Our Eternity*. The attitude throughout is that of the fearless inquirer, who will interrogate death and eternity boldly, narrowly, eloquently. He would attain, in Crashaw's fine words, to

> Life that dares send
> A challenge to its end
> And when it comes say, welcome friend.

But men, he says, will not allow themselves to think of death until they have no longer strength to think ; and then they are afraid. "All the forces which might avail to face death we exhaust in averting our will from it." And now every day is contradicting him. Two years have seen the brightest and the happiest giving up of life without base fear or apprehension, for a love, an idea, even for a land that has been to many

of them a harsh and cold parent. Men do not *talk*
of death, by an unspoken covenant of reticence ; but
they think, as most of us know from small solemn things
said doubtfully in moments of loss or the remembrance
of loss. " Death is the one event that counts in our
life and in our universe." He heads his first chapter,
" Our injustice to death," because we impute to death
the tortures of the last illness, and overwhelm it with
the evil done before it. There is much to the same
effect, and you soon believe that what your author
most of all rejoices in is a kind of solemn logomachy
directed to proving that things are not what they seem.
—As if they ever were ! In a later chapter he urges that
we should regard death as a form of life which we do
not yet understand.

An essay upon death alone, its secrecy, its cruelty,
its kindness, its enormous fantasticality, would have
been an eminent subject for Maeterlinckian fantasies ;
but our author will not be circumscribed by time or
bullied by eternity. He has bridled his fantasy and
used his most serious thought, being concerned not
with death, but also with that unknown to which he
believes death yields entrance. Will that unknown,
he asks with sudden urgency, be dreadful or not ?
Apart from the solution of religion, which he very
cordially dismisses, there are " four imaginable solu-
tions :—total annihilation, survival with our consciousness of to-day ; survival without any sort of consciousness ; lastly, survival in the universal consciousness,

or with a consciousness different from that which we possess in this world." It is to the last that his mind slowly moves, after many rejections, after testings of theosophy, spiritualism, and doctrines of transmigration. There is penetration and judgment in his view of many of these topics ; he has an eye for buckets that will not hold water and hills of sand that sink. From the mere infinity of creation, infinity of time and of thought, of chance and revolution, he concludes that human consciousness will in some way survive.

> It would not be at all astonishing if the consciousness of the universe, in the endeavour to form itself, had not yet encountered the combination of necessary chances and if human thought were actually supporting one of these decisive chances. Here there is a hope. Small as man and his brain may appear, they have exactly the value of the most enormous forces that they are able to conceive, since there is neither great nor small in the immeasurable.

He suggests that it is a mistake to believe that a supreme intelligence directs the universe ; it may be some other force, having no imaginable relation to the mind. This is but to quibble about names. . . . On a wave of exalted eloquence, behold us, he cries, in infinity ; what will be our fate—the fate of such imperfect consciousness as we are allowed to bear through death's gate ?

It is in the persistence of such personal questions that the difficulty of Maeterlinck's inquiry seems to lie. The speculative is entangled with the ethical. Passages of serious thought end with, for example,—

Maurice Maeterlinck

" We must maintain our confidence in a world which knows nothing of our conceptions of purpose and progress, because it doubtless has ideas whereof we have no idea, a world, moreover, which could scarcely wish itself harm." The old Maeterlinck peers through with his familiar " doubtless." He mingles the moral with the speculative almost quaintly when he says, " Every hypothesis is permissible and every question, provided it be addressed to happiness. . . . Infinity is nothing if it be not felicity." I confess that such a confusion of subjects leaves me stupid ; stupider still when I read a little later that it is childish to talk of happiness and unhappiness where infinity is in question. Apart these propositions are as distinct as Monday from Saturday ; but one ringing on the heels of the other makes for bewilderment, and this is thickened by a suggestion that consciousness is not indispensable to eternal happiness. " Happiness ? " one whispers. It is the old theme. " The unknown and the unknowable are necessary and will perhaps always be necessary to our happiness." Perhaps—happiness ; the words themselves are like coloured balloons, bearing in them the whole of the buoyant Maeterlinckian philosophy. " Incomparable mystery," is his phrase for the infinity which he is persuaded can be nothing but a sea of joy. It would be coarse and ungracious to refuse without reflection such faint lights as our author offers in place of the false light which he sees running out into the dark from the " citadel of religion." He invokes human reason and uses it faithfully as far as he can. He is a poet, and in these matters he seems to me like a poet who invokes the powers of metre when he has nothing definite to say. Earnestness and accomplishment cannot even conceal much less supply the want of inspiration either to a poet when he essays philosophies, or to a metaphysician when he essays poetry. What Maeterlinck is seeking is not, you feel, whatever his untrammelled thought may lead him to after many adventures, but something that Maeterlinck, the author of a dozen remarkable books, may be expected to find. It is surely unnecessary to add that he is as unconscious of this bias as any man is unconscious of the trick of eyelid and voice and gesture by which his father is revealed in him. If he so oddly finds that the gravest charge to be made against the positive religions and especially against Christianity is that it narrows the mystery of the universe, he mitigates our surprise by suggesting that we can ourselves make that mystery as large as we please. Whether it is the metaphysician or the moralist that is speaking here I cannot easily guess.

V

The genius of Maurice Maeterlinck, so far as it is notable and valuable, is an entirely distinct and personal genius. Let this be said clearly, since it would be both unfair and foolish to suggest that his work shows nothing beyond an unusual development of general talent.

Maeterlinck is often called a mystic, and himself uses the word so freely that you might well think it the title he chiefly covets. Perhaps no other word has been more generally or more stupidly abused. It has become the ready counter of a cheap, thoughtless currency, so that its proper meaning has dimmed away in the general indistinctness of the hack vocabulary. Only an unheeding acceptance of impressive words will lead one to accept Maeterlinck as a mystic. He writes mysteriously, but there is nothing mysterious in mysticism. To be vague is not to be mystical, for mysticism often presents things and visions with intolerable sharpness. Nor is a mystic necessarily uncertain, abstract, inconsequent, unintelligibly impressive, eloquently bewildered. Even personal goodness has nothing to do with mysticism. Mysticism is essential spirituality, and the difference between a good man and a mystic does not lie in the superior goodness of the mystic, but in his finer spirituality.

When Maeterlinck is called a mystic, I imagine the reason to be that it is not easy to find another equally effective, hasty distinction. In truth, I note in his work very little that points to the spiritual profundity which is thus inadequately named. He has a large and carefully cultivated sense of "the mystery of things," and, for all his explicit disavowal in *The*

Buried Temple, is fonder of discovering than of resolving mysteries. He sees the world as a vast perplexity, beauty at odds with misery, life with destiny, and eternity cloud-like enfolding all. Seeing this, he writes beautifully, importantly, sometimes wisely, with infinite qualifications and hesitancies. Nay, more : he writes cheerfully, consolingly, with a constant simple exhortation to happiness. In this, where is there a touch of mysticism ? For his plays, he presents a state of impregnable grief, a state of sorrowful love, a state of blindness, a state of loyalty ; and these are seen beneath a wonderfully cunning veil of sorrow, loneliness and darkness. But where is there more than a hint of mysticism ?

The mystic is simple, direct, urgent. He speaks by preference of plain, apparent things, and only by great persuasion of dark unapparent things. When he tells of mysterious things, he tells of them not because they are mysterious to him, but because they are not. While they remain obscure and unilluminous he is silent ; he perceives a ray of light running upon them, and needs must speak of the light. He does not communicate his doubts, except in that morbid, over-sensitive condition which leads him to talk of his diseases. St. Paul was a profound mystic, not because he was aware of so many spiritual mysteries but because he read them ; not in so far as he saw in a glass darkly, but in so far as he saw face to face. The mystic tries to say plainly what he sees plainly, to say it as plainly as his complex sense of a plain thing will let him. He uses the language of St. Augustine, of St. Francis of Sales and Bunyan, of Newman and Patmore, of Browne, Donne, Taylor, Crashaw and Blake. . . . Need I go on to say that the mystic is pre-eminently distinguished by his faith ? Only faith of a high energy will make possible that intenser, far-seeing spirituality which is what we suggest by this poor word mystic.

If this is right, then, clearly, Maeterlinck is as far from being a mystic as he is from being a foreign missionary. He is concerned with the same subjects as the true mystical writers, but his concern moves on a lower plane and is inspired by a fainter energy. It is because he has no faith, neither Christian nor Pagan, neither Buddhist nor Theosophist, and because the lack of Faith means the lack of light and foothold among dark places, that he can claim no higher tribute than we yield to a merely influential writer upon serious matters.

In another respect he is distinguished as well from the really profound and noble writers of our day, as from the mystics ;—I mean in the quality of his thought. So often it seems to cost him little, and to yield little to the reader. There is a general diffused thoughtfulness over all his work, but it rarely crystallizes into a memorable, precious truth. He occupies the same place among thinkers as among play-writers, or as Anatole France holds among novelists. His work can no better sustain the common comparison with Emerson's than with Plato's ; it bears less ripe fruit among all its branches than you may pluck from a single ruddy bough of Meredith. How fresh and lively, how rapid and responsive, is the thought of a poem or a novel of Meredith, by the side of the laborious wavering texture of an essay of the Belgian writer ! . . . Maeterlinck has a singular delicacy of thought and manner, but it is not the delicacy of resourceful, perfectly controlled strength—as is a surgeon's—but the delicacy of carefully preserved weakness—as is an artificial flower maker's. . . . You wander among the frail trammels of his essays, longing for a severer logic and a harder grasp. Maeterlinck's very doubt is as delicate and uncertain as the piety of narrow-minded converts. His essays, with all the frequent fascination of his subject, are hard to understand ; to read them is like looking at unfamiliar buildings in a fog. Had he but subjected himself to the sharper exigence of verse-form, he might have given us something as compact and decisive as Pope's steady couplets. Prose exposes his unthrifty faults.

If you turn to his plays, you wonder that plays of so slight a dramatic force should have won so wide an admiration. Not often is there even such heat in them as you may discover in *Pelleas and Melisanda* or *Monna Vanna*, or such tensity as in *Interior*. Take Conrad's novel, *Under Western Eyes*, and read the amazing scene where Razumov is trying to confess

to Miss Haldin his betrayal of her dead brother. A
grave excitement burns in your heart as you perceive
the immense, tragical disquietude throbbing in Razumov's breast, while he looms swaying before the
adored girl. *There* is the true instinctive " static "
drama which Maeterlinck endeavours to present,
and succeeds in presenting in how much smaller a
measure !

What, then, and where, after these large disqualifi-
cations, is the distinct and personal genius of Maeterlinck ? I find it in the creation of an impression for
its own sake, an impression of pure sorrow, love,
terror. Shakespeare wonderfully creates such an
impression, in the opening of *Hamlet*, for instance, in
Macbeth, and elsewhere ; his contemporaries did the
same scarcely less subtly. But the pure impression
is not Shakespeare's end as it is Maeterlinck's. I
know that this may be thought a childish achievement
in the later poet. How often, unconsciously, has it
been achieved in telling a story to children ! You
tell them some simple, odd thing with elaborate
circumstantiality and, little by little, their whole
attention is absorbed, and at some immomentous
phrase or mere insignificant gesture they will burst
into sudden tears or shiver in strange terror. . . .
This is the effect that Maeterlinck prepares ; he has
this secret of our breasts, this sly key. He turns it,
and we are as responsive as children to his slightest
movement. He does this inerrably in *Interior*, almost

as surely in *Pelleas*, less surely in other plays. It is the chief justification of his claim to be an imaginative writer. This small, narrow, intense power, and this alone of all his powers, is his unique portion.

HENRY JAMES

I

TANTALIZING enough is that remark of Coventry Patmore's, answering the question of his biographer, " I don't know what your opinion of Henry James is ? " He replied, almost in a tone of reproach, " Think of him ? Why, of course, I think that he is incomparably the greatest living writer of fiction." The remark was made not long before Patmore's death in 1896. One wonders how faithful a reader Patmore had been, and whether his admiration of Henry James extended to the later novels published before his own death—*The Tragic Muse* (1890), *The Lesson of the Master* (1892) and *Terminations* (1895) ; one wonders, in fact, what it was in Henry James's singularly specialized and rarefied work that could so surprisingly have appealed to an artist not less rare than himself and not less individual, yet so plainly alien. The remark testifies very happily to the novelist's power, and the testimony is oddly contrasted with another dictum of Coventry Patmore's (for which I have to rely upon the poorest memory), that he thought it almost " mean " for anyone to read women as Meredith read them. Had such an opinion conceivably referred to Henry James his own answer would have been ready—the answer which would have sufficed him for any number of querulous objections, and is the particular defence of *The Sacred Fount*.

> To nose about for a relation that a lady has her reasons for keeping secret is made not only quite inoffensive, I hold, but positively honourable, by being confined to psychologic evidence. . . . Resting on psychologic signs alone, it's a high application of intelligence. What's ignoble is the detective and the keyhole.

A reader of the novels will have small scruple in changing this from a dramatic to a personal reference.

Inevitably any present writing upon this novelist's achievement must take the tone and form of a tribute to his genius, a tribute practically unencumbered with questions and hesitancies. For a " study " that should attempt more than a rough tribute a row of books not less numerous than the volumes of the collected edition of his novels would be necessary. The influence of Henry James upon criticism and upon the imaginative art of our time has made an immense difference both to criticism and creation. I think he had the most original mind of our time ; I think his gift to us was an incalculable one ; I think it almost impossible to express even one's own sense of his mind and his gift without speaking, even though but stammeringly, in his own tongue and under the shelter of his own genius.

II

The task is simplified by yielding to the temptation to pass lightly over the earlier and fix one's attention chiefly upon the later work, since the later work is so characteristically *developed*, so purely individual. The earlier novels are not at all negligible, yet (you might say) it was not a writer of genius that wrote them, but a writer of immense and careful talent. But the later novels are distinct alike in subject and in form from the work of all other writers, as well as from that of the earlier Henry James himself. There is no case here of a man of genius writing all at once like a man of genius—of a Keats or a Shelley springing birdlike into the full beauty and wonder of his performance :— there's nothing of sudden, unprepared or miraculous in the art which we have come to recognize as consummate, and nothing of unconsciousness. I doubt if any other writer has laboured so. at achievement. Deliberate, steadfast, unhesitating, he seems, as you look at his successive books, striving always to attain his end not merely by choice of subject, but equally by means of the form which he is never tired of saying is inseparable from the presentation of subject. He has written unwearyingly of technique, finding such continual interest in the theory of the art of writing as shows—if the proof were needed outside his own novels—how intense was the excitement in his mind of intellectual and emotional things. He had the curiosity of a girl, the imagination of a poet, the reasoning mind of a man. Nothing satisfies him in its simplicity, and he must needs see things both more simple and more subtle than men ordinarily do. The surface attracts him, but it is every inch of a small surface; what is beneath invites him, but his look, though keen and frequent, is brief and startled. The glow of romance bathes whatever he looks at, and it is the glow as much as the thing that he loves to watch. He is imaginative yet narrow, tender yet hard, undidactic yet patiently moral, responsive yet reserved, expansive yet obscure, lucidly elusive ; at once gay and grave, profound and fanciful, concerned with tremendous and with trifling things ; an impersonal impressionist, a master of style mastered by his own style, an artist to whom art was life and life the matter of art, and the finer rather than the coarser strands of life more tractable for his art. From the writing of exquisite but not extraordinary stories, curiously sedate in manner, he proceeds slowly to novels the most extraordinary in manner, in colour and in subject—novels presenting (in a favourite image) a precious liquid in a crystal bowl held calmly, with sudden agitations, in a wonderful light. The liquid may be varying in value, but the crystal is always crystal, though ringing with deeper or thinner note, and the light is always strange. His interest lies neither wholly in character nor wholly in the predicament set forth ; and while the predicament has come to mean more and more for him, character cannot quite honestly be said to have become less and less. He passes from refinement to refinement, until his writing seems at times an accomplished and subtle parody of his singular natural utterance.

III

Yet if all this be admissible it would be unfortunate if the impression be suggested that the earlier work is less than admirable and delightful. The reader of those deliberately discursive autobiographical volumes[1] on which Henry James employed his last years will not need to be told with what ample care the novelist was prepared for the career into which he made his sure entrance. Never was family so bright, and in its members and mutual relations so congenial, as that of which Henry James Senior, philosopher and humorist, was the head and front ; never a career more favourably rooted and nourished than that of the brilliant son. He " practised " with enormous industry and patience. Influences are plain enough and preferences avowed—as Hawthorne, Flaubert, Balzac ; but Henry James possessed his own soul. He chose subjects which required no great experience of affairs, and never allowed his passion for Balzac to thrust

[1] *A Small Boy and Others* (1913), *Notes of a Son and Brother* (1914).

him into enterprises in which he might feel bewildered.
His character is usually the American in Europe, and
the class that of the artistic practitioner. I don't
know into how many of these early stories, short and
long, the atmosphere of the studio does not pour.
Charm and interest mark most of them, and a certain
vigour in the portraiture of unusual character ; but
he would need a keen eye who would detect in their
author the author of *What Maisie Knew* or *The Turn
of the Screw.* The limits of the earlier work, so far as
the subject is concerned, remain the limits of the later,
growing even a little more rigid with almost every
book ; himself vowed to art, art is the increasingly
urgent matter which his flame is meant to kindle.
But if the limits are the same for the earlier and later
novels alike, it must be noted that the earlier books
have the advantage—for an advantage it seems to one
reader at least—of a more substantial story than the
latest. It is scarcely a single one of the last half-
dozen novels that you might wish longer, but I confess
that the situation of, for instance, *Madame de Mauves*
demands a less niggardly treatment than is possible
in a hundred pages. The situation is that of a romantic American girl who falls in love not so much with
de Mauves as with his inordinate lineage, and the
implication of honour and nobility which her husband
proves to be the last man in the world to sustain.
Disillusion brings dismay that will not acknowledge
the touch of indignity ; she declines to palliate her

husband's errancies by indulging, as he suggests, in her own ; and de Mauves—by a touch of that queerness which Henry James loves to impart—teased by her rectitude into tardy and unpropitiating admiration, blows out his brains. Queer, is the word you repeat, recognizing something of excess of novelty in the idea of the story ; but the idea is so excellent, and the meagre treatment so unaccommodating, that you inevitably cry for the fullness of relation which the author in other novels has seldom withheld.

Of nearly a hundred short stories I hesitate to say how many or how very few convey this impression of too-summary development, nor could I easily indicate the restlessness of invention which they from first to last almost equally reveal. For if it be a coarse commonplace to say that their author's supreme gift was imagination, it is an equally obvious commonplace that his next gift was invention, a much more docile, prompt and reliable quality. He had the most ingenious mind, and seems to have found in life, in the guarded parts of it which he attentively watched, an infinite amusement, sometimes a strange excitement. The ingenuity and patience of a spider are not more wonderful than the ingenuity and patience of this novelist in his devisal of a hundred webs to snare the bright things that swim within his ken. . . . Far more exact in its application to the later work is another image, for which Sir James Dewar is to be thanked— I mean the image of the scientist's bubble, carefully blown and delicately sustained for how many weeks, wonderfully preserved from breaking and at last—breaking. With a like skill does Henry James prepare and send afloat his amazing bubbles—delicate, shimmering, responsive to his faintest breath, to an impulse that is sometimes no more than faint ; bubbles so fresh, freakish, fragile, that swim miraculously above your head, and then simply end when the sustaining breath fails. . . . His invention is unfailing, and the short stories of his later period, comprised in *The Soft Side* (1900), *The Better Sort* (1903) and *The Finer Grain* (1910), are as deliciously ingenious in their situations as any of the earlier. The ingenuity, the ingenuity ! you find yourself repeating ; and it sets off the particular feature of each of these volumes. *The Soft Side* is ingeniously queer, and the first story in it—*The Great Good Place*—is the queerest of all. *The Better Sort* is less queer and more entertaining, since it comprises *The Birthplace*—the most amusing of all Henry James's inventions. It presents the morbid conscience of Morris Gedge, keeper of *the* birthplace, who scrupulously diminishes the wonders he is required to enlarge upon. He has become too bitterly sceptical to fulfil the pious intentions of those that made him keeper, and his failure to "pile it on" brings an ominous remonstrance from the authorities. Pressed by his wife poor Gedge knocks conscience on the head with a desperate, *Down, wanton* ! and thereafter romances with extravagant gusto around the meagre

substance of " the Poet's " recorded life ;—with such
gusto that Mrs. Gedge has only too much reason to fear
a second, and final, remonstrance. Sardonic humour
dictates the end of the story, which finds the authorities
as liberal in their satisfaction as Gedge has been in his
desperate flourishes ; only, Henry James disappoints
us of the farther, and deeper, comedy of conscientious
scruple, which inevitably must follow this bewildering
satisfaction. Another of these stories, *The Beast in
the Jungle*, presents so didactic a situation as gives of
itself a surprise that Henry James should have invented
it—the situation of a man who, feeling himself marked
for special splendour or infamy and awaiting it, sees
his friend sacrificed to his waiting, and finds when
she is dead that the unknown, the beast in the jungle,
has sprung and he has not escaped.

> The escape would have been to love her . . . he had never
> thought of her (ah, how it hugely glared at him !) but in the
> chill of his egotism and in the light of her use. . . . It had sprung
> in that twilight of the cold April when, pale, ill, wasted, but
> all beautiful, and perhaps even then recoverable, she had risen
> from her chair to stand before him and let him imaginably
> guess.

Another, *The Papers*, suggests that Henry James tails
in verisimilitude whenever his subject—in this case
a modern journalistic " scoop "—specially demands
verisimilitude. The same suggestion occurs in the
third story of *The Finer Grain*, and the fact that this
story (*A Round of Visits*) ends with something no less
tangible than a revolver and no less positive than

suicide, servss only to emphasize the unreality of the effect. Whether the title of this book, *The Finer Grain*, is used ironically I can't readily guess, but it is clear at any rate that the ingenuity of the stories, which show little but ingenuity, composes only a melancholy picture.

It is in books somewhat earlier than these that Henry James's best short stories are found. Nothing is finer than *The Aspern Papers*, a haunting picture (reflecting Claire Clairmont's predicament) of the jealous guardian of a dead poet's fame wrestling to preserve his "papers" from publicity ; a picture memorable of itself and still more memorable from its Venetian setting, whereby a double loveliness is achieved. That picture and that setting prolong for me, and I hope for others, a beauty and an atmosphere that makes them distinct from any other of our author's. . . . Two of the stories in *The Lesson of the Master* have a singular interest inasmuch as they are sketches in apparent anticipation of *The Turn of the Screw*—false starts in the telling of the grimmest of ghostly stories ; but it is to the two volumes published in 1895 and 1896, *Terminations* and *Embarrassments*, that you must turn for some of the most masterly of Henry James's "lessons." To glance merely at the latter book, *The Figure in the Carpet* has the same interest as *The Lesson of the Master* and presses even more deeply into questions of creative art ; the second embarrassment (*Glasses*) is one of the most simply pathetic stories, one of the very few of our author's which are pathetic and no more. The third (*The Next Time*) is once more an embarrassment of art,—the failure of fineness :

> He'll try again for the common with what he'll believe to be a still more infernal cunning, and again the cunning will fatally elude him, for his infernal cunning will have been only his genius in an ineffectual disguise.

Did Henry James, one might ask, quite know that when the " common " completely eludes the artist it is indeed fatal for the artist ? . . . The fourth embarrassment (*The Way it Came*) is again a queer story, of a man who has seen his mother's ghost, and a girl who has seen her father's. The man and the girl never meet, thanks to the petty perversity of fate ; and when that no longer prevails to make a meeting impossible his betrothed, jealous of their psychic intimacy, prevents a meeting by a sudden lie. The girl, in mute protest, " appears " to him in his room, for the first and last time—and is found, at home, dead of pyschic excitement. The queerness is enhanced by the absence of names—an oddity which so pleased the author that he repeated it in *In the Cage*.

IV

Turn to Henry James's impressions of places and people, or turn to his portraits and impressions of those that have laboured in his own field of imaginative literature, if you would ascertain more surely the richness and the restlessness of his mind. *English Hours* or *French Poets and Novelists* among the earlier books, and *The American Scene* or *Notes on Novelists* among the later, witness to very much the same effect as the earlier and later novels :—they tell of a change which may be hinted at by saying that in the impressions of his first period he gives you the *thing* as you might see it for yourself, and in the impressions of his last period the *thing* as none but Henry James could see it or render it. No one would conceivably read *The American Scene* (1907) to " find out " about America, but read it you must if you would discover Henry James. The " restless analyst," he calls himself and no phrase could be happier. . . . And is it not a triumph of genius, then, that he should give not simply his delicate impression and analysis, nor simply his own ingenious preferences and discriminations, but also some veritable sign and portent of the huge gross scene that amazed but failed to overwhelm him ? What could be more penetrating than this from the chapter, *The Testimony of the Club :*

> It is of extreme interest to be reminded at many a turn . . . that it takes an endless amount of history to make even a little tradition, and an endless amount of tradition to make even a little taste, and an endless amount of taste, by the same token, to make even a little tranquillity.

Than this of Newport what could be more cruelly final ?—

The very air and light, soft and discreet, seemed to speak, in tactful fashion, for people who would be embarrassed to be there—as if it might shame them to see it proved against them that they could once have been so artless and so bourgeois. The point is that they have learned not to be by the rather terrible process of exhausting the list of mistakes.

He can be blunt enough, as when he declares the main American formula to be, to make so much money that you don't mind anything; and tender enough, as when he visits the Confederate Museum at Richmond; and lofty enough, as when he looks upon the pretentious Pullman and, in an unusual apostrophe, accuses it of an accumulation of " the unretrieved and the irretrievable "—suggesting inevitably that it is the vast eastern half of the continent itself that he sees spread before him when he speaks. You see by the time his flight is ended that it has given him something quite different from the sentimental pleasure of revisitation; if he returned to smile, the smile became wry, and all his fancifulness of phrase, all his swift scintillation, does not quite hide a shuddering distaste. But the richness of his impression remains, and the vivacity, and the eagerness with which he turns hither and thither, and the sensitiveness with which he confronts scenes the most various, and the unfailing security with which he weighs and judges a world of which the changes, wonderful as they appeared, were less strange than the movement of his own mind.

Of *Notes on Novelists* (1914) it is more difficult to speak, since it covers a period of seventeen years and subjects so congenial as Flaubert and so uncongenial as the younger novelists of our own day. His tribute to Flaubert is a model that should serve for a writer on Henry James himself :

> There are countries beyond the sea in which tracts are allowed to settlers on condition that they will really, not nominally, cultivate them. Flaubert is on his romantic ground like one of these settlers ; he makes good with all his might his title to his tract, and in a way that shows how it is not only for him a question of safety but a question of honour. Honour demands that he shall set up his home and his faith there in such a way that every inch of the surface be planted or paved.

As sure and right is his phrase for D'Annunzio, when he speaks of that novelist's intensely difficult subject in *L'Innocente* :

> We of course never play the fair critical game with an author, never get into relation with him at all, unless we grant him his postulates. His subject is what is given him—given him by influences, by a process, with which we have nothing to do ; since what art, what revelation, can ever really make such a mystery, such a passage in the private life of the intellect, adequately traceable for us ? His treatment of it, on the other hand, is what he actively gives ; and it is with what he gives that we are critically concerned.

I cannot but fall back on these sentences with something of relief when I am tempted to marvel at the subject of *What Maisie Knew* or *The Golden Bowl*. . . . How important a congenial theme is to Henry James himself is shown pretty plainly by a paper which is

unattractive because the subject is not congenial—
The New Novel. He is so concerned to disguise his
comprehensive failure to enjoy the younger novelists
of our time that the disguise—a very miracle of looped
and windowed raggedness—flutters from every page.
It is thus the most difficult thing in the world to read,
as it must surely have been the most difficult thing in
the world for so scrupulous and so generous a man to
write.

Scarcely less difficult to read are the two volumes
of reminiscences—*A Small Boy and Others* and
Notes of a Son and Brother—in which Henry James's
impressionism (if the term will pass) is carried to the
last refinement. Recalling, recovering, clutching at
and missing a shadowy host of memories and portraits
of antique date, darting upon tiny specks and peering
along narrow beams of brilliant light, sweeping away
and down again, and perpetually weighing in critical
scales the value of this, that and the other, he has
extended to a thousand pages the relation of what was.
If it is hard to put the book down, it is equally hard
to take it up again :—the flickering light both excites
and fatigues. Style so exactly responsive to motions
so capricious makes but small account of the weakness
of the common mind ; and it is by contrast as much
as by virtue of their own bright delight that the
portraits of Henry James Senior, William James and
Mary Temple shine out so purely when you turn the
last page.

The Moderns

V

To linger over the shorter stories and the purely critical writings is to evade, as I fear I must still evade, the yet more difficult and yet more delightful task of considering in detail the longer novels, with which by a curious mental association *The Turn of the Screw* (1898) is in my own memory always involved. I think of *The Other House* (1896), *What Maisie Knew* (1897), *The Spoils of Poynton* (1897), *The Ambassadors* (1903) and *The Golden Bowl* (1905) with amazement at what is yet a mere fraction of ten years' work ; and I find myself saying now, the imagination, the imagination ! For these and other novels of the decade strengthen vastly the sense which the earlier books have aroused, the sense, namely, that Henry James is above all a creator, a poet still resisting, though as time passes with diminishing success, the tendencies that had grown as he grew and that went on growing so inordinately. There are characters as well as types, there's passion as well as speculation, strength as well as subtlety, simplicity as well as mystification.

The Turn of the Screw might be reckoned the most typical of Henry James's stories, since it expresses most completely his isolation from all contemporary writers. In his own phrase, it is " the real right thing " among I don't care to count how many contemporary efforts at the merely weird or the merely unpleasant. It is a ghastly story, this relation of the imaginative—which is the moral and spiritual—defilement of two children by apparitional criminals. Nothing more horrible has been conceived. " It gives a very echo to the seat where love is thron'd," and makes love sick ; so that not even the courage of the children's defeated governess, confronting these infernal shades with desperate half-obscure understanding, renders the thing less horrible, though leaving it, I suppose, more wonderful. Whether the courage of this poor woman outweighs the debasement of the wretched children, a question that has not gone unheeded, is a question which I must leave untouched.

The Other House is followed so closely by *What Maisie Knew* that the subject-matter being so intensely odious in each is made doubly odious by the repetition. The universal eroticism of the former is matched by the intervolved erotomania of the latter, and if it were permissible to cavil at a writer's choice of subject, here assuredly were abundant ground. But it is not permissible, mainly for a reason which Henry James himself quite simply and finally states (as I have already shown) in his vindication of D'Annunzio, and partly because no artist conceivably " chooses " any subject at all. It chooses him, and only then *his* choice begins. There is immense passion, clear and smoky, simple and confused, in *The Other House* : to resort to a term which used to have a meaning, it is the " strongest " of the novels, and the strength is predominantly that of character. Rose Armiger has every beauty but the beauty of honour, and she burns with so deadly a flame that you do not stay to ask— as under a weaker fascination you might ask—if she is from top to toe perfectly credible. Nor do you pause to remark too curiously the singular restlessness of the book, the nervousness of nearly every character, the perpetual business of entry and re-entry which has the effect of incessantly repeated stage-directions. You pause, in fact, for nothing until the rapid fire of the conception has burned through the tragic group called so vividly before you.

Moral sickness might well be the result, again, of a slow thoughtless immersion in the clinging complexity of *What Maisie Knew*. Divorcees who loathe one another, and loathe or love one another's successors, who struggle for Maisie's possession so that they may poison her mind with stories of one another, and then cordially disclaim her—" What a set ! " you murmur in Arnold's old phrase. But it is the special success of Henry James—who could succeed, you would say, precisely in proportion to his difficulties—that all these complications are more than endurable, are indeed fascinating as much as they are odious ; the child growing the more vividly sweet as the complications darken around her.

Of *The Spoils of Poynton* and the rest what can be said at once briefly and wisely ? Some of these novels, in which the later Henry James dims into the latest, are among the most wonderful of his labours; but a slow change comes until you find you have passed from the rapid and deadly currents of *The Other House* to the iridescent still waters of *The Golden Bowl*. Style at last wreathes itself around conception like a snake, and the result is a wonderful thing—a wonderful immobility, with life's colours not yet gone, but with life itself, its passion and freedom, in stifled suspense and the brain dizzying into darkness. So powerful is this impression that it checks much that I had meant to say—of the prose that is only too consummate and only too wildly idiosyncratic; of the contacts with the material world and the religious heart of man only too delicate and only too securely restricted; but for these things, almost unimportant in relation to the general impression which is all that is here attempted, I have neither space nor inclination to speak. Not by me shall the devil's advocate be briefed.

For the change is clear. That vivid intelligence might not rest, but if it could do no more it could revolve. It seems to me, and I speak with hesitation, that Henry James came at length to write from no impulse but that urgent one of beguiling the restlessness, even the loneliness, of his mind. He revised even his recent work with the tiniest particularity, sometimes only for the sake or with the result of inserting such a favourite phrase as, " she wound up," or making the elaborate style more elaborately colloquial. Death or time looked over his shoulder, and to forget, and to keep his restless thoughts from resting on that chill apparition, he wrote some of the things we have been looking at with an eagerness too rude, a curiosity too raw, but with an affectionate reverence which his work and the beauty of his spirit alike evoke.

VI

Let it merely be said, then, that Henry James is a creator, a dramatic poet, a model, an influence. There is a singularly fine note in all his work, a note of such personal fineness that it becomes a powerful moral note. *Noblesse oblige*, he murmurs to himself in a superfluous reminder. The point of honour is the point around which his energies move, and the theme he is driven repeatedly to illustrate. It has a double reference—to the narrow, austere obligation of the imaginative writer towards his private genius, and to the obligation upon civilized men and women to live freely, sensitively, finely, with a rightness never merely rigid or cold.

He served his own master, his own ideal, with a passion as faithful as Keats gave to poetry. He conceived nobly and might well have said :

> My love is of a birth as rare,
> As 'tis for object strange and high.

Strange and high his object always was, and he had a special gentleness for his fellow adventurers in the passionate quest. Hence so many of the stories (as a single volume, *Terminations*, may show), distilling a great tenderness into his presentation of the literary artist, have almost too frankly professional a concern. His defeat is made the defeat—alack, the inevitable defeat, in Henry James's view—of some precious, imperfect, fragile thing that only wanted silence, or time, to come to ripeness. He is defeated because of his high aim, or because of his wife, or because he must earn money, or because the world is blind to the real object of his work, the central light, " the figure in the carpet," or death surprises him and blots the page just when expression has at last leaped the old gulf and touched lips with conception. Again and again is the subject taken up, with a passion sometimes wistful, sometimes merely sad, occasionally a little perfunctory ; though, in this, failure shows even more clearly than success how closely the whole tremulous subject is lodged in the author's heart. . . . Merely to glance again at his lavish *obiter dicta* is to see, easily enough, how intense and how penetrating was his apprehension of the truths which are the final truths for writer and reader alike :

> Observation's a second-rate thing, it's only a precaution— the refuge of the small and timid. . . . But to have the thing you mention, and above all not to have imagination, is simply not to have tact, than which nothing is more unforgivable and more loathsome.

Elsewhere he writes :

The Moderns

There is no complete creation without style any more than there is complete music without sound.

And in that teasing, significant study, *The Figure in the Carpet* :

Isn't there for every writer a particular thing . . . the thing that most makes him apply himself, the thing without the effort to achieve which he wouldn't write at all, the very passion of his passion, the part of the business in which, for him, the flame of art burns most intensely ?

But his chief emphasis—if emphasis is not too vulgar a word—is upon the point of honour in its universal reference to the lives of men and women. This highest moral note is plain enough in *The Altar of the Dead*, and indeed in that perilously poised story gives weight just where weight is needed ; it is nowhere clearer than in *The Spoils of Poynton*, which the magnificent Fleda Vetch dominates as a mountain dominates its world. That book is itself a signal and a tribute to honour. The best must be sacrificed to the worst for the sake of the best, because it is the best, and the proof must be asserted in the teeth of the worst. The best may not fall an inch below itself for the merest fraction of time. Here and always conduct is *every* part of life, and manners the beautiful, sparing dress of conduct. . . . Even from the entanglement of *What Maisie Knew* the clear moral impression rises, in the repugnance of the child to the subdual of the one it loves to evil things ; and the slow-revolv-

ing drama of *The Golden Bowl* exalts the tragic pride
that redeems Charlotte from the plot which " passionless passion " spins, and leaves something of other
greatness shining in her beauty as she passes.

JOSEPH CONRAD

I

MR. CONRAD'S work is distinguished from that
of his contemporaries by the quality of its
life. He did not start to write until the best of Meredith and the best of Mr. Hardy's prose had been given
to a still half-oblivious world. With contemporaries
so various as Henry James, Mr. Kipling and Mr.
Hudson he has nothing in common save the " zest for
creation " which Mr. Hugh Walpole in his recent study
of our author's work swiftly recognizes. The quality
of *What Maisie Knew* and a dozen of James's other
books is as utterly remote from the quality of *Heart
of Darkness* and *Chance*, as Chelsea is from the Congo.
The bright world of the one writer swims serenely far
from the ken of the other. More obvious is the comparison with Mr. Kipling, but scarcely more rational.
Mr. Kipling has not created a world of his own, or an
atmosphere for the common world of men ; his is not
that gift of all gifts. Nor, again, could there well be
a greater gulf than that which the all-wise Creator
has fixed between the mind that discovered the world
of *A Crystal Age*, and *Green Mansions*,—crystalline
and Eve-like and warm with human breath,—and

the mind that discovered the tragedy of *Nostromo*. There is, indeed, no one with whom the author of *Nostromo* and the rest can be compared, and he is in the true sense an original writer whom none has been so foolish as to copy.

Twenty-one years ago, his first book was published, and a year ago his last—*Victory*. The first was a stone in but a small still pool ; the last was a voice adding its echoes to the considerable reverberations of *Chance*. *Chance* it was that brought him such fame as an original writer may at length expect. Meredith's letters have told us, with a querulousness perhaps not quite unnatural nor quite unsurprising, of the effect upon a sensitive mind of long years of coldness. Small consolation was it to him that only in such frigid winds of neglect do the tender flowers get strength. For him the result was to make his manner more unfortunately a mannerism and to drive him into a defensive wilfulness which was of small service to him or his readers. From such an error Mr. Conrad has been saved, even as he has been spared the full temptation. His first novels could not but attract and compel, and to have waited nineteen years for the larger recognition means only that the hearers of a new voice must needs be born as well as discovered. His first book, *Almayer's Folly*, would delight us now far more generally than it delighted readers in 1895 ; but to have it to-day as a new book, with all its eighteen successors behind it, would be disconcerting—I mean, in short, that it *begins,* in essence as well as in procession, the long row of novels to which we now return again and again not only with repeated surprise and admiration, but also with clear affection.

Almayer's Folly, then, is the seed from which this wonderful field has sprung to ripeness. It has the strangeness, the passion, the pity, the sadness, as well as the slight exoticism and casual extravagance, that mark the whole Conrad line. The writer has told us in his *Reminiscences* of its origin—how it grew simply from a haunting image :

> Your name was the common property of the winds : it, as it were, floated naked over the waters about the Equator. I wrapped round its unhonoured form the royal mantle of the tropics and have essayed to put into the hollow sound the very anguish of paternity.

Yes, it is a haunted book, haunting its author years and years after so that he dwells with candid absorption on the opening of the tenth chapter :

> " It has set at last," said Nina to her mother, pointing towards the hills behind which the sun had sunk. " Listen, mother, I am going now to Bulangi's creek, and if I should never return——"

In such a suspense does the whole book swing. The sun has set upon Almayer, and leaves only a tragical after-glow upon actors and scene alike ; pouring its later magnificence and its threat over the unilluminable forest darkness. There's nothing that is not strange and something beyond itself—a symbol of something unseen that is more strange, something isolated and insignificant. There is that impressive scene of the interview between Dain Maroola and the chief Lakamba and his crafty minister, Babalatchi, in the uncertain light of ¦smoky torches. A thunderstorm roars and recedes and returns.

The thunderstorm was recommencing outside, the heavy clouds hanging low overhead now. There was a constant rumble of distant thunder punctuated by the nearer sharp crashes, and in the continuous play of blue lightning the woods and the river showed fitfully, with all the elusive distinctness of detail characteristic of such a scene. Outside the door of the Rajah's house Dain and Babalatchi stood on the shaking verandah as if dazed and stunned by the violence of the storm. They stood there amongst the cowering forms of the Rajah's slaves and retainers seeking shelter from the rain, and Dain called aloud to his boatmen, who responded with an unanimous " Ada ! Tuan ! " while they looked uneasily at the river.

Into the sinister night goes Dain, flying from the Dutch authorities ; and the Rajah and Babalatchi meditate upon his possible escape.

Babalatchi stretched himself yawning, but Lakamba, in the flattering consciousness of a knotty problem solved by his own unaided intellectual efforts, grew suddenly very wakeful.
" Babalatchi," he said to the exhausted statesman, " fetch the box of music the white captain gave me. I cannot sleep."
At this order a deep shade of melancholy settled upon Babalatchi's features. He went reluctantly behind the curtain and soon reappeared carrying in his arms a small hand-organ, which he put down on the table with an air of deep dejection. Lakamba settled himself comfortably in his arm-chair.

"Turn, Babalatchi, turn," he murmured, with closed eyes.

Babalatchi's hand grasped the handle with the energy of despair, and as he turned, the deep gloom on his countenance changed into an expression of hopeless resignation. Through the open shutter the notes of Verdi's music floated out on the great silence over the river and forest. Lakamba listened with closed eyes and a delighted smile. Babalatchi turned, at times dozing off and swaying over, then catching himself up in a great fright with a few quick turns of the handle. Nature slept in an exhausted repose after the fierce turmoil, while under the unsteady hand of the statesman of Sambir the Trovatore fitfully wept, wailed, and bade good-bye to his Leonore again and again in a mournful round of tearful and endless iteration.

By such grotesquerie does Mr. Conrad at once relieve and enhance the gathering intensity of picture and suggestion. So, again, when the chase is renewed and Almayer's daughter, Nina, is resolved to go with Dain to the ends of the earth and beyond, the tragical Almayer hears her speak:

"You told me yesterday that I could not understand or see your love for me: it is so. How can I? No two human beings understand each other. They can understand but their own voices. You wanted me to dream your dreams, to see your own visions—the visions of life amongst the white faces of those who cast me out from their midst in angry contempt. But while you spoke I listened to the voice of my own self; then this man came, and all was still; there was only the murmur of his love. You call him a savage! What do you call my mother, your wife?"

"Nina!" cried Almayer, "take your eyes off my face."

—so even here the painfulness is at once diminished and sharpened by the perception of Almayer's forlorn absurdity, making his loneliness no more than merely pathetic :

> " I am a white man." He broke down completely there, and went on tearfully, " I am a white man, and of good family. Very good family," he repeated, weeping bitterly. " It would be a disgrace . . . all over the islands, . . . the only white man on the east coast. No, it cannot be . . . white men finding my daughter with this Malay. My daughter ! " he cried aloud, with a ring of despair in his voice.
>
> He recovered his composure after a while and said distinctly, " I will never forgive you, Nina—never ! "

None of the brilliant, errant or evil people that move with so individual a gesture through all these vivid books is, you feel, rendered from a more intimate vision.

The true spirit of comedy, again, lightens the somewhat clinging darkness of *An Outcast of the Islands*. Almayer appears here also, but as a figure subsidiary to the dishonest and detected mercantile clerk, Willems. A genius for treachery, a passionate ingratitude, a gutter-bred assertiveness, a pathetic craving for respectability and security—these are the elements of a creation more elaborately conceived and fashioned than Almayer, but scarcely more faithful. Moreover, Willems is not so generously dealt with as Almayer ; he is not left to go on his way to right or to left as his own will suggests, but is touched with something oddly like contempt. No one can hate Almayer, his author least of all ; but the author of this Willems has not quite forgiven the haunting of his mind by whatever restless ghost companioned Almayer's as it drifted on the winds. Yet here too is the same blending of those universal characteristics of human life—the pathetic with the absurd ; a combination of which Mr. Conrad is continually aware in his scrutiny of men.

I pass by such books as *The Nigger of the Narcissus* and *Tales of Unrest* because their special virtues are found in other novels which it gives me greater pleasure to dwell upon ; and, too, because I want to step quickly to *Lord Jim.* This is, I suppose, the most simply human of all the novels, the most purely Conradian. Nina Almayer is prompt to remind me that Mr. Conrad has never been indifferent to that feminine portraiture which from Chaucer to Henry James has given a special glory to the imaginative work of English writers ; but in the earlier books of our author this interest is an entirely subordinate one, and in *Lord Jim* almost entirely wanting. Jim, the mere type of clean, honest and vigorous youth, flashes his brilliant, marred personality around the situation in which he has been caught in a single unwary moment. The story, for all its subtlety and indirectness of telling, is simple. Cursed with an over-acute imagination, Jim is dazed by anticipated disaster ; he leaps into a boat which others have cast out, leaving his ship to sink, crammed with helpless pilgrims. It does not sink, the betrayal is discovered, and Jim solitarily faces the bleak wind of an inquiry

determined to say quite plainly (if aught in mortal life
is plain) what happened ; thereafter to pass into
merciful obscurity while he recovers, by a romantic
and audacious fidelity, the lost faith in himself and
of the helpless in him.   He meets death proudly, now,
the spiritual indignity of that earlier failure forgotten,
tranquil in his re-established individuality ; while
round him stand those he has befriended, uncom-
prehending and henceforth unguided natives :

> He passes away under a cloud, inscrutable at heart, for-
> gotten, unforgiven, and excessively romantic . . . an obscure
> conqueror of fame, tearing himself out of the arms of a jealous
> love at the call of his exalted egoism.   He goes away from a
> living woman to celebrate his pitiless wedding with a shadowy
> ideal of conduct.

What may be crudely called the moral interest, the
spiritual value, of imaginative work is at its highest
in *Lord Jim* and two other novels—*Nostromo* and
Under Western Eyes.   Mr. Conrad gives you not merely,
of course, the event, nor merely the motive ; but also
and no less clearly the *value* of incident and motive—
the human effect of the psychology underlying both.
Life has taught him many things, and the great charge
of those that travel the seas has taught him one thing
mainly, that fidelity to a trust is the supreme triumph
and its betrayal the supreme dishonour of a man's
life.   Honour, loyalty, faith, crown his conceptions,
and he involves in them whatever beauty and strength

is discernible in man's desire and achievement. I am not sure that this simple and tremendous moral impression is not of all Mr. Conrad's effects the most weighty and lasting. I am quite sure that it is the most characteristic. He sees life as a conflict: in *Victory*, the latest novel, the conflict of one disdaining strife with spirits of absolute evil; in *Chance*, the conflict of a girl's tragic bewilderment with a man's magnanimity; in *Nostromo*, the conflict of pride with the spell of treasure; in *Under Western Eyes*, the conflict of a passion for independence and order with a base fear. Chiefly, as in *Lord Jim*, it is the inward clash of human aspiration with secret falseness that fascinates his imagination:—and which of us has never known that conflict to be set before the eyes of that audience—most critical and most tender—of which we ourselves are the sole member? It is there that Mr. Conrad finds his witnesses, in those personal recollections of perpetual strife between fear and honour. *Noblesse oblige*, might be inscribed in all his books as in those of Henry James; for they form, in a very real and direct sense, a Song of Honour.

In every book, I repeat, this moral brightness shines. It is conspicuous in that excellent short story, so excellent in its spirit of comedy, *Youth*—a simple recital of the death of an aged ship whose crew have pumped immeasurable water out of her when she leaked, and pumped it back when she burned. " Profane scallywags," the crew, rising quite simply to the incredible, making painful efforts that they knew to be vain.

> It was something in them, something inborn and subtle and everlasting. . . . There was a completeness in it, something solid like a principle, and masterful like an instinct—a disclosure of something secret—of that hidden something, that gift of good or evil that makes racial difference, that shapes the fate of nations.

—" Racial difference . . . that shapes the fate of nations." One delights to apprehend now an unintended significance in the words. The brightness is steady in *Typhoon*, and clearest, as Mr. Conrad loves to show it, in touches half ludicrous, half tender : as— when the immovable Captain McWhirr orders his chief mate to pacify the hundreds of coolies raging below deck and pick up their scattered coins. The minute scrupulousness of this care, and the vast anger of the typhoon, are exquisitely remembered. . . . Like a star it shines over all the passionate confusion of *Nostromo*. Nostromo's fall from fidelity serves but to mark the height of the great argument of the book. He conceals the silver, and permits the owners to think it lost, only because his wearily cynical comrade in the task of saving it has (in the last despair of loneliness) stolen four ingots and drowned himself with them. It is this breach in the wholeness of the treasure that leads to Nostromo's defiant, melancholy secrecy, and the final tragedy. . . . It burns like a sombre fire in *Under Western Eyes*. Razumov has betrayed the man who, in the misprision of sympathy, has forced confidences on him, confidences which his own aspiring spirit abhors yet can't refuse ; and before the sister of his victim he expiates, in a scene that is pure immitigable agony, the greatness of that fall from human fidelity.   Here, there and everywhere is an impression of nobleness, of dignity, honour and enduringness, an impression that not only diminishes the sharpness of the common first sense of melancholy which is so easily remarked in Mr. Conrad's books, but persists and deepens long after that superficial first sense has dimmed away.   For the charge of sadness and moral enervation—to put quite plainly what has been put more delicately—is hardly more than absurd when not simply individual destiny or the course of incident is observed, but the whole of character, its essence rather than its visible success or failure, is taken into the reckoning.   That the noblest fails, that Heyst and Nostromo and Captain Whalley die while worse men live on, is surely not now to be taken as evidence of their creator's cynicism, or disabled faith.   Though the noblest fail, that they are the noblest, that they are the object of their author's patient honour, remains indisputable.   The strife, the assertion, the *being*—there is the triumph of that inward eternal radiance of which an imaginative writer must needs be the prophet, if he is not himself to be false to his high calling.   Need a thing so simple be said in words so simple ?—by that which endures is a writer's conception to be judged. In the case of Mr. Conrad's work, it is honour that endures and defeats the night of blackness.

II

It has been the luck of few writers to bring to their task a richer experience of life and nature than Mr. Conrad has gained. Of the value of experience, even if it be only that of the circumscribed life of the streets and the mean adventures of poverty, Dickens bears witness and Dostoieffsky no less amply. What distinguishes our author's work is the interspersion of scenery and natural phenomena with the recollection of men among whom he has himself moved for many years, and whose visible life has been used so cunningly for the foundation of these imaginative histories. There is even something elemental—epic is the term, is it not ?—in the characters of some of the men thus revivified. You have in *Typhoon* and *Heart of Darkness* and *The End of the Tether* (all in a single rich book) this note of the elemental—not simply of scenery but of personality ; you have, indeed, clearly and freely, those full epic characters with which Victor Hugo attempted so easy and false a familiarity. That is the gift of movement among men of large, incurious mind, amid vast spaces of sea and sky, and the yet vaster loneliness of tropic forests and hills, Mythopoetic is Mr. Conrad's imagination, making

elemental characters in human likeness out of the
east wind and the west wind, in a passage which, even
mutilated as I give it, seems to me as noble a specimen
of heightened prose as any of the moderns has uttered :

> The end of the day is the time to gaze at the kingly face of
> the Westerly Weather, who is the arbiter of ships' destinies.
> Benignant and splendid, or splendid and sinister, the western
> sky reflects the hidden purposes of the royal mind. Clothed
> in a mantle of dazzling gold or draped in rags of black clouds
> like a beggar, the might of the Westerly Wind sits enthroned
> upon the western horizon with the whole North Atlantic as a
> footstool for his feet and the first twinkling stars making a
> diadem for his brow. . . . The West Wind is too great a king
> to be a dissembler ; he is no calculator plotting deep schemes
> in a sombre heart ; he is too strong for small artifices ; there
> is passion in all his moods, even in the soft mood of his serene
> days, in the grace of his blue sky whose immense and unfath-
> omable tenderness reflected in the mirror of the sea embraces,
> possesses, lulls to sleep the ships with white sails. He is all
> things to all oceans ; he is like a poet seated upon a throne—
> magnificent, simple, barbarous, pensive, generous, impulsive,
> changeable, unfathomable—but when you understand him,
> always the same. Some of his sunsets are like pageants
> devised for the delight of the multitude, when all the gems of
> the royal treasure-house are displayed above the sea. Others
> are like the opening of his royal confidence, tinged with
> thoughts of sadness and compassion in a melancholy splen-
> dour meditating upon the short-lived peace of the waters.
> And I have seen him put the pent-up anger of his heart into
> the aspect of the inaccessible sun, and cause it to glare fiercely
> like the eye of an implacable autocrat out of a pale and fright-
> ened sky.

Forgiveness will not be withheld from a chronicler
who yields so lightly to the temptation of quoting a

piece so noble as this. It demands its contrasting portrait of the East Wind :

> But the other, crafty and unmoved, nursing his shaven chin between the thumb and forefinger of his slim and treacherous hand, thinks deep within his heart full of guile : " Aha ! our brother of the West has fallen into the mood of kingly melancholy. He is tired of playing with circular gales, and blowing great guns, and unrolling thick streamers of fog in wanton sport at the cost of his own poor, miserable subjects. Their fate is most pitiful. Let us make a foray upon the dominions of that noisy barbarian, a great raid from Finisterre to Hatteras, catching his fishermen unawares, baffling the fleets that trust to his power, and shooting sly arrows into the livers of men who court his good graces." . . . The East Wind, an interloper in the dominions of Westerly weather, is an impassive-faced tyrant with a sharp poniard held behind his back for a treacherous stab.
> In his forays into the North Atlantic the East Wind behaves like a subtle and cruel adventurer without a notion of honour or fair play. Veiling his clear-cut lean face in a thin layer of a hard, high cloud, I have seen him, like a wizened robber sheik of the sea, hold up large caravans of ships to the number of three hundred or more at the very gates of the English Channel.

Only prose which reaches a noticeable height is capable of a fall. Sometimes Mr. Conrad's fails in vividness, sometimes it is wanting in movement, sometimes it is not lofty but merely inflated, ill-sustained by lavish latinisms. So much must be admitted, with the reservation that these are casual faults, incidental and not essential. The body of this prose is masculine and quick.

In *Lord Jim* Mr. Conrad speaks of finding " at every

turn the magnificence which besets our insignificant footsteps in good and evil." This it is that beckons to him. The word is a favourite word, and the quality is that in which his tragic figures—lofty, mean, absurd—leap into their finest activity. He is obviously a romantic, just as obviously as his method is in several books realistic : of the latter *The Secret Agent* remains, for example, a sinister, unendearing book. . . . At heart romantic :—and I mean by this simply to suggest the element of strangeness, of surprising beauty, rich and curious and passionate, the apprehension of which is a specially modern quest. It neighbours tragedy, and that word suggests promptly enough one superb illustration of the romantic tragedy with which Mr. Conrad is nearly always preoccupied. The story is that short one called *A Smile of Fortune*. From a medley of details of ships' goods, sugar bags, brutalities, provincialisms, there emerges—pure and potent as a candle in the dark—the strange primitive figure of Alice Jacobus, staring forsaken into the night that sweeps even common things with sadness ; in the same moment awakened and forsaken, infinitely desirable yet undesired ; profound and unvalued. She is touched to life, and left ; and the man who leaves her goes on his way with a surprisingly profitable cargo of potatoes, and an unendurable sickness at heart, Magnificence broods here, like a splendid sunset ; the magnificence that a man puts by in the blindness or the meanness of his heart.

The later books do not profess a concern with life so exclusively romantic, they betray an inclination, daring yet successful, to give the reins of romance to realism. Let it be admitted, here, that these abstract terms are hardly more useful than any of the common terms by which thought or its absence is concealed. What I mean is, that Mr. Conrad has more and more steadily bent himself to touching ordinary life as he conceives an ordinary man sees it ; but without struggle and without difficulty the old magnificence bathes the scene—and like a flower from a muddy pond there grows (as in *Chance*) such a delicate, courageous, extraordinary figure as Flora du Barral, such a painfully impressive one as Captain Anthony ; or as in *Victory*, against the unpleasant hard shadows of Mr. Jones and Ricardo (so hard as to be strangely immobile and scarcely even " realistic ") Lena spreads the magnificence of her own spirit—the only magnificence in a book which would have been easily enriched with a little more. It is not romance that Mr. Conrad has to fear.

III

All this points to one plain fact, that Mr. Conrad is a poet in all but the shaping spirit of verse. He has been oddly compared with Browning, for the moral rather than the purely poetic character ; and the comparison on either ground is astonishing. He is an Odysseus among poets, passing lonely, half-glimpsed

and unrecognized through the people of his own
creation. Amid a rich and vigorous dark forest they,
evil and splendid and unquiet mortals, live and move
and have their being. *They have their being*—that is
their tribute to Mr. Conrad's creativeness. Not
invention nor description but imagination marks his
quality, making him a poet among prose writers. He
has something of the careless reproductive power of
natural life, something of its intensity, something of
its variety, something of its mystery. His interest
is as keenly fixed on characters of pure evil as on
Lord Jim or Heyst; he is not concerned to judge
or condemn or excuse, for there is always something
that he cannot explore, a darkness he cannot pierce.
" When it comes to human beings, anything, anything
may be expected." He is not concerned to " present "
to use our modern word; he has no " case " to state;
there is assuredly too little rather than too much of
design and shape in his novels. He is prodigal, various,
intense, mysterious, just as life in men is; and his aim
is to have no aim but to go on creating and reproducing
with the capricious ease of life itself.

But he is not a careless writer. Indirect as his
method is, I do not think it is ever merely clumsy.
He can tell a plain thing plainly—yes: but how few
things are capable of plainness! In *Chance* his
method is perhaps most conspicuously indirect, but
really simple. Of all his books it is the richest in
intuition, the clearest in its reading of the unusual

and remote ; and Mr. Conrad gives its very definite and complex story as an inordinate conversation, immediate or reported, one speaking now, another then, with the inconsequence of interrupted conversation but also with the vivid intimacy of talk between intimates. From a casual encounter between Marlow —subtle interlocutor of more than one story—and another ship's officer, and their discovery of common knowledge concerning Flora and Captain Anthony, the whole story springs :—and how life-like in its casual origin, its wanderings, its tributary narratives, its overhanging brushing commentary, its steady purpose and progress. To Marlow, said Mr. Conrad, years before *Chance* was written :

> The meaning of an episode was not inside like a kernel but outside, enveloping the tale which brought it out only as a glow brings out a haze. . . .

The value of Mr. Conrad's method is that his story has not one life but many lives. He tries to apprehend character in action. So you have the briefest description of Lord Jim, but his actions and his influence (his character *in being*) are detailed with immense patience. You are to feel his impression upon the Commission of Enquiry, upon Brierley (to whose self-security Jim's fall comes overwhelmingly, robbing him of his will to live) ; upon Marlow, the native chiefs and their people, and the desperado through whom Jim dies. They form " a dome of many-coloured glass," through which Lord Jim's personality pours its triumphant ray. Mr. Conrad seeks to involve his reader in his narrative, to bring you to the table where men talk still of these things ; to appeal to your recollection, your apprehension, your sympathy ; for it is his passion that you should possess the whole story, not simply as a procession of events or as an unfolding of character, but as a web of events and characters acting and reacting as living things. Not everything can be told ; sometimes you may but guess, and in one extraordinary scene in *Chance* Marlow himself can only guess dimly what happened, what *must* have happened, when the two sinister characters of his story talk together at night after Flora's fortunes have collapsed like sand. You hear Marlow's voice sink to a dry whisper as he tries to show you the silent horror of that imagined unmasking of evil and disappointed hopes.

Marlow looked at me with his dark penetrating glance. I was struck by the absolute verisimilitude of this suggestion. But we were always tilting at each other. I saw an opening and pushed my uncandid thrust.
" You have a ghastly imagination," I said.

It falls on your ears with a touch of the genius of Defoe.

IV

Every writer, I suppose, cherishes in secret, formulated or formless, a theory or a creed of his art. Lofty

or petty, an unconfessed conception is hid within every
character, and breathed upon by the artist ; and by
the virtue of that conception the virtue of the art is
determined. What is there *central*, one asks, in the
work that is offered to us ? what does it hide and what
does it reveal? We are not children, thirsting to
know what Front de Boeuf did, but men wanting to
know what Mr. Shandy was. " Something human is
dearer to me than the wealth of all the world," says
Mr. Conrad on the title-page of *Youth* ; and speaks
elsewhere of " that spirit of piety towards all things
human which sanctions the conceptions of a writer
of tales." More largely illuminating is another passage
from the same book in which, pondering over " the aim
of creation," he writes :

> I would fondly believe that its object is purely spectacular :
> a spectacle for awe, love, adoration, or hate, if you like, but
> in this view, and in this view alone, never for despair. Those
> visions, delicious or poignant, are a moral end in themselves.
> The rest is our affair—the laughter, the tears, the tenderness,
> the indignation, the high tranquillity of a steeled heart, the
> detached curiosity of a subtle mind—that's our affair ; and
> the unwearied self-forgetful attention to every phase of the
> living universe reflected in our consciousness may be our
> appointed task on this earth—a task in which fate has per-
> haps engaged nothing of us except our conscience, gifted with
> a voice in order to bear true testimony to the visible wonder,
> the haunting terror, the infinite passion and the illimitable
> serenity, the supreme law and the abiding mystery of the
> sublime spectacle.

. . . Nothing but life itself pouring through human

personality—personality heroic, absurd, simple, mean, obscure, plain—nothing but the confused richness of life will content him. And he sees that the spectacle is a symbol as well as a spectacle. He perceives the secret animation of what are called inanimate things; and when he speaks of them even familiar things have a mark of strangeness. Air and sea, space and silence, forests and streets and narrow rooms become alike the accomplices of his living characters.

Of a hundred things unsaid one must be said. These notes are written while all ears are tingling with news of the battle of Jutland. In the last chapter of *The Mirror of the Sea* Mr. Conrad, a Pole using the English language with a care and a power revealing equally his own genius and that of our tongue, has paid tribute to the seaman—so covetous of honour!—who is still the starry hero of England's history. It has given me excellent pleasure to read again, under the title of *The Heroic Age* :

Those who from the heat of that battle sank together to their repose in the cool depths of the ocean would not understand the watchwords of our day, would gaze with amazed eyes at the engines of our strife. All passes, all changes : the animosity of peoples, the handling of fleets, the form of ships ; and even the sea itself seems to wear a different and diminished aspect from the sea of Lord Nelson's day. In this ceaseless rush of shadows and shades, that, like the fantastic forms of clouds cast darkly upon the waters on a windy day, fly past us to fall headlong below the hard edge of an implacable horizon, we must turn to the national spirit, which, superior in its force and continuity to good and evil fortune, can alone give

us the feeling of an enduring existence and of an invincible
power against the fates.

Like a subtle and mysterious elixir poured into the perish-
able clay of successive generations, it grows in truth, splendour, and potency with the march of ages. In its incorruptible flow all round the globe of the earth it preserves from the
decay and forgetfulness of death the greatness of our great
men, and amongst them the passionate and gentle greatness
of Nelson, the nature of whose genius was, on the faith of a
brave seaman and distinguished Admiral, such as to " Exalt
the glory of our nation."

COVENTRY PATMORE AND FRANCIS THOMPSON

I PLACE their names together because, notwith-
standing a most marked individuality, there is
in the work of Thompson a kinship with the work of
Patmore. No mere imitation or thinning echo of
Patmore is discernible in Thompson's writings, but
yet there is a spiritual link which makes it impossible
to speak duly of Thompson without reference to the
elder poet of whom, indeed, he was a " dear son of
memory " as well as a faithful disciple. So I put them
together here, and will say no more than is necessary
to remind the reader that the visible likeness of their
attitude is not the result of literary posturing by the
later poet, but rather the manifestation of their joint
spiritual fidelity. For another reason, I may explain
here that the influence of Patmore upon our time is
partly direct, and partly exercised through Francis
Thompson.

*   *   *   *   *

COVENTRY PATMORE

I

When a writer starts an essay by saying that a poet
has always been misunderstood, and that the true

significance of his work is to be found here rather than there, you may justly suspect this to be merely the prelude to a more ingenious misunderstanding. This I see clearly enough, yet still think that Patmore has been imperfectly understood, if only because he has not been studied sympathetically enough, or even closely enough. There have been articles here and there by Mrs. Meynell, who knew Patmore well, and who writes with that absolute comprehension which is the sure mark of her best work, as of all supremely penetrating work. Then there was a wonderful essay by Mr. J. L. Garvin some years ago, for which you must search the files of the *Fortnightly Review*. But beyond these there is scarcely a line in modern criticism to show that in Patmore we have a poet of a quality so rare and intense as to be almost unique.

Formal criticism is not, of course, the purpose of these discursive papers ; yet the temptation to formal criticism of this poet's work is hard to put by. But let me ask why it is that his work has been so inadequately regarded. A man of genius is usually studied in proportion to the obscurity or the romantic fascination of his personal character, or in proportion to the obscurity or the imaginative profundity of his work. Lamb and Johnson and Shelley charm us all by virtue of an immense personal fascination, quite distinct from the appeal of their writings. Blake and Wordsworth, on the other hand, steal our hearts away by virtue of the imaginative profundity of their work.

And there are one or two other writers, such as Shake-speare and Bunyan, whose appeal is imperative for both reasons. But undoubtedly the appeal of personality is the more ready and compelling. It is this that gives distinction to FitzGerald and Borrow. Clothe Crabbe in FitzGerald's oddity ; or ascribe to this plain parsonical man the adventurousness of the pugnacious bible-seller, his vagrancy, his boastfulness, his amusing intolerance, his overgrown childishness :— and how much more interesting would the dullest of Crabbe's *Tales* seem ! Yet would their value, as poetry, be unaltered.

Here is Patmore's initial disadvantage : his is not an irresistibly alluring personality. Put Patmore's Odes among Verlaine's work—itself claimed as intensely " symbolist " and mystical ; or into Patmore's life read the tragical unhappiness of Gerard de Nerval's, who sweetly led a lobster upon a blue ribbon through Paris :—do this, and who would not search then more earnestly the azure-like lines of *The Unknown Eros,* and assign a new symbolism to the plainest things ?

Yet is it, after all, a disadvantage that Patmore's poetry is to be read simply as poetry ? Is it not rather a great advantage, an advantage which is enhanced when you return to the poetry after surveying the man, and find in it but the luminous expression of a character luminously profound ? Not on his sleeve would you find Patmore's heart, but in his poems, his essays and letters, even in his singular, irreparable suppressions. A character reserved, flame-like intense, at once confident and humble as every mystic's must be ; a character to be understood as much in its restraint as in its freedom ; a character whose passiveness is but inward-burning energy ; a character—in this quite unsurprising to any student of poets or mystics—of notable practical capacity :—this is what appears suddenly and capriciously here and there among the material before us.

II

It is unnecessary to recapitulate the calendar of Patmore's life, and I will only refer to such events as it may be necessary to mention in looking at his work. *The Angel in the House*, his first important poem, enjoyed and exhausted a popularity which has since in some degree returned, and returned for reasons more surely connected with its merit as poetry. It is this poem which has earned for its author the title of " gentle amorist " ; and I can imagine that the fatuousness of the phrase would have provoked anew in him that arrogance sometimes evident in the pages of the " Life." *The Angel in the House* was popular in the days when verse-stories were popular, and a far worse poem would probably have secured as much attention. Tennyson's *Princess* was published in 1847, Patmore's poem between 1854 and 1856 ; and with all the immense advantage of Tennyson's far more general prestige, it is doubtful whether for those who begin to read poetry now *The Princess* will have as much intrinsic interest as *The Angel*. Passion is within the reach of most poets, its ingenious simulation within the reach of all ; and illicit passion offers, alas ! for the lesser imaginative writer, the line of least resistance. Not in this way could Patmore run. He kept as far from the easy pathos of *La Dame aux Camélias*, as from the difficult ardours of *Modern Love*. Yet with his invincibly sedate theme—the love of a languid Wrangler and a Dean's daughter—he succeeds in attaining a level of high poetry which few love poets have surpassed. He shows that normal love poetry can be as wonderful as abnormal ; the common highway gave him the ecstasy for which other poets have sought in perilous dark byways. It is this ecstasy, this puissant transfiguration of spirit, which gives birth to great poetry, and which poetry so greatly conceived in turn communicates :—ecstasy, that has the same primal miraculous energy whether won in the street or upon a mountain. Ecstasy !—even this rare thing appears in Patmore's sober poem, sweetening it with immortality. He himself saw well enough the sobriety, and also the wider opportunity of his tame subject :

> To me, though born so late,
> There does, beyond desert, befall
> (May my great fortune make me great !)
> The first of themes, sung last of all.

It is a discreet, orderly world that he writes of,

pleasant with the ideal security of a deanery, into which no hint of the buttressing care and labour of the world ever strays. Something, he sees, that abode endued—

> With temple-like repose, an air
> Of life's kind purposes pursued
> With order'd freedom sweet and fair :
> A tent pitch'd in a world not right.

In this second decade of the twentieth century we are all concerned with the world not right, at least as much as with the tent secluded from it. We think but little of ladies who, like the Dean's daughters, keep laws which seem to be merely

> The fair sum of six thousand years'
> Traditions of civility.

. . . But it would be absurd to quarrel with this poem for reflecting the placidity of 1856, instead of the tragic energy of 1916. What exalts it beyond such foolish cavils is, for one thing, its constant tribute to ideal womanhood. There is that famous remonstrance (so admired by Ruskin) which every unreasonable, idol-making lover has felt a desire to repeat :

> Ah, wasteful woman, she who may
> On her sweet self set her own price,
> Knowing man cannot choose but pay,
> How has she cheapen'd paradise ;
> How given for nought her priceless gift,
> How spoil'd the bread and spill'd the wine,
> Which, spent with due respective thrift,
> Had made brutes men and men divine.

When Honoria accepts Felix, and his soul is sick with
bliss, is it indeed with bliss, he asks, or

> ——with remorse and ire
> Of such a sanctity as this
> Subdued by love to my desire ?

Love, for Patmore, does not inherit the vast inane.
He sees it as an earthly-rooted thing and asks :—

> How long shall men deny the flower
> Because its roots are in the earth ?——

finding the food of love in the common delights of
common life, and so tasting " nothing but spiritual
joy." Love is a universal revelation, waking men—

> ——once a lifetime each ;
> They lift their heavy lids and look ;
> And lo, what one sweet page can teach,
> They read with joy, then shut the book.
> And some give thanks, and some blaspheme,
> And most forget ; but, either way,
> That and the child's unheeded dream
> Is all the light of all their day.

Over all the poem there is a " glittering peace,"
heightened with those intimate visions of nature
which are as felicitously recaptured by Patmore as by
Tennyson, and undisturbed even by the changes
of note which at times seem almost too sudden. There
is to me something quite wonderful in the way in which
this poem sweeps in a line or two from the height
of :

> One of those lovely things she was
> In whose least action there can be
> Nothing so transient but it has
> An air of immortality . . .

to such matter-of-factness as :

> Her ball-dress seem'd a breathing mist.

This immense transition is curiously unludicrous. There is, I need not point out, something strikingly matter-of-fact in most fine poets, and though it creep into their poetry there is nothing more odd or intrusive in it than in a child's smile in a church. It is, like good-humoured laughter, the mere effect of simplicity.

But the special value of *The Angel in the House* is that it is prelusive to the vastly greater poetry of the later odes. Between the Angel and the Odes, however there is a significant link—*The Victories of Love*, the first section of which (*Faithful for Ever*) appeared in 1860. This really forms part of *The Angel in the House*, but is separated by time and difference of form. A farther and more notable difference touches both form and matter :—the maturity that comes swiftly with years gives the later poem more suppleness and a range of deeper feeling. Here for the first time appears that deeply human characteristic which is so finely distinctive of Patmore's contribution to English poetry—simple poignance. True there is a passage in *The Angel in the House* where, in a causeless, foreboding grief, Felix lives over an unmet sorrow and repeats, without failure of simplicity or sincerity, the expression of unreasonable, intolerable fear which Wordsworth (in *Strange Fits of Passion Have I Known*, for instance) has intensely realized. Elsewhere in *The Angel in the House* this new note is not sounded ; but it is throbbingly persistent in *The Victories of Love*. In the later poem you have a glimpse of the satisfaction of Felix and Honoria, but its chief concern is the marriage and subsequent happiness, smouldering but not less pervasive, of Frederick Graham, a disappointed suitor of Honoria. It is significant that Patmore himself married thrice and that his first wife died before the publication of the second part of *The Victories of Love*. From his earliest days the married relation possessed for Patmore a pure sacramental character ; and it is this austere view in particular that *The Victories of Love* suggests. Graham, declining from impossible rapture to homeliest content, finds that content has a voice sweet and enthralling as the voice of the beloved evening thrush. His rejection by Honoria he cannot but regret : she had roused and transfigured him until rest was impossible

> For the proud brain and joyful breast
> I have of her. Or else I float,
> The pilot of an empty boat.
> Alone, alone with sky and sea,
> And her, the third simplicity.

But not for him the high prize ; he has to discover that " less than highest is good and may be high."

It is Jane, at whom others ignorantly smile, who satisfies his soul with her unfathomable simplicity, and is the desired completion of his else unfulfilled life. . . . All this and more is developed in this poem, which is as wonderful in its reward of close technical examination, as of a survey of its spiritual idea. But the supreme value of *The Victories of Love* is after all in this : that it leads directly and boldly into that difficult region of " mystic " love in which is rooted Patmore's profoundest spiritual conception. Speaking plainly of " married love " he speaks also of Christ's marriage with the Church which is, he avers, more than a metaphor ; and he touches here, too, casually, and almost fearfully, that " doctrine of virginity " to which in his later work he attaches so grave and secret a meaning.

III

Between the publication of *The Angel in the House* and *The Victories of Love*, and the publication of the first of the odes, much happened to Patmore. His first wife died, and his conversion to the Roman Catholic Church and marriage to his second wife followed two years later. Some of the odes were privately circulated as early as 1868, but not until another nine years had passed was *The Unknown Eros* published. A silence of fourteen years is indeed, in the public memory, a long sleep ; but Patmore knew himself well. How wisely did he write :

> I believe that no amount of idleness is wrong in a poet. Idleness is the growing time of his harvest—and the upcome of a year can be reaped in one fine day.

A just pride speaks in that brief preface to the collected edition :—" I have never spoken when I had nothing to say, nor spared time or labour to make my words true " ; and in a letter quoted by Mr. Champneys :— " I am the only poet of this generation, except Barnes, who has steadily maintained a literary conscience." In these quiet years he prepared himself for the more subtle work which he alone of his generation could give. Had he left only *The Angel in the House* and *The Victories of Love* we should have admired and assumed not unreasonably that the very finish of those brilliantly perfect poems was a sign of the premature exhaustion of the writer's faculty. We should hardly have been able to forecast his possible ultimate greatness. Mr. Champneys has given considerable extracts from Patmore's correspondence, and these form a valuable commentary upon the genesis of the Odes. " I work steadily about eight hours a day in preparation for the still more unknown ' Eros ' . . ."

> " I have been continually engaged in studying and meditating the proposed subject of my next poem. The idea has, from time to time, for years past, fixed my imagination ; but it has always seemed too great, when really approached, for my powers. I have not as yet the least idea whether I shall

ever write a line of it, beyond those two or three ' Odes '
which are really part of it."

" Lights are constantly breaking in upon me and convincing
me more and more that the singular luck has fallen to me of
having to write, for the first time that anyone even attempted
to do so with any fullness, on simply the greatest and most
exquisite subject that ever poet touched since the beginning
of the world."

" I mean to call my collection of ' Odes ' *Religio Poetae*
meaning that region of religion which is inexpressible in human
language to the human heart."

This title was used for the volume of essays dealing
with themes akin to those of the odes.

In its final shape *The Unknown Eros* comprises
forty-three odes, many of them quite unconnected
with any discernible scheme. The proem contains his
excuse for long silence, but now that he sings again
he will be no whit discouraged if none attends :

> Therefore no 'plaint be mine
> Of listeners none,
> No hope of render'd use or proud reward,
> In hasty times and hard ;
> But chants as of a lonely thrush's throat
> At latest eve,
> That doth in each calm note
> Both joy and grieve ;
> Notes few and strong and fine,
> Gilt with sweet day's decline,
> And sad with promise of a different sun.

With Miltonic solemnity he prays for the satisfaction
of the Inspirer and ends his beautiful invocation with
a cry which has even a little human laugh in its echo :

Coventry Patmore

This grant, Clear Spirit; and grant that I remain
Content to ask unlikely gifts in vain.

The whole of the first part of *The Unknown Eros*
consists of odes various in subject but alike inde-
scribable in beauty. It is not till you reach the second
book that you are launched upon the unknown flight.
The last ode of the first book, *Vesica Piscis*, bears
obscurely a hint of the difficulty present to Patmore's
mind :

> In strenuous hope I wrought,
> And hope seem'd still betray'd ;
> Lastly I said,
> " I have labour'd through the Night, nor yet
> Have taken aught ;
> But at Thy word I will again cast forth the net ! "
> And, lo, I caught
> (Oh, quite unlike and quite beyond my thought,)
> Not the quick, shining harvest of the sea,
> For food, my wish,
> But Thee !

and the charge comes :

> . . . Be dumb,
> Or speak but of forgotten things to far-off times to come.

Of these forgotten things he sings with a more urgent
music than he has elsewhere commanded.

His endeavour is to shadow forth, by the perfect
relation between lover and beloved, the soul's occult
relation to God ; and since the mere cold statement
of analogy reveals but little of the warmth of the

277

imaginative apprehension with which this profound idea is to be received, he suggests it by parable. He takes up, for instance, the legend of Cupid and Psyche, and has indeed defended—if defence be needed—the use by his church of similar sources of illustration. Any brief indication of his conception would inevitably conceal as much as reveal it ; and I confess that I hesitate to speak of ideas which may seem in their enunciation arrogant, as well as in their implication esoteric. But in this which is Patmore's chief concern there is so much more than the mere visible words suggest, so quick and intense a vitality quivering just beyond even the utmost intention of words, that to treat the idea as less than esoteric, or as easily apprehensible, would be foolish. And so, I am afraid, any explanation in weak prose of what Patmore has sought to surprise in noblest verse—and verse at its highest is how much clearer and surer than prose !—will be hardly better than none. All that can be done is to show, by the help of a few passages, where Patmore has alighted here and there in his strong-winged pursuit of a plain mystery.

And in noting his brief precarious foothold, there is some help in certain of the prose writings. God is the Divine Lover and the soul the Bride. So purely spousal does he judge this relation to be that (quoting St. Francis of Sales) he writes : " She," the soul, " must serve none, not even her Divine Lover, of whom she is not a servant but a spouse." To a great

man and a God, he goes on, a little love is a great
thing ; and in the spontaneous subdual of the great
to the little love, he notes an analogy with God's
relation to the little ardent soul—"felicity in ex-
tremes." Even in the delicate imperfections of human
love, the wounding inattentions and quick suspicions,
he perceives the hindrances of the Divine relation ;
and, more obviously, in the elaborate symbolism of
earthly love, marks an analogy with the profound
symbolism of heavenly love. Again there appears, in
the sense of self-revelation and completion which the
lover brings to the beloved, a most notable likeness to
the revelation and completion which the soul discovers
in God. More surely than aught else, Patmore finds
the indissolubility of perfect union alike in human
and Divine love. He sees that in the initial state of
illumination, or of constraint, fidelity of correspondence may fail ; but when love " reaches the sensible
affections and has been crowned in mutual and ineffable
complacencies, there is no longer any practical danger
of separation " ; and he proceeds upon the most subtle
suggestions of likeness in this delicate personal relation.
Admitting possible exceptions, he declares that there
is no vital characteristic of natural love which has not
its likeness and development in Divine love ; adding,
even, that the natural perfection of love demands
habitual reference to the spiritual.

" All properly human instincts," Patmore writes in
the essay, *Dieu et Ma Dame*, from which I have been

quoting, " are no other than the lineaments of God."
Look now at the odes, and see there some clearer hints
of the true lineaments which he discerns in these
analogies. In *Sponsa Dei* he writes :

> What is this Maiden fair,
> The laughing of whose eye
> Is in man's heart renewed virginity ;
> Who yet sick longing breeds
> For marriage which exceeds
> · The inventive guess of Love to satisfy
> With hope of utter binding, and of loosing
> endless dear despair ?
> . . . Who is this only happy She
> Whom, by a frantic flight of courtesy,
> Born of despair
> Of better lodging for his Spirit fair,
> He adores as Margaret, Maude, or Cecily ?

Answering this, he writes indeed not of analogy but
frankly of identity, and, in fact, in the essay just
mentioned, prefers to speak of identities rather than
of analogies :—

> What if this Lady be thy Soul, and He
> Who claims to enjoy her sacred beauty be,
> Not thou, but God ; and thy sick fire
> A female vanity,
> Such as a Bride, viewing her mirror'd charms,
> Feels when she sighs, " All these are for his arms ! "

Is this overbold ? Not so : in the next ode he writes :

> For, ah, who can express
> How full of bonds and simpleness
> Is God,

How narrow is He,
And how the wide, waste field of possibility
Is only trod
Straight to His homestead in the human heart.

The body itself is " Creation's and Creator's crowning
good " :

Little sequester'd pleasure-house
For God and for His Spouse.

He rises into less lightly-breathed air in *Deliciae
Sapientiae de Amore,* singing of love's festival " in the
glad Palace of Virginity." Here occurs the extension
of his doctrine, upon which his thoughts so often
dwell. His ode echoes :

The nuptial song,
Song ever new to us and them, that saith,
" Hail Virgin in Virginity a Spouse ! "
Heard first below
Within the little house
At Nazareth ;
Heard yet in many a cell where brides of Christ
Lie hid, emparadised.——

And ends :

Love makes the life to be
A fount perpetual of virginity ;
For lo, the Elect
Of generous Love, how named soe'er, affect
Nothing but God,
Or mediate or direct,
Nothing but God,
The Husband of the Heavens :

And who Him love, in potence great or small,
Are, one and all,
Heirs of the Palace glad,
And inly clad
With the bridal robes of ardour virginal.

Let it be noted, in passing, that there are called to the festival even those " in whom living love yet blushes for dead shame " ; which may be paralleled with this from the essay : " Past corruptions that are really past and no longer active are so far from hindering love that they act as manure in which the seed of Divine Love and the seed almost divine of a pure and fervid mortal affection flourish wonderfully." Far from Patmore's spirit is any narrow, ungenerous Calvinism.

Then, as I have said, he takes up the subject by parable, three long odes being devoted to Psyche. " O Mortal," cries Eros, " I craved but to be caught " :

Wanton, it was not you
But I that did so passionately sue . . .
'Tis but in such captivity
The unbounded Heav'ns know what they be !

God, writes Patmore in *Religio Poetae*, is the synthesis of " Infinite " and " Boundary " . . . To her immortal lover Psyche sings, " The whole of life is womanhood to thee," and, humble with extreme bliss, avows herself " nothing . . . but now a no more void capacity for thee." The spiritual parallel need not be pointed out.

I must admit, nevertheless, that despite lines of

dazzling brightness, these three odes are not clear
to me in more than a general sense ; indeed, it seems
that the symbol becomes now too particular, and
now too dark, for the concealed doctrine. The
" mystery," however, is one of those of which Patmore
himself was probably thinking when he asked that he
might so possess it that he would not desire to understand it.

There remains one of the mystical odes, *The Child's
Purchase*, which calls for separate notice. This is his
long-meditated tribute, " the ode on the great subject " as he termed it, quick with the urgently invoked—

> . . . steady heat
> Of thought wise, splendid, sweet,
> Urged by the great, rejoicing wind that rings
> With draught of unseen wings,
> Making each phrase, for love and for delight,
> Twinkle like Sirius on a frosty night !

The whole is instinct with love and reverence, chiefly
expressed in the universal sex-metaphor. He appeals
to the Virgin as the " Desire of Him whom all things
else desire,"proffering the splendours of his song to her
as a young child returns to his mother the coin she has
given him. *Ora pro me* he murmurs, breaking the
impetuous flood of grave song again and again with
an intimate filial cry. It is the superbest of his odes
of this kind, summing up his loyalty in a sustained
outpouring of the devoutest adoration of subtle mind
and full heart.

The Moderns

To speak more of the doctrine of *The Unknown Eros* is unnecessary, and indeed I doubt if it be wise to attempt to say so much, since there will be many to whom that doctrine will seem too fantastic, and some to whom it will seem too profane, and a few to whom it will seem too secret, to be uttered aloud. Patmore himself has occupied an essay with reasons for silence upon the profounder things of the spirit ; and some of his poems seem not so much direct statements of his meaning, as mere hints of an attitude before that profound darkness in which these spiritual things live and move and have their being.

IV

Even if we pass hastily by these severe utterances upon dark and serious themes, there is yet a body of Patmore's later poetry claiming equal attention for more purely human reasons. That sharp note which was remarkable in *The Victories of Love* is heard more troublingly in the odes—more acutely, more troublingly than elsewhere in the whole of our wonderful English poetry. Profound humanity beats in the most instinctive work of this poet, who sought to fuse human with divine affections. Odes such as that famous confession *The Toys*, *Departure*, *The Azalea*, and a dozen others, are of an intensity unique in the whole range of our literature. The sadness of parted love, the agony of loss, the bitterness of severing death

284

Coventry Patmore

—with these familiar infinite sorrows is his song occupied. For my own part, this is the only modern verse, other than some lines of Shakespeare, Burns and Keats, which I find it hard to read without tears; and though I have read these odes a hundred times I know not where, precisely, the secret of their unfailing poignancy is lodged, or how it is to be described :—just as, though I have watched them a thousand times, I know not how to explain the acute poignancy of a sea-bird's flight or the scream of a swallow. Many of these singular utterances are the expression of personal experience; but even where this is not óbviously the case, Patmore's psychology of love and grief, of the ingenious cunning of sorrow, is as true as it is subtle. In *The Azalea* he dreams that she he loves is dead; he wakes, and for a delicious moment is thankful it was only a dream—until he is reminded, by the breath of the azalea, that indeed, indeed, she *is* dead. In *Departure* he reproaches her for going the "journey of all days with not one kiss or a good-bye," seizing upon the lesser grief as a shield against the greater. With *The Toys* every one is acquainted, and also, perhaps, with the following little piece which is only printed here in order that Patmore may speak fitly for himself :

IF I WERE DEAD

If I were dead, you'd sometimes say, " Poor Child ! "
The dear lips quivered as they spake,

285

And the tears brake
From eyes which, not to grieve me, brightly smiled.
Poor Child! Poor Child!
I seem to hear your laugh, your talk, your song.
It is not true that Love will do no wrong.
Poor Child!
And did you think, when you so cried and smiled,
How I, in lonely nights, should lie awake,
And of those words your full avengers make?
Poor Child! Poor Child!
And now, unless it be
That sweet amends thrice told are come to thee,
O God, have Thou *no* mercy upon me!
Poor Child!

If any criticism might be ventured upon, in considering such an acutely painful poem, it would be that this stark rehearsal of intimate grief is intolerable. Just the same absolute note is heard in *A Farewell*, mitigated by those casual touches of pure beauty which make even such grief endurable, and by the remote hope of rencounter (to quote one of the most magical of single lines):

> Seasoning the termless feast of our content
> *With tears of recognition never dry.*

Distinct from *The Unknown Eros* yet naturally ranging itself with the other odes, there is one for which Patmore himself had an especial regard—*Amelia*. This holds the same position in relation to his other poems as the *Epithalamion* holds to the other work of Spenser—Spenser who is a precursor of Pat-

more in passionate devotion to ideal womanhood. . . .
No poet but Patmore would have opened an ode with
such a line as

> Whene'er mine eyes do my Amelia greet ;—

but from this tame start proceeds one of his loftiest
tributes, in which is embalmed not a little personal
history.   Here gleam those starry lights of imagination
upon which in his later years Patmore seemed able—
sign of matured power !—to focus surely and at will.
The beauty ranges from such a Corot-like picture as
this of Amelia :

> ——for fairness shown
> Like a young apple-tree in flush'd array
> Of white and ruddy flow'r, auroral, gay,
> With chilly blue the maiden branch between ;—

to the more sombre colour of :

> ——her pensive footstep stirr'd
> The darnell'd garden of unheedful death.

Amelia, in short, shows Patmore's genius in its purely
lyrical exercise, disengaged from the rather solemn
contemplation in which he became more and more
completely engrossed.

*   *   *   *   *

Henley somewhere remarks that all fine poets, as
their genius grows more confident, become impatient
of the formal restraints of their medium ; and he
instances, I think, the change in Milton from the form

of *Paradise Lost* to the form of *Samson Agonistes*, and the change in Tennyson from the form of *The Idylls* to the form of *Rizpah*. It is an acute observation, and is illustrated most sharply by Shakespeare, whose whole work is a lesson in the free development of poetic expression under laws of its own imposition. The study of Patmore's technique further supports Henley's idea. If a fault is to be urged against the verse of the earlier poems it is that it is too flawless, too neatly perfect. Yet one may well be tempted to pause upon that verse, and note how exactly correspondent the form is to the emotion, and how, if need be, the scrupulous monotony of its movement is quickened :

> Then is my sadness banished far,
>   And I am like that ship no more ;
> Or like that ship if the ice-field splits,
>   Burst by the sudden polar Spring,
> And all thank God with their warming wits,
>   And kiss each other and dance and sing.

Just so are the prim couplets of *The Victories of Love* burst with the storm that

> . . . the blood prick'd and a blinding flash
> And close coinstantaneous crash
> Humbled the soul, and the rain all round
> Resilient dimm'd the whistling ground.

Even within normal iambic limits it has an extreme and sensitive beauty ; but it is in the later work, and there alone, that you find the firmer, more impulsive, incontinent beauty which is inalienable from the due utterance of Patmore's spiritual apprehensions.

These " irregular " odes are not without precedent, but Patmore himself speaks of them as of his own discovery. Crashaw, indeed, has the very Patmorean note sounding in the very form of the later poet's odes. There are passages from the *Hymn to St. Teresa*, etc., which might well be ascribed to Patmore, who yet knew little or nothing of Crashaw's work until long after his own was complete. But Patmore's verse is instinct with a more delicate life, controlled by a more accomplished art ; it has a certain likeness—in rhythm, sweetness and grave strength—to those most magnificent poems of the unpraisable Spenser, the *Prothalamion* and *Epithalamion*. His own phrase describes it—" wedded light and heat," or the metaphor so constantly present to his mind, of the song and flight of a bird at evening, He forsakes the precise simplicity of the octosyllabic line of *The Angel*, for a rhythm released from apparent bond and restraint, but demanding a secret firm integrity in the writer for its salvation from over-sweetness on the one hand, and the trailing shapelessness of much " irregular " verse on the other. You find a line of such unfaltering fine music as :

Through delicatest ether feathering soft their solitary beat—

and anon such a consummate sense-echoing passage as :

She, as a little breeze
Following still Night,
Ripples the spirit's cold, deep seas
Into delight ;
But, in a while,
The immeasurable smile
Is broke by fresher airs to flashes blent
With darkling discontent ;
And all the subtle zephyr hurries gay,
And all the heaving ocean heaves one way,
T'ward the void sky-line and an unguess'd weal :
Until the vanward billows feel
The agitating shallows, and divine the goal,
And to foam roll,
And spread and stray
And traverse wildly, like delighted hands,
The fair and fleckless sands ;
And so the whole
Unfathomable and immense
Triumphing tide comes at the last to reach
And burst in wind-kiss'd splendours on the deaf'ning beach,
Where forms of children in first innocence
Laugh and fling pebbles on the rainbow'd crest
Of its untired unrest.

No one who has essayed the subtle and difficult art
of verse, will fail to recognize with sudden delight the
subtle and difficult art concealed here.   Once and but
once, in the third ode (*Winter*) he resorts to the device
of a rhymeless ending, where the escape from form
is more exquisite than any observance of it might be.
" I have hit," he writes, in a moment of enthusiasm,
" upon the finest metre that was ever invented."
Here is no space for the close analysis of the metrical
form of these odes, but few studies in the art of verse

could be more fruitful than an examination of Patmore's later style ; nor could a finer instance be found of the inseparableness of form from substance, which is the insistent assertion of every poet.

V

" That's telling secrets," said Father Gerard Hopkins to Patmore, after reading the manuscript of a little treatise called *Sponsa Dei*, which Patmore promptly burned, though saying that it was " the work of ten years' continual meditation " upon the main idea of his writings. But throughout them all he was telling secrets. That the secrets are not clearly told, or not clearly heard, is because they are in their nature remote, profound, all-but inaccessible. Or more exactly I might say, in the words of Emily Patmore to her father, " I think the Odes are very like Holy Scripture in being so simple that anyone might imagine they understood all there is, and so profound that few will really do so. They are also like Scripture in the way Shakespeare is, viz., in being intensely human, and in not saying the words allowed to express the thing, but the *thing* itself." First and last Patmore was a mystic, in the strict sense in which St. Augustine and St. Francis of Sales and St. John of the Cross were mystics. The word is not one which he was fond of using, for his care—as is inevitable with men whose thought is unusually profound—was ever for the definite and the precise. He has that intimate, searching and confident view of the soul which Meredith has of nature and her proper kingdom. Meredith discovers relations and dependencies between the soul of man and nature, which it is a spiritual education to perceive ; and of all his legacies to us, this is perhaps the most personal and enduring. And Patmore discovers relations and dependencies between the soul of man and God, and unfolds these in an analogy so close and sharp as to be almost inadmissible by those who do not perceive it for themselves. " None will learn from my book," he says, quoting Aristotle, " anything but that which is already known." But there is so much knowledge lodged unrecognized in our hearts, that until we hear we do not know that we know. This is the secret of the appeal which so much modern poetry makes to us : it reveals our knowledge to us. Shakespeare makes us feel that ours has been the experience of Lear and Goneril both, of Hamlet and Iago, of Desdemona and Ophelia ; and so enlarges infinitely our narrow personal understanding of humanity. Meredith helps us to perceive in ourselves the invisible threads of communion with nature, quickening them into electric sensitiveness, until we feel our identity with nature more or less complete as our responsiveness to his touch is more or less delicate. And so Patmore, to a soul thus steeped in the Shakespearian humanity and the Meredithean nature-communion, brings this final illumination of the

Coventry Patmore

spiritual world. As faith in humanity distinguishes Shakespeare's plays, and faith in nature distinguishes Meredith's novels and verse, so faith in God is the high distinction of Patmore's work :—the faith of each being (need I say !) no mere effort of belief, but a steady constant illumination. No man can study Shakespeare attentively without coming to a warmer and wiser understanding of human glory and grief, passionate love and infidelities. No man can study Meredith attentively without coming to a closer knowledge of the enfolding intimacies of what he knows to be " the spirit of the earth." Nor can any man study Patmore attentively without coming to an apprehension of the existence of spiritual mysteries, and thence to an apprehension of their nature, truth and urgency. The result of study in each case is not the acceptance of any particular doctrine or theory, but the approximation to an angle of perception. He is not a profound influence who merely suggests specific remedies for specific ills, or a speedy panacea for all ; but rather he who assists us to an attitude, a position " where we shall need no glass," but be able to see for ourselves and in true perspective our relation to man, to nature, and to God.

It is in this finer and positive sense that Patmore is an influence upon the thought of our day. He stands for the unknown, and confronts the affirmations of the material with the affirmations of the spiritual. Few turn to him, but fewer still leave him. His words

293

are persuasive only to those who will receive them.
He is an excellent instance of the wisdom of Wordsworth's admonition :

> You must love him ere to you
> He will seem worthy of your love.

This is a fact which neither poet nor reader can alter,
a fact inherent in the very rarity and fineness of the
attitude towards which Patmore and his confederates
move. In his remote yet imperative meditation he
has avoided that worst of faults, vagueness. He
knows how very easy it is to " speak splendidly and
profusely about things which transcend speech " ;
and the very precision and brevity of what he says
upon some of the high themes of his odes seem at times
startling. He disdains to speak loudly, or loosely
upon matters that can only be thought of in intense
quietness, with intense concentration. Just because
things are obscure will he be sparing of his words upon
them, and he regards it as a private obligation not to
confuse by many words the vision he may perhaps be
able to hint at in few. So he becomes more and more
epigrammatic, starlike, till the silences grow and he is
dumb not because he has said all, but because there is
so much to say :—as lovers speak more and more
quietly until they are hushed, and as purest love-
poetry, aspiring to yet more insustainable heights,
passes into silence. After such speech, silence is
eloquent and wise ; and as St. Augustine knew (in that

marvellous passage of meditation with his mother in the *Confessions*), is how much more intimate than words ! In some of the odes, Patmore seems to be trembling before the invasion of silence ; the rhythm of his lines, even, that else are so swift and bold, quivers with its imminence. . . . It is strange, yet not very strange, that a poet of affirmations, of positive meanings, should be a poet whose song falters upwards out of hearing, as a bird soars out of sight :—not very strange, I think, when you consider, even detachedly, the nature of this that he seeks to convey. It is the final witness to the integrity of his sight and the fidelity of his report.

FRANCIS THOMPSON

Patmore and Thompson are like two noble headlands overlooking a wide bay. You may look at each headland narrowly, studying them as it were foot by foot ; but to see them properly and in proportion you must look across the bay from the one to the other and so complete your understanding of each from the eminence of the other. Thompson will not be fully apprehended unless you see him from the point of view which Patmore's work affords ; and in turn, to look back at Patmore from the height of Thompson's achievement, is to observe more surely the singularly lofty and pure attitude with which he confronts the mortal sea and immortal sky.

I

Let us look first at Thompson closely, before looking from any distance. He speaks of himself more frankly and often than does Patmore, and this gives a sharp autobiographical interest to much of his work. And, too, the personality expressed is one of such interest and large power, that the faintest autobiographical hints are valuable. Full intimacy with any man, however, is only to be shared by the very few whose spirits are exactly attuned to his. Imperfect sympathies exist everywhere, and it would be stupid to pretend that Thompson's personality or work could mean as much for the many as it does for that small circle of people who knew him well and loved him faithfully.

But they are few to whom this poet will not make a more or less powerful appeal. Do not believe that " men of the world " always sneer at what they do not understand, or cannot attain. The sneer of artists at men of the world is every whit as unintelligent and as inexcusable as the sneer of men of the world at art. There is no attitude so incapable of illumination as the attitude of contempt, but I fear it is the choice and careful study of the artist far more often than of the Philistine. Men respect that which they cannot understand, when they think their not understanding is due to some shadowy deficiency of their own. They have no hostility to genius, and are only too ready to believe its report. When, then, they see a character in which pride and humility exist together ; where faith in spiritual things is matched by quiet indifference to temporal things, and where a high active genius is content with a very little space for its eternal manifestation ; how can they but wonder and hold that character and genius in a respect that lacks little in sincerity, however much it may be wanting in understanding ? Thompson's strangeness, his simple removal from common aims, his unconquerable vagrancy, the purity of his energy, the conspicuous splendour of his genius—all these are elements in the attraction which he is casting upon men now that he has left them. Just in proportion to the delicacy and rarity of an idea, must be the delicacy and rarity of its expression :—and is there a more constraining utterance, a more persuasive embodiment, of delicate and powerful ideas, than the simple one of personality ? A poet may utter his conceptions in verse, and his life may be a farther symbol of their truth and beauty. How often, indeed, has it happened that the life is an essential complement of the work, or even a key to it ? Questions of personality inevitably interest us all intensely, for this plain reason. Hence the fascination of the continual attempt to discover the personality of Shakespeare, and the many discrepant endeavours to build his image anew. With Shelley, again, one feels that half only is told in his poems ; the other half is to be disengaged from the fiery tumult of his visible path on earth. . . . If this is true of any artist, I think it especially true of Thompson. He tells many things more or less plainly, more or less urgently, in his writings ; he conveys them again, silently, implicitly, in his life, in his attitude towards the world, in his clear adorations, in his quick personal faith.

But I do not propose reducing to a few pages what Thompson's biographer has presented in a volume. I would rather look at this poet's work with the purpose of observing there the ideas and the attitude which his personal life rendered over again for those privileged so to receive them. And let me say clearly here, that it would be foolish to regard any study of Thompson as a light study of a minor poet :—in him we have a poet of superb and as yet half uncomprehended genius. This, indeed, is the justification of the present essay.

If his first book (1893) remains his finest, it is because it includes *The Hound of Heaven* ; and if that be held to be one of the most wonderful lyrical poems in our language, it is because it expresses an intense personality and a unique spiritual ardency. Never has a poet broken more suddenly and magnificently upon our silence ; never was a dead year more deliciously startled with spring. Did Thompson ever write an immature, an incomplete, an unrealized poem ? I do not know which it is among those of his first volume. Of all his writings he has left nothing of a finer pitch than *The Hound of Heaven* ; and it is good to note, in passing, that this is the most popular of them all. Popularity is so often contemned by those who seek a private and narrow success, that it is well to remember that what is popular is not therefore inherently bad. When the judgment of the many is in concurrence with the critical judgment of the few—so much the better for the many, but, equally, so much the better for the few. Let it be admitted that he who runs may no more read the finer works of Wordsworth and Thompson than a dialogue of Plato or a discourse of Coleridge. Yet there is a music, clear, plenteous, plangent, which falls arrestingly upon the ears even of those who run ; and if *The Hound of Heaven* rings with this music, then so much the greater honour to Thompson, who achieves with noble superfluousness what (probably) he did not consciously attempt. The poem is a striking instance of the co-existence of the two sincerities—the personal and the artistic ; the joint activity of two motives—one spiritual and one poetic. Forget, if you can, that it is verse, and you will yet note the extraordinary spiritual earnestness of the whole cry. It is a Confession of St. Augustine done into English verse ; and if you read it so you will feel humbled at the sight of this unshrinking, self-accusing spirit, acknowledging those infidelities, confessing those denials and mortal errancies, which, in memory, are like knives thrust

under the ribs of sensitive life.   The burning sincerity
of the sudden onset of the poem :

> I fled Him, down the nights and down the days ;
> I fled Him, down the arches of the years ;
> I fled Him, down the labyrinthine ways
> Of my own mind ; and in the mist of tears
> I hid from Him, and under running laughter.
> Up vistaed hopes I sped ;
> And shot, precipitated
> Adown Titanic glooms of chasmed fears,
> From those strong Feet that followed, followed after.
> But with unhurrying chase,
> And unperturbèd pace,
> Deliberate speed, majestic instancy,
> They beat—and a Voice beat
> More instant than the Feet—
> " All things betray thee, who betrayest Me "——

—this is maintained right onward through stanza after
stanza to the grave quietness of the close.   I am loth to
emphasize unnecessarily the perfectly evident veracity
of Thompson's rendering of the Divine pursuit.   No
one who has felt those spiritual misgivings which we
seldom speak of directly will fail to remark the rightness
of this :

> . . . Yet was I sore adread
> Lest, having Him, I must have naught beside——

or of this plea :

Ah ! must Thou char the wood ere Thou canst limn with it ?

or the truth of :

> Lo ! naught contents thee, who content'st not Me.

Francis Thompson

The pursuit of the soul by its " tremendous Lover " has never been more purely or more powerfully suggested, even by the seventeenth-century poets with whom Thompson has so often been compared. Not Crashaw's self, vehement and storm-like as was his worship, has reached the sublimity of this tribute.

And then, forgetting this, read the poem if you can simply as verse and note the height to which Thompson's muse so easily rises. He suggests, as few English poets do, speed, energy of flight, rapture. He uses repetition to sharpen the sense of pursuit ; you hear the very wind of speed, feel the beating of swift wings, are conscious of disturbed heights of air. Who since Shelley has moved more securely than Thompson among the large metaphors and images into which earthly and spiritual phenomena are resolvable and through which alone they are intelligible ? Thompson rejoices in the spaciousness of imagery almost too great for comprehension. He is perhaps unique among poets of our generation who are masters of the sublime. Sublimity has, I know, fallen a little into discredit of late years. It is, indeed, exposed to grave perils : the higher the ascent, the greater the fall. Only a poet of terrible earnestness and unchallengeable power dare attempt those fine-breathed flights in which anything short of perfect success is presumptuous failure. Thompson moves in the loftier altitudes with an ease which is in itself really impressive and absolute, the mark of royal inheritance. It is his native region as certainly as it was Shelley's ; he scarcely breathes in the valley where others work at their neater and smaller but still sincere imagery. And as the false-sublime or the faulty-sublime is proof of insincerity or want of firm intelligence, so the true, the unrelapsing sublime is proof of a spiritual integrity that may seem incomprehensible, but only because it is lofty ; remote, but only because it is undefiled. . . . I insist on the exalted sincerity of *The Hound of Heaven* because this must be remembered equally in considering the substance and the movement of the ode. Without it, the idea would be incapable of its due embodiment, and the form incapable of its due elevation. Another sign of its impassioned integrity is the fact that the poem remains unimitated and inimitable. The more profoundly personal things cannot be imitated. Thompson has put his soul so simply and urgently into his poem that the very simplicity and urgency make imitation, how adroit or devout soever, quite impossible. It is the large, the overwhelming, that alone is secure from any praise but that of wonder.

Let us look a little more closely at *The Hound of Heaven*. The first stanza has already been cited, and it would be superfluous to point out how the flight therein described is at first in time, and then followed in the mind, through laughter, hopes and fears. In the second there is the recital, simple and passionate, of the evasion of desired felicity ; in the third, the recital of the vanity of refuge or satisfaction sought in nature ; in the fourth, the recital of the failure of life, of the bitterness of disillusion, of the half-glimpsed, eternal signs ; and at its close, the pursuing cry :

> Lo, all things fly thee, for thou fliest Me !

And upon this there ensues the remonstrance of infinite pity strengthened with infinite love. The flight ends :

> Halts by me that footfall :
> Is my gloom, after all,
> Shade of His hand, outstretched caressingly ?
> " Ah fondest, blindest, weakest,
> I am He Whom thou seekest !
> Thou dravest love from thee, who dravest Me."

Thompson has not simply given here (to return to an earlier point) an intense, individual utterance of surpassing value ; he has rehearsed the flight which every human, free soul attempts. Some men never escape from the labyrinthine ways of their own minds ; some avoid only too successfully their pure felicity and live melancholy, arctic lives ; or yield themselves delightedly to visible nature, and there for them all flight and pursuit end.[1] But some pass on to the acceptance, the abnegation, the fulfilment, which Thompson has faintly suggested towards the close of his ode. To put it briefly this poem, for all the apparent

---

[1] Conspicuous witness of this is Richard Jefferies, whose nature-love, for all its acute fervour, seems ever to be a defeated substitute for some other love.

exclusiveness of its subject, has really the universality of a great human conception, in which all men may see something, and many see more than the whole, of their private experience.

Even this narrower analysis leaves, I fear, something untouched. Every true poem has in it that which defies searching, that which will speak for itself and of itself, or not at all. What is it that is thus disengaged from the wonderful web of this verse ? To me it is an impression of the loneliness of Thompson's spirit. Through all the haste of flight and pursuit, the perplexed soul runs solitarily intent. Others' faces, children's faces, appear, but leave unmitigated the solitude of flight. This, maybe, is an impression which was unsought by the poet, though it speaks so plainly in his poem. It forms, I think, the *invisible* burden which is the last token of every poem's veracity. Reading the lines attentively, you find that in the unconscious suggestion of loneliness it is instantly true ; for however appealingly we may look to others, however we may comfort ourselves by their words, only in the loneliness of our own spirit is the eternal flight and pursuit experienced, and the eternal goal found.

II

From *The Hound of Heaven*, then, we may gather some hint of the experience of mankind, and, almost as clearly, some hint of the private experience of

Francis Thompson

Thompson himself. Other poems there are, which
extend or repeat the burden of this one, but it would
be merely tiresome and provoking to treat them all in
detail. Few poets have spoken so frankly of themselves. It is not so difficult to speak of one's love,
desire, regret ; of common tangible things. Cowper
and Byron, for example, had no difficulty in revealing
what it would have been perhaps harder to conceal.
They, and many other writers of lesser or larger charm,
are eager to tell us that which we do not greatly fret to
know. But when the question is of spiritual things, of
the soul's life and love, silence falls. Of the few who
have much to tell, few have told us much. Leave
aside those, saints and preachers, whose peculiar office
it is to utter their persuasions of these things, and they
are but few, writing in English, who are one with them
in this lofty concern. Browne, Donne (in his verse),
Crashaw, Vaughan—they form a sudden unmatched
starry cluster ; after them there is but a name here
and there, and a silence almost unbroken from Bunyan
to Newman.

> " I have not spoken of these things
> But to one man, and unto God,"

says Loniel Johnson. It is Thompson's simply
inappraisable gift that he tells to all the things which
most others, if indeed they know and speak, tell only
to God. As in *The Hound of Heaven*, when he speaks of
himself he speaks for others also. Few pleadings are

more nobly pathetic than *To the Dead Cardinal of Westminster*—pathetic with profound sorrow that is only not quite despairing.

> But I ex-Paradised,
> The shoulder of your Christ
>   Find high
>   To lean thereby. . . .
>
> I have no thought that I,
> When at the last I die,
>   Shall reach
>   To gain your speech.
>
> But you, should that be so,
> May very well, I know,
>   May well
>   To me in hell
>
> With recognizing eyes
> Look from your Paradise—
>   " God bless
>   Thy hopelessness ! "

" Call, holy soul," he cries, and tell the angelical hosts of one :

> Who measureth world's pleasure,
> World's ease as Saints might measure ;
>   For hire
>   Just love entire
>
> He asks, not grudging pain ;
> And knows his asking vain,
>   And cries
>   " Love ! Love ! " and dies ;
>
> In guerdon of long duty,
> Unowned by Love or Beauty ;
>   And goes—
>   Tell, tell, who knows !

Aliens from Heaven's worth,
Fine beasts who nose i' the earth,
 Do there
 Reward prepare.

But are *his* great desires
Food but for nether fires?
 Ah me,
 A mystery!

And if they tell, send some high gold embassage, he pleads, to teach my unripe age. The experience here is not wholly a strange or remote one ; but its expression is rare and searching. Thompson is in fact telling open secrets about the profoundest motions of the soul, of which the experience is far more common than the utterance. In a later poem, *Any Saint*, he returns to this " high speech," with a yet more piercing intimacy ; soon losing, however, the simple personal note in the general assertion of the wedding of human and divine in man.

 Not to me, not to me
 Builded so flawfully,
  O God
  Thy humbling laud !

Not to this man, but Man—
 Swinging-wicket set
  Between
  The Unseen and Seen.

 Lo, God's two worlds immense,
 Of spirit and of sense,
  Wed
  In this narrow bed. . . .

Stoop, Stoop ; for thou dost fear
The nettle's wrathful spear,
  So slight
  Art thou of might !

Rise ; for Heaven hath no frown
When thou to thee pluck'st down,
  Strong clod !
  The neck of God.

" Mine eyes saw not, and I saw," he writes, in *The
Mistress of Vision*, and that somewhat constrained,
somewhat too curious poem renders the vision of which
" mine ears heard not, and I heard."

When to the new eyes of thee
All things by immortal power,
Near or far,
Hiddenly
To each other linkèd are,
That thou canst not stir a flower
Without troubling of a star ;——

then there is no more to seek. It is the same vision
as Blake desired :

To see a world in a grain of sand
And heaven in a wild flower ;
Hold infinity in the palm of your hand
And eternity in an hour.

But Thompson knows that for this vision strict and
grave preparation is necessary :

Learn to dream when thou dost wake . . .
Lose, that the lost thou may'st receive;
Die, for none other way canst live [1]——

[1] Thompson's development was of an extraordinary kind.
His attitude becomes one of complete abnegation, at the same

308

that ancient, familiar lesson which is never learned, but only discovered in the journey of the soul. Far from being an easy, casual gift, he sees that it needs the severest discipline before it can be received. Nothing in life can be received freely, however freely it be given. To admit the greater you must discard the lesser. It is a thing one learns but slowly, that to receive is of all acts the most difficult. To receive effectually a new idea, an unfamiliar fact, a strange interpretation—this does not always become more difficult with years, but with years we recognize the difficulty and so learn patience. Life, we discover, is at once infinite and circumscribed.

" Ultima," he calls the last poem in his last book, and the word indeed suggests the whole of his work. He passes by the obvious, the merely immediate, and casts himself into that dark night where eyes see not. He will speak of the secondary wisdom, the wisdom of personal conduct :

> On him the unpetitioned heavens descend,
> Who heaven on earth proposes not for end ;
> The perilous and celestial excess
> Taking with peace, lacking with thankfulness.
> Bliss in extreme befits thee not, until
> Thou'rt not extreme in bliss ; be equal still :
> Sweets to be granted think thyself unmeet
> Till thou have learned to hold sweet not too sweet. . . .

time that his expression of it becomes more and more personal and wilful. Hence the later poems have a less ready and in-stinctive attractiveness than the earlier.

but more absorbedly of the primary wisdom that
concerns man's attitude to God and eternity. This is
the really unique wisdom which we cannot all attain
for ourselves, but which we must even take thankfully
from the securely-adventurous souls of a Dante, a
Pascal or a Newman. This it is that we have seen
equally in Patmore and Thompson. Elder and
younger poet are alike in their secret attitude. That
attitude has a boldness even in its humility, a confidence even in its fear, a joyfulness even in its sorrow ;
and gains utterance as bold, as confident, as joyful.
Both poets are full of intimacies which offend those
incapable of sharing them. Love is not perfect till
it has cast out fear ; and if fear is gone, then, for
many, the plainest sign of love is gone. Patmore's
constant use of the sex-metaphor in his rehearsal of
Divine relations ; Thompson's apprehension of God
as the secret lover—these may seem over-bold, unre-
ticent, impermissible. But true speech of true things
is always bold (even when it is most subtle), delights
in directness, in pure nakedness, knows no shame,
fears nothing but dumbness. . . . Is there not,
indeed, a strange compulsion upon such writers, so
that the things said to God must needs be said to man
also ? It is the men who have nothing which they
cannot suppress, who demur when others whisper the
insuppressible things.

III

But I despair of conveying anything of Thompson's
attitude of which I have failed to give a suggestion
hitherto. Let me rather turn to those of his poems
which are perhaps more accessible in their delight-
someness, the personal tributes. The poems with
which the first volume opens, *Love in Dian's Lap*, form
a most lovely honour of a living ideal. One cannot
but hesitate to speak impersonally of poems so delicately personal ; poems, too, proffered to one who is
herself in the happiest sense a living poet. Thompson
could yield tribute to the poet :

> Whatever singing-robe thou wear
> Has the Paradisal air ;
> And some gold feather it has kept
> Shows what Floor it lately swept ;——

yet not for an instant forget the woman. He pays her
the superb honour of charging her spiritual integrity
with the responsibility of his own soul, declaring
how—

> Like to a wind-sown sapling grow I from
> The clift, Sweet, of your skyward-jetting soul,——

He has the true poet's cunning of compliments :

> Thou dost to rich attire a grace
> To let it deck itself with thee.

Or yet more high and subtle :

> Where a sweetness is complete
> Add not sweets unto the sweet!
> Or, as thou wilt, for others so
> In unfamiliar richness go ;
> But keep for mine acquainted eyes
> The fashions of thy Paradise.

But all his fine things of this sort look pallid before the splendour of *Her Portrait*. One is reminded at once, of course, of the magnificent Donne's [1] *Anniversaries* ; but Thompson's celebration is equal to them in ardour, delicacy and loftiness. This is Donne at his highest :

> . . . Her pure and eloquent blood
> Spoke in her cheeks, and so distinctly wrought
> That one might almost say her body thought.

But Thompson cries :

> Oh, but the heavenly grammar did I hold
> Of that high speech which angel's tongues turn gold!
> So should her deathless beauty take no wrong,
> Praised in her own great kindred's fit and cognate tongue.

Yet how, he asks,

> How praise the woman, who but know the spirit ?

Of her beauty :

---

[1] To Shelley, of modern poets, was Thompson's love chiefly given ; but he discovered in him the inheritor of an earlier school of poetry, the " metaphysical " school, affirming indeed that Shelley is simply Crashaw born greater, the objective of the metaphysical poets' aim. It is of *their* spirit that the most abundant impulses will be found in Thompson.

The immortal could we cease to contemplate,
The mortal part suggests its every trait.
God laid His fingers on the ivories
Of her pure members as on smoothèd keys,
And there out-breathed her spirit's harmonies.

But to speak further of this offering would be quite
impertinent. Let me but say that, never declining
as the glorious *Anniversaries* at times decline, it does
not on the other hand wander into the intense inane
with Shelley's *Epipsychidion*; and but with these
noble poems Thompson's is incomparable.

Of the poems to children I can write but briefly.
Sister Songs, the longest, contain some intensely
valuable reminiscences of his forlorn days ; but their
chief value is in the exhibition of genius pouring out
treasures of love and adoration at the feet of childhood.
And great as is the prize thus poured out, it is enhanced
by the fact that it flows from the lips of the author of
The Hound of Heaven, Her Portrait, and other well-
remembered poems of his three volumes. Nowhere
else are the splendours so profuse, and as you read
through, each time with fresh delight, you recognize
it as proof of Thompson's fine generosity of mind that
much of the most sustained of his best work should
be that conceived as humble and ardent tribute to
the young beauty and promise of others. Here
indeed he is greatly inspired, and the greatness of
the inspiration is abundantly seen in passage after
passage of flagrant beauty, of dominant and enkindling

music, of vision so large and noble as to be at times overwhelming.

One section of Thompson's poetry remains to be noticed—the odes concerned with the interpretation of nature. His attitude is as impassioned as Jefferies'; and if less eager than Meredith's, only less eager because more assured. His faith is a lamp to her feet, and so her journeys and divagations are for him neither quite obscure nor quite hopeless. His positive and secure spiritual perception becomes a protection equally against the sentimental and the gloomy obsessions. He sings an Anthem of Earth, but does not look at earth as at a sentient all-powerful ruler, with whimful cruelties and gaieties the more bitter as they are the more inexplicable. From Rousseau and Wordsworth to Emerson and Maeterlinck, we have heard so much of nature that we forget it is only hearsay. We have not discovered nature, but her name, yet wilfully ascribe to her the most secret and the most mighty potentialities which we deny in God. Infinitely far from this antinomianism is Thompson's conception. Call him a pantheist, but he is a pantheist whose God is infinitely knowable, too clear not to shine in every bud, bush, cloud, hue, water, and too surely infinite not to be manifest beyond all these phenomena of nature. So in his *Orient Ode* he mounts to ecstasy, singing to the sun,

> If I too shall adore
> Be it accounted unto me
> A bright sciential idolatry——

but he asks, if it is indeed to the sun or to Christ that
he proffers his longing verse :—

> . . . For oh, how could it be,—
> When I with winged feet had run
> Through all the windy earth about,
> Quested its secret of the sun,
> And heard what thing the stars together shout,—
> I should not heed thereout
> Consenting counsel won :—
> " By this, O Singer, know we if thou see.
> When men shall say to thee : Lo Christ is here,
> When men shall say to thee : Lo Christ is there,
> Believe them : yea, and this—then thou art seer,
> When all thy crying clear
> Is but : Lo here ! lo there !—ah me, lo everywhere ! "

And so, in the *Ode to the Setting Sun*, he deems his
tributary music raised amiss to the visible sun, outpouring it more wisely, more solemnly, in the " after-
strain " to the " King-Maker of Creation." Nature
may awe but may not bewilder him, for it is within
his power to conspire with God—

> To grasp this sorry scheme of things entire—

and so find nature neither unintelligible, nor dismaying.
He sees her not as lord but as servant, with purposes
vast yet subordinate, powerful, yet less powerful than
thought, unspeakable in wonder and loveliness, and
yet no more than the fluttering garment of the invisible.

IV

I return from this inadequate rough map of Thompson's treasures of verse, to say once more that the value of this verse lies ultimately in its expression of eternal truth. Much could be written upon his form, the " incidental greatness " of his least-considered ways, his strange, Shakespeare-like vocabulary, his richness of metaphor ; much could be written upon the constant and amazing energy of his mind ; but I do not attempt it here. He has another claim upon men and women of 1916 ; he influences the influential. He stands pre-eminent with Patmore among later poets as the asserter of faith, joint-inheritor of the spiritual world, revealer of the unseen. Thompson reveals it often in large and rich images which in themselves are astonishing. " Things more excellent than every image are expressed through images " ; and it is not simply a choice but a necessity for a poet to utter what he would by symbols and metaphors, giving to the unbodied a body. The images of true poetry are never the additament of cunning rhyme, but the expression by picture and analogy of else inapprehensible truth. Every man must be haunted at times by a sense of the strange correspondence of diverse things, by casual intimations of the invisible world. And what is at the centre of them but something of unity and order, of common vitality and common purpose, subtly threading its infinite filament

316

through all the nerves and veins of existence ? Now
Thompson proceeds (as in *The Mistress of Vision* from
which I have quoted) from the recognition of the
casual likeness, which is within the opportunity of all,
to the recognition of the essential likeness, which is
within the power of few. He speaks of nature when
he means God, of a girl's love, when he means the
soul's love. His poetry and Patmore's thus become
antiphonal; but the first song is the song of *The
Unknown Eros.*

Almost alone among later imaginative writers, they
sail out boldly into that spiritual sea which to many is
all but unknown, and by some still held unknowable.
But even to those who sail not with them, groping still
in comfortable twilight, there comes the great inspiration of their song, a consciousness of the purity of
their faith, and at the least the guidance of the white
foam of their course.

ROBERT BRIDGES

I

THE poetry of Robert Bridges seems often the most natural in the world, and sometimes the most cunning in artifice. And that is because, using words loosely, we hardly stay to remember that poetry is an artifice, and that no one naturally uses the forms of verse for common speech. But at least one may say that poetry has never come more near to common speech and yet remained indubitably poetry, than in some of Mr. Bridges's blank verse. For although the form of verse may be quite alien from the form of common speech of most men, it is not so foreign with all men. Exceptions there have been among English poets, and of them it is remarkable that some of the chief instances should be in our own day.

Is there a language of poetry, distinct from the language of prose? Wordsworth denied it, and proceeded both to support and refute the denial in his own work. " Poetic diction " was the centre of the old dispute ; and in truth, those who maintained the necessity of poetic diction in poetry had much to assist

319

them. They could bring in evidence how much of
Shakespeare and Herrick, of Milton and Fletcher !
They could, and did, quote all Pope—and so ruined
a promising argument. " It may be safely affirmed,"
wrote Wordsworth with perfect finality of assurance,
" that there neither is, nor can be, any *essential* difference between the language of prose and metrical
composition." And again :

> Poets do not write for poets alone, but for men. Unless
> therefore we are advocates for that admiration which subsists
> upon ignorance, and that pleasure which arises from hearing
> what we do not understand, the Poet must descend from his
> supposed height ; and, in order to excite rational sympathy,
> he must express himself as other men express themselves. To
> this it may be added, that while he is only selecting from the
> real language of men, or, which amounts to the same thing,
> composing accurately in the spirit of such selection, he is
> treading upon safe ground, and we know what we are to ex-
> pect from him.

A native sincerity, a great desire to be simple and
straightforward in what he said, taught him this that
is to us now so well-worn and accepted a truth. So
in his own best and most truly expressive work, the
language and the construction are plain and direct
There is choice of words, but not of strange words ;
care in construction, but not careful oddity. He is
among the wisest of English poets, and his poetry is
yet of the clearest. As clear as prose, a hater of verse
might grudgingly say.

What is it then that distinguishes it from prose ?

for none could mistake it for prose. The essential distinction is the rhythm of poetry.

I do not say that we of to-day have a better control of rhythm, but I think we have a better understanding of it, than had those for whom science had done little. We perceive it to be one of the secret powers of the universe, one of the palpable forces of the world. We perceive it in the sway of the tides and in the procession of the stars; in the recurrence of the seasons and in the sequence of the physical ages of the globe; in the course of the blood in the veins and the sap in the trees; in the generation of gnats and of thoughts; in the flight of light and sound; in all things material and (only less obscurely because our knowledge is little more than conjecture) in all things spiritual. It is the common note of this world and other worlds, the relating characteristic of dissimilar things. It is even, perhaps, the common note of narrow time and unimagined eternity. There is something, says Goethe, magical in rhythm; it even makes us believe that we possess the sublime.

Confined to the present matter, if rhythm is distinguishable in poetry, it is istinguishable also in prose. Undoubtedly that is the case; but the point to be remembered is, that the rhythm of poetry is different from the rhythm of prose. For one thing, much that is called prose, being a useful, debased, macadamized thing, has hardly any surviving rhythm. It has not been born, but made. It has not grown, but merely been put together ; here a phrase and there a phrase, each ready-made and hastily flung together with a slack conjunctive. Nevertheless, who of careful readers has not sometimes found the rhythm of prose almost as clear as the rhythm of poetry ? In our own earlier prose literature it is most generally observed, for the reason that from the Elizabethans— and earlier times still—down almost to the nineteenth century, prose was commonly written as something heard. With the nineteenth century it became the record of things seen. Until then the natural rhythm of sounds was perpetuated in the language of prose ; and most purely in the prose of the English Bible, of Milton and Browne, Taylor and Traherne. You are aware of it in this of Donne :

> As my soule shall not goe towards Heaven, but goe by Heaven to Heaven, to the Heaven of Heavens, so the true joy of a good soule in this world is the very joy of Heaven ; and we goe thither not that being without joy we might have joy infused into us, but that, as Christ sayes, " Our joy might be full," perfected, sealed with an everlastingnesse :

as well as this more famous apostrophe of Raleigh's :

> O eloquent, just, and mighty Death ! whom none could advise, thou hast perswaded ; what none have dared, thou hast done ; and whom all the world has flattered, thou only hast cast out of the world and despised ; thou hast drawn together all the far-fetched greatness, all the pride, cruelty and ambition of man, and covered it all over with these two narrow words, Hic Jacet !

Johnson's grave and scrupulous English was written

with this obedience ; and of later times, is there any
need to quote the example of Ruskin and Newman ?
I do not speak of Ruskin's earlier magniloquent
manner :—rhythm dominates his later simpler style
no less completely ; and as for Newman, did he ever
write a page not informed with this universal pulse of
life ?

The rhythm of prose is vague, elusive, difficult to
mark : yes !   And when it becomes strict it becomes
lifeless, and shows mechanical in Gibbon and detestable
in Macaulay.   Of the prose of our own time, there is
a curious thing to remark : that it has become pictorial
more than rhythmical, even while poetry has become
more delicately responsive to the laws of rhythm.
It has not proved so easy to exorcise the rhythm of
poetry.   Poetry is often poetry, in general acceptance,
because it rhymes—an easy and charitable distinction ;
but rhymed verse itself may so unfortunately be
rhythmless.   For rhythm, in the practice of verse,
means not simply regular recurrence or precise co-
ordination, but recurrence with infinite slight modification.   Just as, of a myriad dewdrops, no two would
be found precisely similar in the quality of their
reflection ; or of a myriad daisies none in which even
the inexact human eye would not detect a tiny triumphant difference ; so in the rhythm of human language
adapted to poetic expression, continual modification,
" slight novelty," will be found to vary the sameness
of mere recurrence.   Lacking that constant innovation,

poetry is the less surely and the less delightfully poetry. It is indeed, perhaps, simply to a physiological demand that this variability is making its mysterious response; or if it be merely to a narrow æsthetic sense, yet that æsthetic sense is no less vital and imperative than a physiological sense. . . . One touches here on matters which it is difficult even to look at steadily in a short article, and which to consider at length in the writings of others I have felt sufficiently bewildering.

II

I return at last to Mr. Bridges. His work is of an unusual simplicity, and of a very high rhythmical quality. It is free from inversion (that tempting trick of much verse even of to-day), and depends for its impression upon the sense of life conveyed by the naturalness of its movement, by its responsiveness to the thought. Verse becomes, here if anywhere, a natural form of speech. But to say natural is not to say commonplace : the difference between the two is the difference between Mr. Bridges and Cowper. Cowper merely creeps upon commonplace ; Mr. Bridges rises upon natural wings.

But you may compare his verse with that of a far finer poet than Cowper, with Tennyson when Tennyson is not at his rarest, and observe at once how much more natural, how much more instinctively rhythmical, is

the work of the later poet. Take almost any of
Tennyson's blank verse save the earlier :

> " O brother," answer'd Balin, " woe is me !
> My madness all thy life has been thy doom,
> Thy curse, and darken'd all thy day ; and now
> The night has come. I scarce can see thee now.
> Goodnight ! for we shall never bid again
> Goodmorrow—Dark my doom was here, and dark
> It will be there. I see thee, now no more.
> I would not mine again should darken thine,
> Goodnight, true brother ; "

and by the side of this set Mr. Bridges :

> . . . I will go down to the grave,
> And plead my cause before the holy angels,
> Whether it may be permitted for a princess,
> Against her father and faith . . .—Nay, is't not writ
> There is there no vain discourse nor charge of sin,
> But pleasure to the faithful ? And I to die
> With house and kingdom shamed ! How would my crown
> Shine 'mong the blessed caliphs, and the martyrs
> Who fell in fight upon the road of God ?
> How would they look upon me,
> If 'mong their moonbright scimitars I came,
> My child's blood on my head ? and she not there,
> The fair flower of my life, the bud of grace,
> Which my long-withering and widowed tree
> Held to the face of heaven,
> Now from my own trunk by my own hands torn.

One need not be a very exact student of English
prosody to recognize the rhythmical superiority of the
latter. The comparison could be multiplied to tediousness.

    I dwell on this merely technical point because it has

more than a merely technical significance. True that
the appearance of naturalness in verse is not always
easily contrived. Mr. Bridges is a profound student
of questions of prosody, and has for many years been
credited with a knowledge of music unusual, for its
intimacy, among English poets. Such knowledge,
such expertry, forms a great advantage. He brings
to the writing of verse a rare skill in the judgment of
sounds and words, and an ear for delicate cadences,
like the ear which apprehends the tenuous cry of a
bat. What a reticent mastery is his of the teasing
difficulties of the art of verse! There is nothing out
of the Elizabethans of so easy and pure a felicity, no
verse where the shackles of verse are more unconsciously worn. It is like the movement of that other
beautiful and free and strict art, dancing : as gay and
observant as dancing. It is never merely dignified,
though it has the dignity of poetry. It is not made
to look curiously unlike prose, in order that it may
appear the more surely poetry. There are no strange
words, no astonishing transitions. It is pure poetry
by virtue of its secure and unfailing rhythm. Look
again at that passage of Tennyson, and you will
observe a monotony of rhythm, like the tune of the
revolving arms of a windmill. With all his immense and
impressive gifts, Tennyson is without the exquisitely
delicate responsiveness to the interior rhythm with
which all poetry must more or less nearly accord.
To say that Mr. Bridges is a greater poet than Tenny-

Robert Bridges

son would be gratuitous folly, but he assuredly has a
finer sense of rhythm.   The rhythm of his verse is like
that of willows caressing and caressed by the wind,
or like the waves' unmonotonous unceasing tossing.
Keeping as Mr. Bridges does mainly to the fair and
temperate zone of passion, and shrinking from excess
as from blasphemy (which indeed for thoughtful
artists it is), he nevertheless proves his medium
capable of dark and serious things, as in *Palicio*, or
lofty, as in *Prometheus the Firegiver*, or tender, as in
the beautiful *Return of Ulysses*, or familiar, as in *The
Humours of the Court*.   But whether passionate or
lofty, tender or familiar, Mr. Bridges's blank verse
always appears a *natural* form of speech, even though
you know that such fine, felicitous work is never
achieved but by the vigilant cunning of a fine mind.
Coleridge shows yet more of the same accomplished
simplicity, but the verse most like Mr. Bridges's is
found in the Elizabethans—in Fletcher or (as an
anonymous writer remarked some years since) in
Massinger.   More interesting is it, however, to note
the influence of this naturalness upon the work of
living men.   Mr. W. B. Yeats might be thought to
have learned from Mr. Bridges the plain secret of his
simple verse, but for the fact that the origins of his
art are hidden away beyond easy discovery.   Even
in his earlier poems, where the manner is less assured
than in his later, you may note " truth's simplicity " :
and in the later you will find this :

> I think that all deep passion is but a kiss
> In the mid battle, and a difficult peace
> 'Twixt oil and water, candles and dark night,
> Hill-side and hollow, the hot-footed sun
> And the cold sliding slippery-footed moon,
> A brief forgiveness between opposites
> That have been hatreds for three times the age
> Of this long 'stablished ground.

But I think I can read clearer signs of Mr. Bridges's influence in the poetry of one of the most excellent writers of to-day, Mr. Lascelles Abercrombie. And it is the more conspicuous since the character of his verse is very different from the character of Mr. Bridges's. Mr. Abercrombie is brilliant, vehement and bold as Mr. Bridges never is; he chooses subjects far from the elder poet's choice; his expression has little or nothing of the grave gaiety which makes the lyrics of this master treasurable as Mozart's music. But his is the same high rhythmical quality; reading his poetry, you are at once aware that the rhythm has made the verse and not the verse the rhythm. That is to say its form is essential and not arbitrary; his verse is *essentially* poetry.

> This crime is mine.—O cramp is at my heart.—
> I have the guilt. I need not so have grieved
> About your eyes : it was I who was blind.
> I know not how to bear you close to me,
> The touch of your hands will be a fearful thing
> For me henceforth.—Give me your hands in mine;
> The Lord in Heaven knows nothing can be
> To any human soul more horrible

Than these poor dreadful hands : therefore I kiss them,
And may it do for prayer. At Judgement Day
Tell them, my child, you did not make his death.
I will not share it. It is all mine.

Of the matter of Mr. Bridges's dramatic writings
I do not propose to speak in detail. He has written
two plays upon Nero, others upon historical events,
as *The Christian Captives* and *Palicio*; others again
where his scholarship has served him finely, namely,
Achilles in Scyros, *Prometheus the Firegiver* and *The
Return of Ulysses*; and two comedies standing apart
from all the rest and from each other—*The Humours
of the Court* and *The Feast of Bacchus*. The last named
is partly translated from Terence, and is the most
excellently pleasant of all these plays. To suit the
easy comic spirit the author has used a line of six
stresses full of those nice adjustments which Mr.
Bridges so happily contrives. The result is a play as
truly comic as Molière's plays, in a medium of familiar
verse which preserves faithfully the exquisite commonplace and sly humour of the various characters.

I said just now that this merely technical point,
rhythm, had a significance more than technical. The
free naturalness which is the obvious metrical characteristic of each play is the effect of a natural freshness
of vision. Or to go back a little farther, it is closely
correspondent to the human feeling shown everywhere
in them. All these plays are warm and living with
the same human experience, the same directness, only

differing in force as the dramatic requirement demands. Nero, for instance, becomes (especially in the second play on this most maltreated subject) a really credible human figure, cruel, capricious, full of ambition, and ever mortally aware of his loneliness. Ulysses, finding himself in Ithaca and becoming known to his son, utters the very soul of human delight at the recognition of inward-treasured things ; the same intimate remembering delight which Mr. Bridges expresses in many of his lyrics—as " the Silver Thames." Even in *Prometheus the Firegiver*, where the interest is inevitably remote and the whole atmosphere that of a myth, you are yet persuaded that Inachus is a man, and it is in anxious human tones that Prometheus himself foretells the expiatory woes of Io :

> When her wild cries arouse the house at night,
> And, running to her bed, ye see her set
> Upright in trancèd sleep, her starting hair
> With deathly sweat bedewed, in horror shaking,
> Her eyeballs fixed upon the unbodied dark,
> Through which a draping mist of luminous gloom
> Drifts from her couch away,—when, if asleep,
> She walks as if awake, and if awake
> Dreams, and as one who nothing hears or sees,
> Lives in a sick and frantic mood, whose cause
> She understands not or is loth to tell——.

A strict test of poetry is that it should be capable of the most literal interpretation, that it should be *literally* true. It is, I think, surprising how many of the fine, famous things in English poetry can bear the narrowest examination and be found mere truthful statements of facts and impressions. Poetry is not speech upon impossible things ; it is the only form of speech upon certain things that must find expression. It is a purely human utterance upon matters affecting man. The truest poetry is inevitably unextravagant ; among poets there is no such thing as poetic licence. They do not need it : they abhor it, as being false to the spirit of their noble, exacting art. . . . These plays by Mr. Bridges sustain the literal test admirably. They are full of human feeling, full of wise speech upon near and dear things ; and that speech has the natural free rhythm of unmistakable, spontaneous poetry.

III

I must say no more of the plays, since it is not as a dramatic writer that Mr. Bridges is chiefly to be esteemed. He is a lyrical poet, and it is the substance and the sum of his lyrical poetry, as well as its form, that must be noticed now. In the collected edition of his works, the lyrics are all contained in the second volume, and it is necessary to look at them as all parts of one great lyrical poem, as well as individually.

But before doing this I must speak of the sonnet-sequence, *The Growth of Love*, which may be taken as an introduction to the lyrical poems. The sonnets are among the earliest of their author's work. He says that they were not intended for the public ; but now that (thanks to American enterprise and against his wish) they are to be read by the public, we may regard them more or less critically. Taken strictly as sonnets they are sometimes irregular in form, but throughout their beauty is singular. There is a pure morning air over them. They have not been made, but sung while swallows flew and shrilled. In so many sonnets there is stiffness, perhaps wilful, or conscious dignity. Mr. Bridges's are lyrical cries in sonnet form :

> O my uncared-for songs, what are ye worth,
> That in my secret book with so much care
> I write you, this one here and that one there,
> Marking the time and order of your birth ?

Verse written for one's secret book is not always very fine verse, and some of these sonnets hold but little poetic heat. But even at their poorest they have charming personal touches. " I will be what God has made me," he declares ; and in the next sonnet (No. 63) :

> I abide and abide, as if more stout and tall
> My spirit would grow by waiting like a tree.

He has a " careless eagerness," but hides his own thought :

> If I rejoice
> In what is done or doing, I confide
> Neither to friend nor foe my secret choice.

There is, it must be said, little evidence of the " growth " of love in the sonnets grouped under this

title.   Love appears full-grown with nothing tristful,
nothing passionate ; love as the natural fulfilment
of human life is their note. . . .   I quote one here
which is not a love sonnet, but which is clearly the
finest of the entire sixty-nine, and one of the truly
fine sonnets in our tongue :

> I heard great Hector sounding war's alarms,
> Where thro' the listless ghosts chiding he strode,
> As tho' the Greeks besieged his last abode,
> And he his Troy's hope still, her king-at-arms.
> But on those gentle meads, which Lethe charms
> With weary oblivion, his passion glow'd
> Like the cold night-worm's candle, and only show'd
> Such mimic flame as neither heats nor harms.
> 'Twas plain to read, even by those shadows quaint,
> How rude catastrophe had dim'd his day,
> And blighted all his cheer with stern complaint :
> *To arms ! to arms !* what more the voice would say
> Was swallow'd in the valleys, and grew faint
> Upon the thin air, as he pass'd away.

To pass now to the volume of pure lyrics, let me say
that here is seen the proof of the statement made in
the first sentence of this article, that Mr. Bridges's
poetry seems sometimes the most cunning in artifice
of all poetry.   These lyrics, in the first place, show
without displaying an extreme ingenuity of form, a
metrical variety which it would be hard to match in
any other poet.   There is here and there a rondeau or
triolet, which has almost been discovered by antholo-
gists, and one or two eclogues in heroic couplets ; but
leaving apart these forms, I find no fewer than eighty-

three distinct metrical devices in the hundred and twenty-six poems of the volume.

But I do not want to dwell longer upon questions of technique, attractive though they are. What do these poems mean ? What is it that gives them the distinction claimed for them ? Why is the work of this still almost unregarded poet to be singled out for study so disproportionate to his general reputation ? In what is it remarkable ?

Plain questions cannot always get very plain answers ; indeed, answers to questions of art and life can never be quite so simple as the questions. It would not be incorrect to say, for example, that there is nothing remarkable in Mr. Bridges's lyrics, and to add smartly that they are remarkable in that. They have distinction by virtue of their manner, but not only by virtue of that. And as for the sum of their meaning, to ascertain that you must try to gauge the measure of their intention, the depth of their suggestion. I do not mean that there are any well-hidden treasures of wisdom in the remote chambers of these poems : I do not think there are. There is a way that some writers have of giving their readers flash-light revelations, sudden surprises, lights the more vivid from the surrounding darkness. Mr. Bridges does not do this. His meaning is plain, his emotions not curiously refined, his ideas not very often subtilized. But nevertheless there *is* more than the separate meanings, or than the sum-total of those separate meanings : there is the spirit in which he confronts the form of time and the spectre of eternity. Let the metrical diversity be as wonderful as you please, the separate " notes " as charming, the intentions as wise : yet these can make but faint claim on our serious thoughts if there is nothing more.

Well, one thing that is to be remarked is the essential joyousness of life as viewed in the lyrics. Joy pours in with sun and frost, clouds and dews, sleep and dreams. Usually it is a " passionless passion " that glows in these beautifully fashioned braziers, sometimes a " solemn joy " ; but it yet burns undiminishing. He has a beautiful impulsive ode to joy ; he knows that joy is not careless or heartless :

> But they who build thy towers fair and strong,
> Of all that toil, feel most of care and wrong.

He does not regard the world as fashioned for the sole delight of man : God's " old intents we see were never for our joy designed." He watches grief and terror all around, pain and " the grinding enginry of blood and breath " : but suddenly, we know not why, " there comes the happy moment " when life and joy are one. But not always does it appear in these poems as so sudden and unaccountable a visitant : more often it is an abiding presence. Both joy and sorrow are but links of his personal relation to life and the problems of life. His attitude, in short, is one of passivity or quietism. He waits " like a tree," living on hope. He, too, " presents life." He leaves aside the material considerations of life, with which most of us are honourably occupied, and gives his attention to the inward-growing ideas of joy, sorrow, and the satisfactions of the spirit.   Towards the clarifying and the establishing of these does his recent anthology, *The Spirit of Man*, directly and deliberately tend.   With but little immediate moral or spiritual direction, you find in his work a stimulus to finer living.   The *value* of life is enhanced, and the quality of its beauty, its affections and influences.   Even more than joy he desires peace, which hides beneath both joy and sorrow.   Accept, he says in effect :

> O soul be patient, thou shalt find
> A little matter mend all this—

he urges, looking too sorrowfully upon the tumultuary sorrows around.   When he does pass on to direct moral assertion, he writes with great wisdom.   The instance is in the second Eclogue, concerning Giovanni Duprè, a poor woodcarver's son whose bones are laid with those of the mighty Buonarrotti.   Nothing he did deserved great praise, or exceeded the praise it won :

> Yet he made one thing
> Worthy of the lily city in her spring ;
> For while in vain the forms of beauty he aped,
> A perfect spirit in himself he shaped ;
> And all his lifetime doing less than well
> Where he profess'd nor doubted to excel,
> Now, where he had no scholarship, but drew
> His art from love, 'twas better than he knew :

Robert Bridges

And when he sat to write, lo! by him stood
The heavenly Muse, who smiles on all things good;
And for his truth's sake, for his stainless mind,
His homely love and faith, she now grew kind,
And changed the crown, that from the folk he got,
For her green laurel, and he knew it not.

LAWRENCE. Ah! Love of Beauty! This man then mistook
Ambition for her?

RICHARD.   In simplicity
Erring he kept his truth; and in his book
The statue of his grace is fair to see.

LAWRENCE. Then buried with their great he well may be.

RICHARD.   And number'd with the saints, not among them
Who painted saints. Join we his requiem.

Or there is that other brave lyric (interesting, too,
as a metrical study) which bids us call upon an inward
fortitude, and urges the dignity of not begging even
for the removal of dark clouds.

> Weep not to day: why should this sadness be?
>   Learn in present fears
>   To o'ermaster those tears
>   That unhindered conquer thee.
>
> Think on thy past valour, thy future praise:
>   Up, sad heart, nor faint
>   In ungracious complaint,
>   Or a prayer for better days.
>
> Daily thy life shortens, the grave's dark peace
>   Draweth surely nigh,
>   When good-night is good-bye;
>   For the sleeping shall not cease.
>
> Fight, to be found fighting: nor far away
>   Deem, nor strange thy doom.
>   Like this sorrow 'twill come,
>   And the day will be to-day.

337

But in speaking in this general way of Mr. Bridges's book I must not omit to mention one or two particular features not expressly touched upon hitherto. First let it be remarked that he has an earnest and bright love of England, and of her land as being hers and a part of nature. A pure and steady lamp of devotion shines in his reserved unemphatic verse. His feeling for the earth and waters of England is, in truth, filial in its affectionateness ; and his renderings of English landscape—making for me the most complete of all the delight of his verse—are as pure and direct and as truly impassioned as those of Gray and Arnold, and only less moving than Wordsworth's. And the other feature is this—the love which is as prominent a characteristic of his individual work as it is of the whole of English poetry. " Love on buried ecstasy buildeth his tower," he murmurs, and nurses the idea of love the more tenderly for its secrecy. The gaiety, the lightness, of many of his " amoretti " prevents your seeing how warm with eager fire they are, until you are accustomed to give every word its full value, as indeed you must learn to do, if this poetry is to have more than an academic or decorative use. He is painfully aware of the buried ecstasy, yet how tell it ! • Love is Nature's perfect art," is what he has learned ; and in " clothing his thought in forms of sense " man may become godlike.

> But O, have care, have care !
> 'Tis envious even to dare :

Robert Bridges

> And many a fiend is watching well
> To flush thy reed with the fire of hell.

So when he writes of the ecstasy, he must be heedful
of his song. Ecstasy forbids excess, even if his art
had not already forbidden it. He writes, then, with
fear almost, or with reluctance as though, as Donne
says :

> 'Twere profanation of our joys
> To tell the laity of our love.

So, in the seventh of the New Poems, you will find
poetry moving upwards like a lark into full silence,
passing from imperfect speech into perfect stillness :

> I climb the mossy bank of the glade :
> My love awaiteth me in the shade.
>
> She holdeth a book that she never heedeth :
> In Goddës work her spirit readeth.
>
> She is all to me, and I to her :
> When we embrace the stars confer.
>
> O my love, from beyond the sky
> I am calling thy heart, and who but I ?
>
> Fresh as love is the breeze of June,
> In the dappled shade of the summer noon.
>
> Catullus, throwing his heart away,
> Gave fewer kisses every day.
>
> Heracleitus, spending his youth
> In search of wisdom, had less of truth.
>
> Flame of fire was the poet's desire :
> The thinker found that life was fire.

339

The Moderns

> O my love! my song is done:
> My kiss hath both their fires in one.

Is it not the sign of a supreme capacity, when the inadequacy of even a supreme capacity is recognized?

IV

Does it seem foolish to burden a book of such beautiful lyrics with a meaning, a philosophy, or even with main and lesser characteristics? Is it not better to look at them simply as the casual outpourings of a writer whose lyrical gifts are delicate rather than profuse, more pleasant than profound?

Well, one may regard them thus, or even think them Elizabethan miracles repeated, and be not wholly unfair. Only, I do not see why one should not try to weigh the full purpose and the full accomplishment of a volume of lyrics, as well as of the five acts of a play, or the several books of narrative or epic. And there is indeed so obviously a common note in them all, that these poems may well appear to justify at any rate such brief general treatment as I have given them. Their excellence merely as verse is remarkable when it is noted that there is not a failure from the first to the last—scarcely a flawed line. Character is in all these poems; an idea is created of certain fine desirable features grouped into a harmony of life. At once eager and reticent, proud and humble, wise and gay—you recognize the various qualities before

340

you recognize the synthesis of them all, which is like an air flooding these lyrics with life and light. But beneath and beyond all there is that intense power of transfiguration—ecstasy. Yes, buried ecstasy, Mr. Bridges calls it ; but buried as seed is buried, to live again more fruitfully. . . . All his art is offered as tribute to ideal beauty ; all his soul streams out in a creative passion, as he evokes from the silence awaiting the revelation an image of that interior beauty. Do but look attentively at these poems, remembering that the words have their own sure value and relation which must be neither forgotten nor exaggerated, and you will become aware of an influence the more penetrating for its very quietness and stillness. It is like the voice of a sensitive conscience, which we can easily refuse to hear, but which when heard we cannot neglect ; a voice which extorts even from the breastless bosom of ingratitude some throbs of profound recognition.